Instructional Materials for Exceptional Children

Selection, Management, and Adaptation

Joseph J. Stowitschek
George Peabody College
for Teachers
Vanderbilt University

Robert A. Gable
National Children's
Rehabilitation Center

Jo Mary Hendrickson
Continental Systems, Inc.

AN ASPEN PUBLICATION®
Aspen Systems Corporation
Rockville, Maryland
London, England
1980

Library of Congress Cataloging in Publication Data

Stowitschek, Joseph J.
Instructional materials for exceptional children.

Bibliography: p. 319
Includes index.
1. Handicapped children—Education—Audio-visual aids. 2. Educational technology. I. Gable, Robert A., joint author. II. Hendrickson, Jo Mary, joint author. III. Title.
LC4019.S76 371.9'043 80-11730
ISBN: 0-89443-277-X

Library of Congress Catalog Card Number: 80-11730
ISBN: 0-89443-277-X

Printed in the United States of America

2 3 4 5

Dedication

To teachers who know what it means to have struggled with instructional materials, and thought, "Next year I'm really going to get organized."

Contents

Foreword

This book provides educators and others with essential information for the more effective education of children with handicaps. Such help is urgently needed because of this country's commitment to the education of *all* handicapped children. The magnitude of the task is difficult to comprehend.

More than $5 billion are spent annually in educating nearly four million handicapped students. Almost one in ten of all students are handicapped and the average cost for their education is twice that of educating nonhandicapped children. The Education of all Handicapped Children Act of 1975 requires for these children a free, appropriate, publicly supported education in the least restrictive environment. The law also requires a written Individualized Education Program including annual goals, short term instructional objectives, and the proposed strategies to be used to achieve them. The task is great. The resources and good ideas are limited. Instructional materials and educational technology can help enormously. They can be of maximum assistance if they are soundly based in effective principles of learning and teaching; if they are accessible, economical, and relevant to daily use in classrooms where children with handicaps are taught.

The vast investment of resources, the numbers of children being served, the high cost in human resources and time boggle the mind. However, effective education for children with handicaps ultimately comes down to providing programs that enable each child to improve performance in learning.

For these purposes, a materials resource technology making effective use of teaching and learning materials and instructional technology are becoming increasingly available.

For more than one hundred years, the federal government had been supporting the development and distribution of instructional materials for handicapped persons. The Act to Promote the Education of the Blind was implemented in 1879 and today continues to support an essential instructional materials service for visually impaired persons. Since the early 1960s, the federal government has made sizable investments in captioned films for the deaf and media, materials, and educational technology services for all children with handicaps. Among more recent developments is a program of research to generate new knowledge, new methods and materials, and new applications of technology for the improvement of the education of all handicapped children. The provisions of support service, funds for research, and new training programs in media and materials join such other federal support services for education of the handicapped as program assistance grants for personnel preparation, direct financial support and technical assistance to states and local education agencies, and grants for field initiated research and requested proposal research. Thus, current and recent developments continue a more than one hundred-year history of recognition of the essential role of instructional materials in the effective education of handicapped persons.

Surprisingly few books have been written that are of direct help to teachers in making good use of instructional materials. As the title of this book indicates, it provides unique help in selecting, managing, and adapting instructional materials for exceptional children. The book itself is a unique instructional material facilitating the acquisition of skill in selecting, managing, and/or adapting materials. The book also provides a ready reference guide to solving specific problems in using materials. The inclusion in each chapter of objectives, study questions, and self-checks enables the reader to assess his/her own understanding of the work.

Selecting appropriate instructional materials from among the probably more than half a million such materials is not an easy task. Today, the best interests of exceptional children and rising prices, shrinking budgets, and emphases on teacher-accountability make wise choices imperative. Chapter 2 provides effective assistance in the selection of materials based on sound principles of teaching and learning. Chapter 3 provides help on how to get information about materials and how to locate and retrieve them. Chapter 4 deals with the crucial topic of budgeting for these purposes.

Chapter 5 and 7 analyze substantive matters relevant to the use of materials to support individualized educational programs and to managing daily use of instructional materials in the classroom.

It has been said that only about one in one hundred instructional materials have been field tested or learner verified with one or more learners to determine its effectiveness. Chapter 8 deals with the critical matters of field testing and evaluating materials. Chapter 9 provides special help with difficult learning problems and handicaps. Chapter 10 is among the most valuable in the book because it deals with the too-much neglected problem of child-bared evaluation of instructional materials.

Chapter 11 deals in unique ways with the specialized applications of media, materials, and educational technology to the problems of educating children with handicaps.

Educational technology is among the most promising avenues of future development in the field of special education. The information and skills imparted by this book applied to the enormous problems of educating effectively all handicapped children can make a very significant difference in the future of special education. Teachers can benefit from the use of this book through in-service and continuing education. Those who are preparing to teach will serve children better if they have opportunities to acquire the knowledge and skills in this book prior to their placement in careers in special education or "mainstreaming" handicapped children in regular education programs.

S.C. Ashcroft
Professor, Special Education
George Peabody College for Teachers
Vanderbilt University

Preface

This book arose out of concern that the use of instructional materials in the education of handicapped persons appears to be taking a lesser role than its importance demands. In most instances, instructional materials are the common medium for instruction. Whether they are materials used directly by the handicapped learner or guides used by the trainers of handicapped learners, materials do and must continue to play an important role.

Educators, including special educators, are in the process of developing technologies of education, or training, if you will. A *technology* is a process where by tools or materials are employed to provide designed products. The *process* (teaching methods) without the *tools* (instructional materials) is an incomplete technology. Likewise, the tools in the absence of procedures for using them often produce undesirable results. Much of the current literature deals either primarily with the process or primarily with the tools and leaves it up to the teacher to integrate the two. This integration may not occur. Teachers may see little relationship between measurement and the materials used in instruction or between individualized educational programming and the daily presentation of practice materials.

Entwined with the development of a materials resource technology is the development of a technostructure, albeit a miniature one. A *technostructure* involves the management of the technical aspects of any operation. The efficiently operating classroom is a technostructure. The teacher is the manager rather then solely the imparter of instruction.

We know that the methodology for effective teaching is being researched and developed; we also know that effective and replicable instructional materials can be developed. We apparently have yet to learn much about how these two come together in the education of the handicapped. Many teachers have training in effective methodology; still others have training in effective instructional development. Seldom are the two well coordinated. It is like an automobile engine that has all the parts and is running but may be out of tune and "missing" badly. The fine tuning needed in the classroom relates to the coordination of methodology and materials in this technology.

Instructional materials are part of a long process in a child's development, which involves transferring the controlling stimuli from parents in early years to teachers who gradually increase the transfer of stimulus control to materials and eventually to society. Materials are a critical link in this transfer of stimulus control because they are a progressively closer approximation to societal controls (e.g., newspapers, job application forms, checkbooks, purchase receipts, public signs, etc.). With handicapped children two problems often arise. First, stimulus control of the parent or teacher may never have been established before the process of transfer began, thus setting the occasion for failure responses. Second, the process of transferring stimulus control from materials that grossly approximate societal controls to those that more closely approximate them may have been too rapid, with large jumps or gaps in the approximations.

Acknowledgments

The authors would like to extend their gratitude to the following teachers and teacher trainees who asisted in field testing this book:

Maria A. Almeida
Cynthia D. Bearden
Martha Bennett
Donna Boyington
Beth Bruce
Ann Burgess
Elizabeth A. Cattanach
Brenda Cohen
Constance M. Coleman
Anthony Curtis
Kim Dunning
Jean Eppling
Deborah L. Falkoff
Margery E. Flautt
Sandra Frankenstein
Mildred D. Goodall
Cathy Hawkinson
Judi Hebden
Harriett L. Hilley
Elizabeth A. Huber
Christopher R. Jolly
Susan Kennedy
Dorothy L. King
Sheree Kooser
Sara E. Lashlee
Kimberly M. MacDonald
Sally A. Main
Martha McDonnell
Helen Napier
Jennie Noles
Beverly S. Norton
Margaret L. Oakman
Dorothy Ellen Palmer
Glenn M. Penkava
Sally Preston
Denise Raff
Mary P. Reynolds
Challice E. Rickard
Susan M. Schacht
Diana S. Shelley
Antonia G. Smith
Bruce Smith
Barbara L. VanMatre
Cathryn L. Walker
Tamera L. Yonts
Clifford C. Young
Rebecca Zachary
Laura J. Zega

CHAPTER 1

Instructional Materials as a Technological Resource

Objectives

1. Identify the importance of instructional materials in special education.
   - Why are they important for individual education program implementation?
   - Why are they important for individualized instruction?
   - How can materials affect the level of appropriate instruction?

2. Describe the critical elements of a materials resource technology.
   - How well do materials represent principles of instructional technology?
   - How critical is the teacher in this technology?
   - When do materials prohibit the educational progress of handicapped persons?

3. List what can be expected and not expected from this book.
   - Are materials-selection, management, and evaluation skills specific to each category of exceptionality and each curriculum area or can they be generalized?
   - Are teaching procedures independent of materials or are they an integral part?
   - Should I use this book as an instructional text or as a reference guide?

Our society is undergoing a major change in the way handicapped persons are viewed. This change is particularly evident in their education. It will not be long before all handicapped persons are receiving educational services, many of them in mainstream education programs. The change is reflected in several forms. One of these forms is in the requirement for written individualized education programs (IEPs) resulting from the "Education of All Handicapped Children Act of 1975 (P.L. 94-142)". This requirement subjects to careful scrutiny the major elements of instruction that a handicapped person receives in any given education program. Mandated individual programming places renewed emphasis on the importance of instructional materials.

A parallel change is taking place in our economy. The emphasis on conservation of resources is having a noticeable impact on our education system. This impact is most directly evident in the availability of instructional materials. The effect on teachers is twofold: (1) they must become increasingly shrewd and judicious in how they expend what materials funds are available, and (2) more importantly, they must develop skills in using existing resources at a level that heretofore has been attained by only a handful.

Materials are a major instructional resource with which some teachers are able to achieve amazing results. What is it that these teachers do to get materials to work so well for them? Why can't all teachers learn to obtain these results? We think we have some answers to these questions in the chapters that follow.

THE IMPORTANCE OF MATERIALS

After more than sixty years of research in education, there is very little that we can unequivocably say is a critical variable affecting instruction. The one factor that is quite clear pertains to instruction time—specifically, the time that students spend working at educationally relevant tasks. The efficient use of time can be further translated into the degree to which students are allowed to work at the portions of the task on which they require the most practice. James Popham and Eva Baker (Popham & Baker, 1970) called this "the principle of appropriate practice."

Given that practice time-at-task is so critical, we need to analyze how materials play a part. Considering the school day, with lunch, recess, civic awareness, pencil sharpening, coat hanging, assembly, field trips, absences, and so on, a teacher can expect to have his or her students work an average of one and three-quarters to two hours a day at academic skills. Suppose that this teacher were a special education teacher with a lower pupil-teacher ratio (15 to 1) who taught reading, mathematics, spelling, social studies, and handwriting as academic skills. Without materials, the teacher would have to work directly with his or her pupils. Assuming that each student is at different performance levels in the five subjects, the teacher would probably have to work on a one-to-one tutorial basis. Table 1-1 depicts how much instruction time each pupil would receive without instructional materials in two hours out of a six-hour school day, assuming that more time is spent on reading, mathematics, and spelling.

This table serves to underscore how dependent we are on instructional materials, especially if we believe in individualizing instruction (Ashcroft, 1979).

Instruction time is dear, even when materials are used. The availability and use of instructional materials does not guarantee that that time will not be wasted. Many students in an average classroom can be found busily working in materials that pertain to the subject area (e.g., reading) but not to the task(s) on which they need practice. Often, materials are used in a "shotgun" approach where some of the class is working ahead of where they should be, some behind and still others will practice the same task until they are "blue in the face." Often students are practicing on the right level but with the wrong response. They may be circling misspelled words when they should be writing words from dictation. They may be practicing math facts for accuracy when speed is really critical. The efficient management of instructional materials will insure that this time is used to the benefit of the student and not just as some-

Table 1-1 Representative Time Proportions of Individual Teacher Attention per Pupil Spread Across Five Subject Areas

	Instruction Time per Subject	*Instruction Time per Student (n = 15)*
Reading	40 min.	2 min., 40 sec.
Mathematics	30 min.	2 min., 0 sec.
Spelling	20 min.	1 min., 20 sec.
Social Studies	15 min.	1 min., 0 sec.
Handwriting	15 min.	1 min., 0 sec.

thing to be filled to get both teacher and student through the day (now you may wish to try Self-Check 1-1).

A MATERIALS RESOURCE TECHNOLOGY

The technology of instructional materials development has progressed by leaps and bounds in the last two decades. Through this technology, we know how to better relate materials to the entire process of instruction (Smith, Neisworth, & Greer, 1978). There are a growing number of instruction programs that have successfully integrated critical elements of the instruction process into materials. These elements include the following, which incidentally, are now mandated by law in the form of individual education programs:

1. *Objectives*. The precise specification of what the student is expected to do, under what circumstances, and at what level of proficiency are common ingredients in many, although not in the majority of, published materials.
2. *Entry assessment*. Many programs include assessments that permit teachers to determine exactly where in the sequence of materials a student shall be placed, what prerequisite skills are necessary for beginning the program, and how students should be grouped according to their performance.
3. *Task analysis, sequencing, and synthesis*. The breaking down of skills into manageable subtasks is extremely critical to the progress of handicapped persons. The sequencing of these subtasks according to prerequisite order so one task builds upon another is also an important feature of instruction. Finally, the synthesis or combining of these subtasks to ensure that the parts sum up to equal the skill (Johnny sounds his *br* blends well but can he read any better?) is an essential feature that must be represented in materials.
4. *Programming instruction*. Techniques for ensuring that the attempts to perform a task will meet with more success than failure, particularly in the gradual removal of prompts and in the inclusion of procedures for systematically reinforcing correct performances, are key to effective use of instructional materials with handicapped persons.
5. *Progress monitoring and record keeping*. The evidence in favor of integrating assessment with practice as part of the instruction process is overwhelming. The growing use of criterion-referenced testing and recording procedures in instructional materials has instilled in teachers the notion of a different purpose for assessment than merely, "Well, how do these students stand up against last year's class?"

Self-Check 1-1

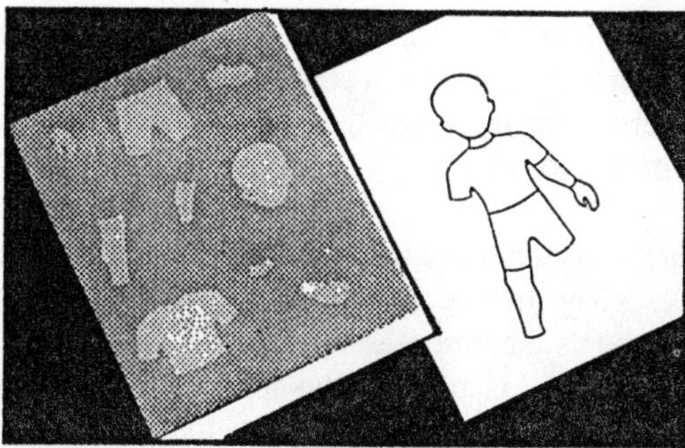

BODY CONCEPT TEMPLATE
The student's first task is to recognize and name the nine outlines on DLM's template of specific body parts. The student is then asked to draw a completely integrated body by tracing the randomly placed outlines, some of which are interchangeable.
The 8½" x 11" plastic, transparent template comes with instructions.
#209 $4.25

Description

The student's first task is to recognize and name the nine outlines on DLM's template of specific body parts. The student is then asked to draw a completely integrated body by tracing the randomly placed outlines.

Instructions

Based on this information, how can this skill be taught without using the provided materials? List as many alternatives as possible.

Response

1. ______________________________
   ____
2. ______________________________
   ____
3. ______________________________
   ____

Compare your response to the sample response in Appendix A.

Source: Reprinted from *Developmental Learning Materials Catalog* with permission of the publisher. 1977-78 by Developmental Learning Materials.

6. *Redirection of instruction.* Many materials contain provisions for alternative practice if one approach does not work. Successful use of these provisions are highly dependent upon whether the materials contain an effective progress monitoring system.

These instruction elements are repeatedly related to instructional materials decisions throughout this book. They are the basis for the materials-selection, management, and adaptation models that are presented.

Although we have seen monumental changes in the application of principles of instructional technology to instructional-materials development, there are two notes of caution. First, the teacher is the technologist (Tiemann & Markle, 1973). Materials are not the panacea that teachers often look for, the one program that will "do it all." The only potential panacea in sight is the teacher. It is the teacher who can make or break an instructional program. It is what the teacher does with instructional materials that determines the successfulness or usefulness of materials. Publishers of teaching machines and programmed instruction spent a fortune learning this fact. During the 1950s and 1960s they attempted to develop "teacher-proof" programs and found that these programs could be fouled up just as easily as could nonprogrammed materials. Teachers could also make programs highly successful when they otherwise would not have been. Teachers *must* be the programmers of materials and not the reverse.

The second note of caution is that the bulk of instructional materials still do not have the six critical elements of instruction described earlier designed into them. Many materials are merely drill and practice pages that the teacher will have to adapt, adjust, and supplement to make them useful for handicapped persons. All materials are purported to have "good things" for students, and they usually look like they do, too. In the end, it is the students' learning that determines whether materials contain "good things." However, some features in materials, such as the six listed above, permit a teacher to predict which materials may be likely to be successful. It is the skillful teacher, and not the lucky teacher, who can predict the usefulness of instructional materials. It is one of the goals of this book to provide teachers with a means of becoming skillful in selecting and retrieving, as well as adapting, instructional materials.

Do Materials Work?

Validity in materials is also an important teacher consideration. What evidence is there that materials are effective, that they produce learning in children? In the early 1970s, it was apparent that less than 1 percent of published instructional materials have been field tested (American School Board Journal, 1975). No compelling evidence suggests that this figure has changed drastically in the last few years. If the information is not available, teachers will have to consider conducting their own field tests.

Prohibitive Materials Prerequisites

With regard to the education of handicapped persons, materials can be particularly helpful or prohibitive, again depending on how they are used. By the nature of their problems, handicapped children usually lack a number of prerequisite skills, and you will find it necessary to compensate for prerequisites that are lacking in order to use many instructional materials. One of the most common prohibitive prerequisites is reading. For example, Julie must be able to read to follow the directions on how to work in a certain time-telling booklet; or, to use a prompting sentence in a spelling drill book, Harry must first be able to read the sentence. Following directions is another problem. Ms. James demonstrates a direction for a workbook exercise and the children begin work but find that directions vary from page to page in this book. Seigfried Englemann (1970) noted that many children who are having trouble finishing their school work are actually able to accomplish the task but they are uncertain which task they are expected to accomplish.

Materials Can Repeat Patiently

Prohibitive prerequisites either must be taught to handicapped students or must be circumvented because materials are so important to them. Handicapped students often require more repetitive practice than do nonhandicapped children on these prerequisites. Materials, particularly media-supported materials, are infinitely more patient for this repetitive practice than is the average teacher. The same instructional stimulus will come out of the spirit duplicating machine (in good working order) every time the work-sheet master is run through it. When using materials, repetition of instruction does not wax and wane with a headache, a cold, or even an argument with a spouse the evening before the school day. (Now try Self-Check 1-2 on circumventing prohibitive prerequisites.)

Materials Aid in Mainstreaming

Instructional materials are also important because they must often serve as a bridge between special-class instruction and mainstreaming efforts. Special- and regular-class teachers have very little time to work directly together. Instructional materials must often serve as a substitute. However, materials will be a poor substitute if the student is unfamiliar with them or if they are so

Self-Check 1-2

NAME ______________________________

The two words above each set of sentences sound alike, but they do not have the same meanings. Pick the word that correctly completes each sentence. Write the word in the blank.

ads **adds**

1. A store owner ______ up how much money she makes.

2. Mary Jo looked in the newspaper for ______ about dogs.

Description

To complete the work sheet shown above, the student must first read and comprehend the directions and then match the correct verb to each sentence.

Instructions

You are given two possible alternative instructions a teacher may use to aid the learner. State three or more.

Response

1. *Read directions aloud to student(s).*
2. *Give an example of work to be done.*
3. ______________________________
4. ______________________________
5. ______________________________

Sample response can be found in Appendix A.

Source: Reprinted from Skilpak for *Inside Out* of the Reading 720 series by Theodore Clymer and others by permission of the publisher. Copyright, 1976, by Ginn and Company (Xerox Corporation)

different in format from what the student is used to. Skills do not necessarily transfer across materials. To expect a handicapped student to perform well in new materials simply because they pertain to the same task is leaving mainstreaming efforts open for failure. As a first step to mainstreaming, the transfer of students' daily work to materials used in the regular classroom must be carefully and systematically programmed. The teacher who is skillful in materials programming will be successful in achieving mainstreaming goals.

Individualized Instruction and Materials

Much has been written about the importance of individualized instruction. Some educators have indicated that materials are important to individualized instruction mainly because children are different. In fact, that is the single most conclusive finding from the years of research on individual differences. Similarly, with the research on teacher characteristics, such as personality, little was learned about teaching except that teachers differ in their personalities and in other facets. But what is the application to instructional materials? Should one match materials characteristics to inherent individual differences or to teachers' personality styles? Is that the essence of individualized instruction?

A growing body of educators view individualized instruction differently. Instead of a singular focus on the learner and his or her inherent characteristics or the materials and their inherent characteristics, many believe it is the interaction between teacher, materials, and learner that is critical to individualized instruction. Poor materials and a failing learner can be offset by good teaching practices (Figure 1-1, top). Likewise, a lack of teacher time to devote to individual learners can be compensated for by carefully sequenced interactive materials and a motivated learner (Figure 1-1, bottom). For this reason the techniques of a materials technology do not focus on materials and their characteristics alone, the types of learners to be dealt with, or particular attributes that the teacher may have. Instead, these techniques are intended to assist in increasing or improving the interaction between:

Teacher ——— *and* ——— Materials
(selecting, adapting)

Teacher ——— *and* ——— Learner
(integrating direct instruction with materials)

Learner ——— *and* ——— Materials
(evaluating materials)

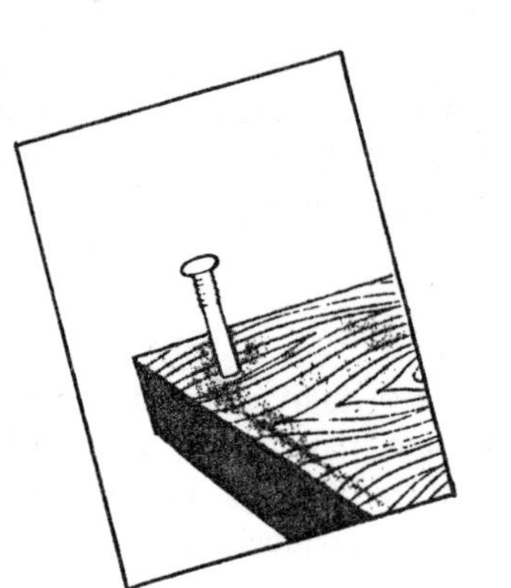

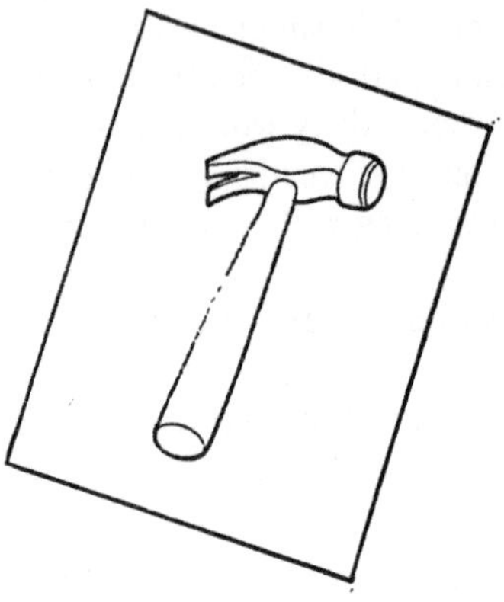

Example A: Flash Cards

SOUNDS

TASK 1 Teaching p as in pat

a. Point to **p.** **My turn. When I touch it, I'll say it.** (Pause.)
Touch **p** for an instant, saying: **p.** Do not say **puuh.**

b. Point to **p.** **Your turn. When I touch it, you say it.** (Pause.)
Get ready. Touch **p.** *p.*

c. Again. Touch **p.** *p.*

d. Repeat *c* until firm.

Example B: Page—Highly Scripted

Figure 1-1. *Examples of Minimally and Highly Programmed Materials*

Source A: Reprinted from *DLM Motor Expressive Cards I* with permission of the publisher. Copyright 1969 by Developmental Learning Materials.
Source B: Reprinted from *Distar Reading, I* by Siegfried Englemann and Elaine C. Bruner with permission of the publisher. Copyright 1974, 1969, Science Research Associates, Inc.

WHAT TO EXPECT FROM THIS BOOK

Generalizable Skills

Materials can be treated in many ways when they pertain to the instruction of handicapped persons. One may decide to examine materials according to how they are used with different handicapping conditions. Another way may be to classify materials according to certain features such as their motivation level or their colorfulness. Curriculum subject area, such as reading, mathematics, language development, and daily living skills, is another approach to the grouping and analyzing of materials. Some writers have attempted to treat materials with respect to an important trend in education such as individualized instruction or mainstreaming.

All of the above possibilities have merit. Some materials must be treated differently for certain handicapped persons, particularly those who have sensory deficits such as a visual impairment or deafness. In many cases some materials have more appeal than others. Curriculum areas such as reading often contain unique requisites for instructional materials that may not be apparent in other subjects. Changing trends in education are placing new demands on instructional materials.

It would have been quite appealing to succumb to one of these approaches in writing this book. It would have made the task much simpler. However, the goals set for this book do not permit us to focus on any one of these approaches. Any single viewpoint listed above would not permit the preparation of a comprehensive procedural text on materials. Although handicapped persons differ in types of handicapping conditions, there is more similarity than difference when one considers basic principles governing the way they learn. This premise is supported by the cross-categorical trend in service delivery and teacher-training programs.

Although certain physical features of materials are important, it is our conviction that the primary focus in analyzing materials should be on the handicapped child and the teacher who uses those materials. Although understanding that curriculum subjects are unique, we again suggest that the similarities, followed by the differences, are important for a focus on materials. Recognizing that individualized instruction and mainstreaming are trends to which materials can contribute, we are also aware that these are not ends in themselves. They must be viewed as a means to achieving other outcomes that are best stated in terms of learner performance.

In their book on *Instructional Materials for Exceptional Children*, Anderson, Greer, and Odle (1978) allude to a materials technology being available. This book focuses specifically on illustrating the use of that technology. The development of a materials resource technology requires a generic viewpoint regarding the tools of this technology. It is our belief that it is more effective and efficient to acquire materials-selection, management, and evaluation skills that span across handicapping conditions, types of materials, curriculum areas, and trends in education than it is to confine skill acquisition to a single focus (Self-Check 1-3 illustrates material adaptability to different disabilities).

Methods and Techniques

Much of the information regarding instructional materials either surveys the broad spectrum of materials or provides isolated pieces of substantive information that may not be easy to pull together. Consequently, preservice and inservice teachers learn to do little more from this information than to peruse materials. Seldom do they learn anything about what to *do* with materials (Brown, 1975).

In explaining a materials resource technology, this book does not attempt to survey materials. Instead, it concentrates on what to *do* with materials. In this sense it is a methods book. Although it deals with materials in a variety of curriculum areas, it is not a book on curriculum content. It is designed to be a bridge between teaching procedures and curriculum content. Materials are the substantive representative of curriculum content. Thus the teacher must have the skills to select, manipulate, augment, and supplement materials to meet that responsibility. He or she must be able to (a) select and retrieve materials that are best able to represent the content, (b) manage the effective and efficient use of available materials, (c) adapt or modify materials that are not being used effectively or efficiently, and (d) evaluate materials to determine their exact contribution to the achievement of learning objectives.

WHAT NOT TO EXPECT FROM THIS BOOK

A Materials List

Other textual materials, resource centers, and computer retrieval systems provide lists of materials. We discuss such resources in later chapters and provide information so you may have access to them. Because our focus is on what a teacher may do with materials, we believe the following chapters must be devoted to that goal.

A Survey of Materials

Information surveys allow people to become familiar with topics or sets of skills but not proficient in them. Our aim is to provide information and exam-

Self-Check 1-3

The Abacus

The abacus is ruled into four 'columns'. Each of these represents a power of the base of the number scale that is being used. As will be seen from the diagram below, the powers, reading from right to left are the zeroeth, first, second and third:

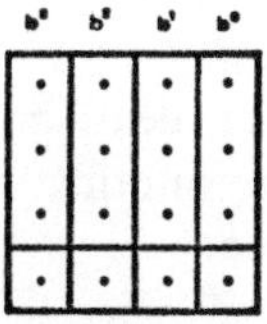

b^3 b^2 b^1 b^0

1000 100 10 1

If work is in the denary scale, that is, the number scale to the base of 10, the columns represent values as follows:

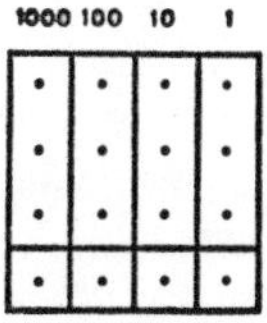

The ruled line at the foot of the abacus indicates the position of the 'answer'.

Instructions

List the necessary changes and adaptations to be made (if any) in order for handicapped learners to use the abacus.

Response

As a calculation aid.

1. Learning disabled ____________________

2. Physically handicapped ____________________

3. Blind or visually impaired ____________________

4. Deaf or hearing impaired ____________________

Compare your response to the sample response in Appendix A.

Source: Reprinted from *Using the 'Invicta Abacus' in Relation to Calculation* by L.G.W. Sealey with permission of the publisher. Copyright 1971, Invicta Plastics, LTD.

ples that are concentrated enough to permit teachers to begin to become proficient in the tools of a materials resource technology.

A Litany of Categories of Exceptionality

This book does not contain chapters for the blind, deaf, physically handicapped, and so on. Chapter 11, however, provides information on applying generic materials skills to different groups of children.

A Rehash of Outdated Information

Except for a brief materials center history, this book refrains from describing materials projects that, although they are interesting, may not be accessible by teachers or useful to them. When materials projects and programs are described, we strive to include only those that are currently available and accessible.

HOW THIS BOOK IS ORGANIZED

This book is organized in three major sections, each of which pertains to what teachers need to do regarding the preparation of materials for instruction or the use of materials in instruction. Because the skills are divided by section, those presented should not be regarded as discrete from one another, nor should they be viewed as what is to be done sequentially.

Section I: Selecting and Retrieving Materials

A wealth of instructional materials currently on the market may potentially be useful in the education of handicapped persons. Much has been done to develop systems for collecting and distributing materials. These systems vary a great deal in their accessibility by teachers. Many options are open to teachers for getting access to materials. The most effective of these options are explored.

The acquisition or purchase of instructional materials, whether by the classroom teacher or by the local or state education agency, will, in all likelihood, continue to be constrained by the reality of limited funds. Such monumental contraints have a potential for affecting classroom learning adversely unless precautionary steps are taken to ensure wise investments. Careful planning and selection of materials appears to be the most promising method for ensuring that an adequate, although possibly Spartan, array of useful materials is available to the teacher. Several activities to be undertaken before purchasing new materials are presented. For example, taking an inventory of accessible materials and available resources for acquiring materials (whether on loan or permanently) are the preliminary steps to purchasing materials. Guidelines for a functional approach to collecting, inventorying, and gaining an overall picture of the available materials and their quality are provided.

The application of materials selection, retrieval, and budgeting for differing classroom conditions as well as selected curriculum areas is also explored. Variables, such as readability of materials and the ability of paraprofessionals to understand and use the materials, are examined as additional selection variables.

Section II: Managing Instructional Materials

In the past, *classroom management* has usually referred to the means whereby teachers sought to establish and maintain acceptable pupil deportment. This somewhat constricted view of classroom management ignores the significant academic as well as social benefits derived from a more comprehensive management strategy. Indeed, careful attention to the planning and managing of diverse classroom components such as the physical arrangement of each area of the classroom and the scheduling of groups versus individuals for instruction, coupled with a variety of different reinforcement contingencies for each learner, has the potential to yield greater gains than does attention to other factors.

This section develops a range of alternative tactics for managing instructional materials systematically and is intended to increase the overall effectiveness of instructing exceptional learners. The importance of the learning sequence as a standard for relating materials to instruction, as well as the relationship between measurement, instruction, and instructional materials, is explored. The intercorrelation of materials with the various stages of instruction is demonstrated through a sample materials-management system. The system proposed in this section is intended to provide the precision of a diagnostic-prescriptive program, yet promote enough flexibility so teachers can bring to bear all resources in the education of handicapped children.

Teachers implement many well-designed materials with every intention of using them appropriately only to find that the ongoing daily hustle and bustle of the average classroom can rapidly erode the fidelity of that use. Daily materials-management strategies and tactics for helping teachers remain faithful to their intentions are also presented in this section, along with a discussion of classroom design and organization to use materials better. Finally, adaptations of these materials-management procedures to specialized situations are presented.

Section III: Adapting Instructional Materials

Teacher-education institutions have apparently done a less-than-adequate job of educating teachers in the importance of field testing during development. One publisher of special education materials with a WATS line for teachers recently stated that "of the hundreds of inquiry calls I have received from teachers regarding my products, only one or two have asked anything about the research or field testing done on them."

The basic questions of significance to any user of instructional materials are "For whom are these intended?" and "How well do they do what they are intended to do?" Evidence that the materials used in the prescribed fashion do lead to predictable changes in student's educational performance is actually preliminary to managing and adapting instructional materials. This section presents a rationale for posing the right questions regarding the validity of instructional materials with respect to saving time and money and toward promoting teacher effectiveness. Besides providing the reader with appropriate questions to ask, such as "What does the author claim for these materials?" and "How were they validated?" a straightforward approach for interpreting these questions in light of the individual teacher's needs is presented.

The best evidence of how useful or appropriate instructional materials may be for any given teacher, classroom, or group of students can be obtained by teacher evaluation of one or two students as they use the materials in daily work. The value of this form of evaluation is a major theme advocated in this book. Means by which teachers may acquire materials for trial periods are explained in earlier chapters. This section presents a precise and straightforward plan for assessing instructional materials within the classroom.

Many instructional materials, with slight modification or supplementation, can be easily adapted for use with handicapped learners. Chapter 2 presents evaluation strategies that are designed to coordinate with later chapters on child-based materials evaluation and on adaptation. Decisions regarding what to adapt and whether a set of instructional materials is even worth adapting are also explored.

Applications of materials management and adaptation to specialized situations pertain to factors such as increasing the potential for student assistance, adjusting physical arrangements of rooms to accommodate multimedia materials better, and scheduling arrangements to increase practice time. Applications of materials management for teachers of severely handicapped persons pertain to the employment of systems to monitor progress across a variety of daily living skills and to adapt materials designed for moderately handicapped persons so they may be used with severely handicapped persons.

CHAPTER ORGANIZATION

The chapters are organized in this book to serve two purposes. First, a reader may use the chapter content as an instructional material to acquire skill in materials-selection management or adaptation. Second, the reader may use the book as a quick reference guide regarding specific problems that occur in using materials.

For organizational purposes, each chapter contains objectives at the beginning of the chapter. Periodically through the chapters, self-checks using hypothetical exemplary situations help the reader determine the extent of his or her understanding of critical portions of the chapter content. Wherever possible, materials checklists and other forms are included to assist the teacher in transferring materials-selection, management, and evaluation skills to classroom use.

For purposes of quick reference and as an aid in problem solving, the questions at the beginning of each chapter serve as an outline of the content of each chapter or as a "trouble shooting" guide to help readers determine whether the information contained in the chapter pertains to a particular problem of interest. The appendix contains three additional types of information: (1) sample answers to chapter self-check exercises, (2) materials-selection, management-adaptation, and evaluation forms that may be duplicated for classroom use, and (3) selected materials references and resources.

I
Selection and Retrieval

CHAPTER 2

Selecting Appropriate Instructional Materials

Objectives

1. Identify critical instructional variables important to the selection of instructional materials.
- What measurement variables help determine whether a material is appropriate for an individual prescription?
- What planning activities must be carried out before materials can be systematically selected?
- How do decisions about the types of teaching formats to be used depend on the types of materials available or to be selected?

2. Select appropriate materials for an entire class of learners.
- What must I know about the curriculum I am responsible to teach before I can select materials for my class?
- What must I know about the materials I already have available before I can select materials for my class?
- Can I select appropriate materials sight unseen? What information sources are there?
- How do I go about thoroughly reviewing materials?
- Can I organize the information I accumulate about materials for easy access and later use?

3. Select materials that are appropriate for an individual prescription.
- Where do I get an individual prescription?
- How do I go about matching the information I have on the learner with the information I have on the materials?

A recent publication indicated that there are over 300,000 commercially produced instructional materials available (Ashcroft, 1979). Many of these materials are potentially related to the educational needs of handicapped persons. How does a teacher cope with this overwhelming array? With a limited supply budget, it is imperative that teachers develop and use means of selecting materials that are the most beneficial to his or her learners in the most needed areas of the curriculum.

A number of strategies have been presented to aid teachers in the selection process. Some are thorough to the point of having little practical utility because of the immense amount of time involved. Other selection strategies are terse to the point of providing little information. Be assured that there is a complete array between these two extremes. Important materials-selection considerations are embodied in most of these strategies (Ensminger, 1970; Wiederholt & McNutt, 1977; Standard Criteria.., 1977). Deciding on a materials-selection strategy depends upon one's ability to identify the most important factors in sound instructional practice. It is only logical that the criteria one must judge materials against are at least the same criteria that one must judge good instruction against. There are direct and obvious criteria and there are peripheral criteria. At first look, all of these criteria appear to be of equal importance. This is definitely not the case. To treat them equally would produce a monumental task. Since the time that teachers can devote to analyzing, critiquing, and selecting materials is limited, it becomes imperative to sort out the most important from the peripheral criteria.

The two major questions to be answered about materials are (1) what will do the job and (2) what is practical to use. Assuming that the job is to teach a learner to perform a skill, we must identify the most useful criteria for helping us decide whether the material will do the job. The most useful criteria can be drawn from the literature on teaching, learning, and curriculum design. Writers such as Ralph Tyler, Robert Gagne, B.F. Skinner, and James Popham have repeatedly laid down principles for effective teaching and learning. It is only logical that these principles should be reflected in the materials one uses in teaching. These principles relate to three areas of instruction—planning, measurement, and direct teaching—and each can be well represented or poorly represented by materials.

PRINCIPLES OF TEACHING AND LEARNING LEADING TO CRITERIA FOR SELECTING MATERIALS

Planning

Objectives

The need to specify precisely what learner performance is expected is gaining common acceptance in education. In special education, this principle is part of law (P.L. 94-142) and is embodied in the short-term objectives of an individualized education plan. When a teacher knows exactly what a learner is to do, under what conditions, and to what level of competence, he or she has three powerful tools for gauging the usefulness of materials.

Sequence

What comes first and what comes next are two decisions for which a teacher must have an organized plan of attack. Many skills, such as those used in mathematics, require prerequisites that must be taught first. Other skills, such as spelling or sight word recognition, contain so many items that they must be broken down into manageable units or subskills. One point about sequencing is that a subskill or step in the sequence should be mastered by the learner. This may seem to be an obvious statement but it often goes unheeded. The sequencing of materials gives teachers some of the greatest headaches.

Redirect

With the emphasis of objectives on the learner and on task mastery, greater planning time must now be placed on solving the problem of what happens when instruction does not work. We cannot be satisfied with one pass through a skill area and say that whatever the learner picks up is his or her lookout. We have two redirection options: repeat instruction or change instruction. The decision between the two is extremely important. Various materials supply both options or one option but many materials supply neither.

Measurement

Initial Assessment

To decide which objectives to teach, we must know which objectives have and have not been previously met. An increasing tendency on the part of the modern teacher is to rely on tests that have a close correspondence between test items and teaching objectives. The use of criterion-referenced tests have substantially increased the teacher's ability to pinpoint learner entry levels and place them appropriately in instructional sequences.

Progress Monitoring

The decision regarding how well instruction is going should not be after the fact. How much time a child spends on a given task should be dependent upon his or her progress. To make these decisions, a teacher must use sensitive and frequent measures of progress. Some materials have progress tests embedded within the sequence; others do not.

Mastery Assessment

The ultimate measurement function is to determine whether the learner is competent, possibly proficient, and has maintained this level regarding a given skill. Many materials supply mastery tests. Seldom is review or maintenance assessment systematically built into materials.

Direct Teaching

Appropriate Practice

Regardless of the instruction format or method, the learner should be given the opportunity to practice the behavior specified in the objective. No matter what the teacher does or what the material does, it is how much time the learner gets to work at the task that counts. This is probably the single most important materials-selection variable.

Reinforcement

By far the most empirically documented instruction tactics relate to the reinforcement of desired behavior. Reinforcement tactics are difficult to build into an instructional material. However, some programs do provide supportive materials for systematizing reinforcement.

Prompting

Various prompting techniques that reduce errors and serve to lead a learner gradually to respond under the conditions of the terminal objective have been developed and empirically tested. Many of these techniques have been programmed into materials. In some cases teachers must employ these techniques in the adaptation of materials. Self-Check 2-1 provides the reader with the opportunity to examine the relationship between these instructional variables and materials.

Self-Check 2-1

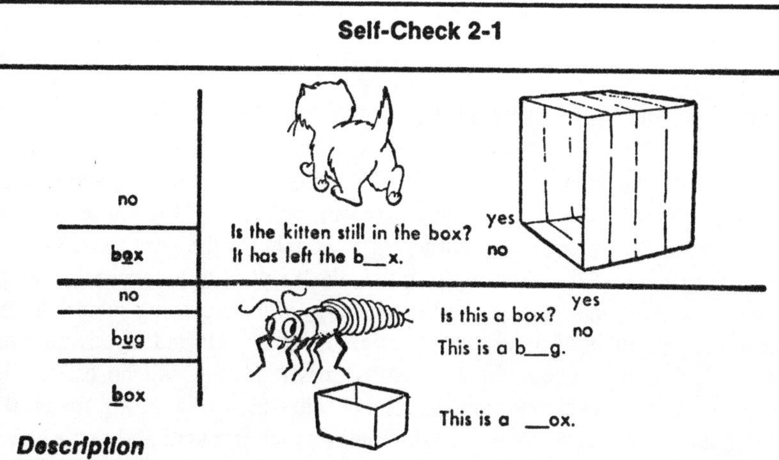

Description

Programmed Reading consists primarily of 21 programmed books and a teacher's manual. A test places students at the beginning of different readers and end-of-book tests for each of the 21 books. A student who meets the criterion (95% correct) goes to the next book; a student who does not starts the book over again. Behaviors that are to be performed in the program are precisely stated. There is careful, step-by-step programming of subskills. New tasks are slowly and systematically introduced. Reading responses consist of learners circling printed words that match with pictures or writing in missing letters for words. A correct response is acknowledged by the learner checking his answers (slides a mask down the left side of the page). Each frame has cues or hints to ensure that the learner makes the correct response.

Instructions

From the information given above, circle *only* the instruction elements listed below that you do not think are well represented here and indicate why.

Response Instruction Elements

Objectives ____

Sequence ____

Redirect ____

Initial assessment ____________________________________

Progress monitoring ___________________________________

Mastery assessment ___________________________________

Appropriate practice __________________________________

Reinforcement _______________________________________

Prompting ____

Compare your response with the sample response in Appendix A.

GROUP MATERIALS SELECTION

The procedures detailed in this section of the chapter are for the teacher who is selecting materials to set up a new classroom, trying to fill in some gaps in the current year's instruction, or reordering materials for the next year. Often, teachers of handicapped children are given the responsibility for organizing new programs. This includes selecting, ordering, and purchasing materials on a limited budget. In both cases the materials must be selected in advance of having any knowledge about the learners with whom they will be used. Although it seems the most important information needed for selecting materials is missing, this is the most common situation in which teachers find themselves for selecting materials. Many guidelines are available to aid in this process, and some are described below.

Group materials selection

1. Examine (or develop) a scope and sequence of subjects taught in your class.
2. Inventory classroom materials.
3. Review and critique materials presently in the classroom.
4. Pinpoint material needs.
5. Complete preliminary selection.
   a. Study catalogues and brochures (Chapter 3).
   b. Use available information retrieval system summaries (Chapter 3).
   c. Examine textual resources.
6. Determine if a purchase can be made at this point (if yes, go to 8; if no, go to 7).
7. Obtain and critique actual materials.
   a. Through local materials centers.
   b. Through other teachers (see teacher interview).
   c. Through loan by publisher representatives.
   d. Through trial approval (usually ten days to two weeks). From the publisher.
8. Match selection information with budget information (Chapter 4).
9. Set priorities and decide whether to purchase now or store for later reference.
10. Purchase material.
11. Store information (see Figure 2-1).

SCOPE AND SEQUENCE—WHAT YOU TEACH

Before looking at new materials acquisitions, the thoughtful teacher first examines what skills must be taught, what materials are already available to teach

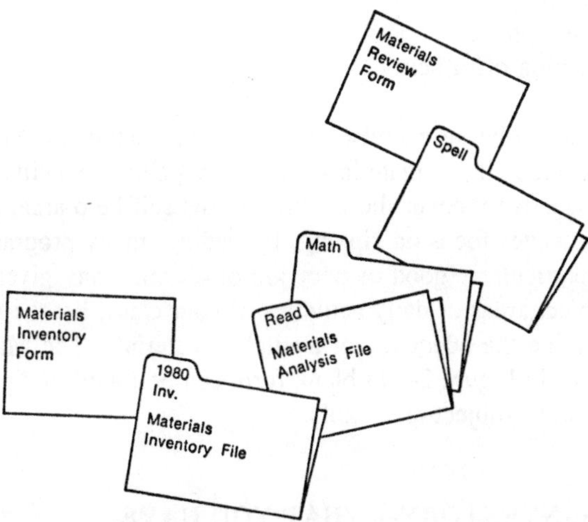

Figure 2-1. *Materials-Analysis File Including Materials Inventory, Review, and Budget Information*

those skills, and what the greatest materials needs are. To accomplish this, the teacher must have listed at least the major skills in each subject area to be taught. For instance, in reading, major skill areas may be:

- Sound-symbol relationships
- Word attack
- Sight word recognition
- Oral reading
- Comprehension

Often it is preferable to have these skills broken down further, either by subskills or by levels. The main purpose is to try to cover the range of skills that will be taught for the year. In some skill areas such as those taught to the moderately to severely handicapped, the skills must be broken down further:

Dressing
- Putting on-taking off underwear
- Putting on-taking off pants or dress
- Putting on-taking off shirt or blouse
- Putting on-taking off coat
- Putting on-taking off socks
- Putting on-taking off shoes
- Shoe tying-untying

- Zipping-unzipping
- Snapping-unsnapping
- Putting on-taking off a belt

This is not meant to be an exercise in detailed task analyses. Skills should be listed in enough detail so materials can be matched to skills to determine whether they effectively cover those skills. In the self-help area, self-contained instructional packages focus on zipping. In reading, many programs span skills but may do a particularly good or poor job of teaching any given skill. So for each of the subject areas or daily activities of your class, list the skills that will help you determine the adequacy of available materials. The Materials Inventory Form shown in Figure 2-3 (a blank form can be found in Appendix B) has a column for listing subject-area skills.

MATERIALS INVENTORY—WHAT YOU HAVE

At first glance it may seem that some classrooms are so ill-equipped that an inventory would yield nothing. Unless it is new, a classroom usually contains several materials. They may be stashed away in a closet and covered, or they may be something not thought of as instructional material. A carefully conducted inventory of these materials will assist in the following ways: (1) it will provide a clear picture, through a permanent record, of what materials one does and does not have for a given skill; (2) it will help avoid purchasing unnecessary new materials; (3) it may bring to light old materials that, at the time, had no use, were stuck away, and now fill an instruction need (e.g., Figure 2-2); and (4) it provides the teacher with a start on a list of materials that needs only to be updated when new materials are acquired.

The inventory may be completed all at once, say, on an inservice day, or it may be filled out one subject at a time after school. All materials for that subject must first be located. As each material is examined, several decisions must be made. First, its title or name must be entered beside the skill(s) that it teaches (see Figure 2-3). At this point you are not evaluating the materials; you are simply listing what you have for a particular skill. Evaluation will come next. If the material teaches several of the skills in succession, just abbreviate the title beside the next skills. Second, write down the storage location for each material so it can be easily found. Third, enter other materials you have for each skill. Four places have been allowed on the form for any given skill. The next two columns on the form—"Analysis Showed Them Useful?" and "Materials Pinpoint Need?"—are for later use after you have critiqued the materials.

Enter all types of materials including comprehensive programs, kits, teacher-

TEACHING
ARITHMETIC
to Young
Children

Figure 2-2. *Example of a Potentially Useful Material That an Inventory May Uncover*

Source: *Teaching Arithmetic to Young Children* by Abraham Feingold with permission of the publisher. Copyright 1965, John Day Book Company.

MATERIALS INVENTORY FORM

Subject Area Reading

Curriculum Sequence	Material #1	Location	Material #2	Location	Material #3	Location	Analysis Showed Them Useful?	Material Pinpoint Need?
Word Attack	1) vowel cards	bottom file cabinet drawer	1) programmed Reading books 1–27	back shelf	1) Basic Reading	wall shelf		
Sound Symbol	2) Distar Reading I	back shelf	2) Basic Reading	wall shelf	2) Ideal consonant and vowel cards	bottom File Cabinet drawer		
Compre-hension	3) Reading Spectrum Series	wall shelf	3) Basic Reading	wall shelf	3) Teacher Worksheet 13.A	2nd File Cabinet drawer		
Sight Words	4) Basic Reading	wall shelf	4) phrase word cards	bottom File cabinet drawer	—			
Oral Reading	—		—		—			

Figure 2-3. *Examples of Materials Inventoried by Subject Area*

made materials, work sheets, drill pages, flash cards, and manipulatives. Remember, this is something you will have to do only once. From the first time on, all you have to do is update the inventory.

REVIEW AND ANALYZE AVAILABLE MATERIALS

Can these materials help me teach what I want to teach? This is probably the most important decision regarding selection that a teacher can make. To make this decision a teacher must be able quickly and systematically to evaluate materials and must be able to refer back to these evaluations. Many critique forms and procedures have been devised for evaluating materials. In boiling down the multitude of factors involved in reviewing and analyzing materials for use in our file system (see Figure 2-1), two principles take precedence. First, the most important variables regarding instructional materials are those that relate directly to instruction. Second, practicality considerations demand that it be possible to review and analyze each material in from 5 to 15 minutes depending upon the material. This does not suggest that teachers should not do a more careful review of some materials. They should, particularly those that have some probability of being used.

We chose the standard file folder as our basic format for collecting materials-reviews and analyses. The main reason for this choice is its flexibility. Folders can be easily added to or replaced; information is economized so it can be quickly referred to, and if the teacher prefers, materials can be sorted by analysis factors and transferred to card sort systems.

Throughout the remainder of this chapter and succeeding chapters, this main review and analysis procedure is developed. Variations to it and supplements are also illustrated but the basic format as laid out in this section is addressed.

This Materials Review Form (Figures 2-4 and 2-5) and set of procedures represent evaluative factors adapted from Educational Products Information Exchange Reports (EPIE), the National Media Materials Center for Severely Handicapped Persons (Menhusen, McGonigel, Alexander, Smith, Tremblay, Carruthers, Griffin, Grafton & McClure), and other sources. A blank materials review form is provided in Appendix B.

The top third of the front side (Figure 2-4) of the review form is for noting general information regarding where to locate the material, its purpose, including the date reviewed, the subject area, age or grade level, and whether the program is comprehensive (intended to teach an entire subject area), across skills (teaches to several skills within a subject area), or single skill (teaches one skill, subskill or task within a subject area).

For many materials there is not just one cost; there are several costs, and each must be considered.

Title " Lunch Box " Subject Hand writing Date Reviewed 7/79

Publisher Science Research assoc. Level 2nd - 3rd grade ? Scope: Comprehensive ___

Address 259 E. Erie st., Chicago, IL 60611 Across Skills ___

Brief Description Cursive letter and word writing Single Skill X

Costs: (See Chapter 4)

Initial cost $49.00 Comment (Are the cost factors within reason?)
cost per student $49.00 divided by # of students

Replacement cost $49.00?
portion consumable (%) ___
portion reusable (%) 100 if overlaps are used

Initial cost low? NO high for a simple skill

Replacement cost low? NO

Hidden costs? yes must replace all material?

Time Involved:

(A) Time to complete in program (estimated)
weeks 10-15 days ___

(B) Daily time required
of teacher 5 min? of learner 20 min?

Comment will have to frequently inspect student's work

Other:

Response(s) required in the material Trace and copy letters, numbers, words

Prerequisites required ___

Student ability to use media equipment None required

Comment (prohibitive learner prerequisite?) Seems to yes, if learner can manipulate writing instrument

Preparation:

Initial preparation/training involved None

Daily preparation involved ___

Preparing materials None

Comment (Are you willing to expend the effort required?)
yes

Physical Characteristics:

(A) Media/hardware required.....NONE
available.....___
obtainable.....___
non-obtainable.....___
alternatives?.....___
service warranty?.....___
local service?.....___
can get on loan?.....___
requires special training?___

(B) Duplication required.....NONE
mimeo.....___
xerox.....___

(C) Extra materials required.....NONE
locate.....___
make.....___

(D) Sensory mode required
visual.....X
auditory.....___
tactual.....___
olfactory/gustatory.....___

(E) Safety
toxic.....N/A
non-toxic.....___

(F) Durability of manipulatives
durable.....X
non-durable.....___

Comment (Are there prohibititive physical characteristics?) ___
easily lost - must have system to keep track of cards when the period is finished.

Figure 2-4. *General Characteristics of a Material as Noted on the Front Side of the Materials Review Form*

Instructional Characteristics:

Format

	Self Instruction	One to One Tutoral	Small Group	Group
Initial Instruction	___	___	___	___
Drill and Practice	X	___	___	___
Enrichment	___	___	___	___

Comment Left open to teacher

Planning

1. Objectives: specific___ general___ not stated X
   Comment Tracing and writing manuscript and cursive letters, numerals and words!
   (Do the stated or implied objectives match your intent for the materials?)

2. Sequence: complete___ gaps X not determinable___
   Comment whole letter practice
   (Is the sequence thorough and in logical order?)

3. Redirection: can recycle___ can vary instruction___
   no redirection specified X
   Comment massed practice

Measurement

4. Initial assessment: placement___ pretest___
   no initial assessment X
   Comment maybe able to use the progress assessment as a pretest-?

5. Progress assessment: daily ? weekly___
   summary chart or graph___ none specified___
   Comment just circle letters mastered no criteria!

6. Mastery assessment: same as initial assessment___
   same as progress assessment X
   new assessment___
   no mastery assessment___
   Comment definitely!
   (Are you going to have to supply another assessment?)

Direct Teaching

7. Appropriate practice: all pupil work is appropriate___
   some pupil work is appropriate ?
   no pupil work is appropriate___
   Comment just massed drill

8. Reinforcement: general instructions___
   specific instructions___
   none specified X
   Comment definitely!
   (Are you going to have to design and implement your own reinforcement?)

9. Prompting: errorless responding possible___
   fading of prompts
   no prompts provided X
   Comment almost no instructions

10. Amount of adaptation required (number of characteristics) 7

Field Test Results:

Subjective	1	expert appraisal..............	___
	2	publisher testimonials.........	___
	3	teacher testimonials..........	___
	4	marketing research............	___
	5	no field tests reported........	X
	6	individual learner verification	___
	7	one group field tests (pre--post-tests).............	___
	8	controlled study comparing one material to another........	___
	9	controlled study comparing material to objectives (validation research)..........	___
Objective	10	performance warranty..........	___

Figure 2-5. *Instructional Characteristics of a Material as Noted on Side Two of the Materials Review Form*

Initial cost may be the only expenditure you will make if the material is reusable and can be used with several students. This is the total purchase price of one set.

Cost per student is another way of determining cost. Divide the number of students who will be using the material into the total cost of the materials. This will provide a cost-use factor that will help determine if the cost will be worth the purchase. Also, if a program can be used for, say, up to five years, the total cost could also be divided by the number of years of use.

Replacement cost per student refers to what portion of the material is consumable—will be used up by the students—and what it will cost to replace that portion for each student. When the larger proportion of the materials is reusable; then replacement costs may be minimal.

Whether or not the initial costs or replacement costs are low depends upon the benefit the material will provide against its cost. This consideration is discussed further in Chapter 4.

Hidden costs are additional costs that teachers may often foresee at the time of purchase. Calculators require batteries, loose materials require containers or organizers, and so on. Try to project whether the material is completely self-contained or whether you may have to supply something additional. Hidden costs are discussed in more detail in Chapter 4.

Remember, the form shown in Figures 2-4 and 2-5 is designed for flexibility of use. Record as little as necessary in each category. An X or a check (√), a yes or a no, or a single word or phrase are often sufficient. You must be able to come back to the form later and quickly scan it to obtain the information you need. This form is simply a composite description of the salient portions of a material based on what the publisher states and on what your inspection reveals. You will often have to make assumptions, estimations, and downright guesses about some categories. In these cases, follow your responses with a question mark (e.g., see the item on replacement cost in Figure 2-4.)

The next section of the form (''Preparation'') helps assess the teacher effort involved in training to use the material and in preparing materials.

The section of the analysis form entitled ''Time Involved'' helps teachers estimate what will be required in scheduling and teaching time, how long it will take to complete the program, and how much daily teaching time is involved.

The section entitled ''Other'' pertains to reviewer notations of learner responses (e.g., write letters, say words, sort chips, and so on), what learner prerequisites are necessary to begin the program or manipulation of media (e.g., operate a tape player or teaching machine).

The last section of the front side provides information on the physical characteristics of the material. It allows the teacher to assess what media, duplication, extra material, special sensory mode, and safety considerations pertain to those materials. Self-Check 2-2 allows you to check your understanding of the front side of the form.

The back side (Figure 2-5) of the Materials Review Form gets down to cases regarding the instructional qualifications of a material. The planning, measurement, and direct teaching components that are critical to sound instruction are assessed in this section.

Under "Format," the type of grouping and the stage of instruction are checked. *Self-instruction* pertains to materials that a child must practice on without constant teacher attention. Often these materials are placed in "desk-work" or "seat-work" activities while the teacher moves from student to student. *One-to-one tutorial materials* are those in which a teacher must work with one child constantly. *Small group* refers to a program in which the teacher interacts with a group of from three to five (seldom more) learners. *Group interaction* refers to a program in which the teacher lectures, discusses, or carries out other instruction with an entire class of learners.

The *stage of instruction* refers to the instructional purpose of the material. *Initial instruction* pertains to materials designed for learners who have little or no responses (in regard to the objectives) in their repertoire. *Drill and practice materials* are for learners who can demonstrate the desired response but are not at a level of proficiency. *Enrichment materials* are for learners who have mastered an objective but are in need of a broader range of application. This section may contain one X or several, depending upon the nature of the material reviewed. The Lunch Box program appears to be primarily drill and practice to be used during desk-work activities.

Planning

Objectives

— *Specific:* A behavioral statement regarding what the learner will do as a result of instruction.

"Pupils will write the numerals 1 through 10."

— *General:* Not stated in behavioral terms, may even not refer to the learner.

"To present the concepts of spatial relationships."

— *Not stated:* Many materials do not include goals or objectives but simply identify the topic of the material.

"Teaches higher order thinking skills."

Self-Check 2-2

Instructions

Using the brochure excerpt below, fill out the portions of the Materials Review Form shown below. If you cannot find sufficient information to answer an item, try to make a best guess on it. If there is no information on an item, simply skip it.

Oregon Math **is a highly structured program to teach computation skills which has been specifically developed for retarded children and children who have severe learning problems. *Oregon Math* employs a teaching method which gives the students simple rules to remember for addition, subtraction, multiplication, and division, and a procedure for incorporating the rules together with use of their fingers to arrive at the correct answers. The program provides constant review, actively involves the students, and can be easily administered by aides. *Oregon Math meets the requirements of new federal legislation for handicapped children.***

HERE'S HOW *OREGON MATH* WORKS: First, each student is given a placement test to decide where he fits into the program from number writing to long division. He must do reading, counting, and writing of numbers, and then computation (if he can) with addition, subtraction, multiplication and division. The teacher then places him in a small group of up to five students, and begins him at his own level of ability in the program.

Each day for 30 minutes, the student is actively engaged in learning mathematics. After his lesson is presented, he does a "lesson sheet" which contains three trials of three problems each, representing skills learned in the day's lesson. After he has successfully completed a trial, he goes to his desk to work the seat work sheet of 25 problems.

MANUALS

- includes complete objectives and record forms which meet all IEP requirements
- no preparation time is necessary--all instructions for each lesson are clearly presented
- totally individualized
- 300 lessons
- can be used in self-contained classrooms, resource rooms or for individual students
- appropriate for elementary through junior high grades

Oregon Math + − manual plus 10 Student Record Books Cat. No. 241 Price: $59.95
Oregon Math × ÷ manual plus 10 Student Record Books Cat. No. 341 Price: $59.95

STUDENT RECORD BOOK

- pretest/placement test + − and × ÷
- posttest + −, posttest × ÷
- Daily Lesson Point Chart and Individual Profile
- each page is perforated for easy removal

Student Record Books (pkg. of 10) Cat. No. 441 Price: $4.95

F.O.B. Beaverton, Oregon 97005
Add $1.50 or 10%, whichever is greater, for shipping and handling. We will pay postage on all prepaid orders.

Oregon Math Workbooks

workbook #1 lessons 0-39 reads numbers 0-10
through
adds 1 column numbers sums less than 20
Cat. No. 242 Price: $3.75

#2 40-76 counts backwards 10-0
through
adds 2 place + 1 place without carrying
Cat. No. 243 Price: $3.75

#3 77-114 adds 2 place + 2 place without carrying
through
adds 3 or more place numbers without carrying
Cat. No. 244 Price: $3.75

#4 115-159 subtracts 3 or more place numbers without borrowing
through
subtracts 2 place − 1 place with borrowing
Cat. No. 245 Price: $3.75

#5 160-199 subtracts 2 place − 2 place with 1 borrow
through
correctly solves any addition or subtraction problem
Cat. No. 246 Price: $3.75

#6 202-242 counts by 2's
through
multiplies by 9's
Cat. No. 342 Price: $3.75

#7 243-274 divides by 2's 1 step without remainder
through
divides by 9's 1 step without remainder
Cat. No. 343 Price: $3.75

#8 275-300 multiplies 2 places × 1 place without carrying
through
multiplies 3 or more places × 1 place with carrying, and divides 1 place divider, 3 steps
Cat. No. 344 Price: $3.75

WORKBOOKS

- you buy only the workbooks your students need
- contain lesson work sheets
- contain seat work sheets
- contain skills tests
- each page is perforated--you tear out the daily lesson and seat work sheets

Response

MATERIALS REVIEW FORM

Title ________________ Subject ________________

Publisher ________________ Level ________ Scope: Comprehensive ____

Address ________________ Across Skills ____

Brief Description ________________ Single Skill ____

Preparation:

Initial preparation/training involved ________________

Daily preparation involved ________________

Preparing materials ________________

Comment (Are you willing to expend the effort required?)

____

Physical Characteristics:

(A) Media/hardware required..... ____
available.................. ____
obtainable................. ____
non-obtainable............. ____
alternatives?.............. ____
service warranty?.......... ____
local service?............. ____
can get on loan?........... ____
requires special training?____

(B) Duplication required....... ____
mimeo...................... ____
xerox...................... ____

(C) Extra materials required.... ____
locate..................... ____
make....................... ____

(D) Sensory mode required
visual..................... ____
auditory................... ____
tactual.................... ____
olfactory/gustatory........ ____

(E) Safety
toxic...................... ____
non-toxic.................. ____

(F) Durability of manipulatives
durable.................... ____
non-durable................ ____

Comment (Are there prohibititive physical characteristics?) ____

____

Costs: (See Chapter 4)

Initial cost ____
cost per student ____

Comment (Are the cost factors within reason?)

Replacement cost ____ ________________
portion consumable (%) ____ ________________
portion reusable (%) ____ ________________

Initial cost low? ____ ________________

Replacement cost low? ____ ________________

Hidden costs? ____ ________________

Time Involved:

(A) Time to complete in program (estimated)
weeks ____ days ____

(B) Daily time required
of teacher ____ of learner ____

Comment ________________

Other:

Response(s) required in the material ________________

Prerequisites required ________________

Student ability to use media equipment ________________

Comment (prohibitive learner prerequisite?) ________________

Compare your response to the sample response in Appendix A.

Source: Reprinted from *Special Offerings for 1978-79* (advertisement) with permission of the publisher. Copyright 1978, C.C. Publications Inc.

Sequence

— Complete: The sequence of tasks or activities in the material appears to be adequate.

— Gaps: Some skills or subskills in the material are not taught. The jumps from one step to another are too large.

— Not determinable: Some materials do not reveal their sequence without first attempting to use them.

Redirection

— Can recycle: The materials contain provisions for having the student repeat part or all of the instructional sequence.

— Can vary instruction: The materials contain alternative instruction exercises for students who do not succeed in the main program.

— No direction specified: According to specifications, the materials are used once, regardless of learner performance.

Measurement

Initial assessment

— Placement: Does the material contain assessments that allow pupils to be placed in the sequence of instruction?

— Pretest: Is there a pretest that establishes a level of learner performance but does not place the learner into the program sequence?

— No assessment: The materials contain neither pretests nor placement tests.

Progress assessment

— Daily: Provisions are included for daily assessment of programs.

— Weekly: Provisions are included for weekly assessment of programs.

Summary chart or graph: The materials include some sort of charting or graphing procedure for visually displaying progress.

Mastery assessment: Same as initial assessment.
Same as progress assessment.

	New assessment: The mastery assessment is a different test from that used elsewhere in the material.
	No mastery assessment.
Direct teaching	
— *Appropriate practice:*	How much opportunity is there for the learner to practice the behavior(s) specified in the objective(s)?
Reinforcement	
— *General instructions:*	Is motivation loosely referred to with no mention of a contingent relationship between response and reinforcement?
— *Specific instructions:*	Procedures for reinforcing appropriate learner responses systematically and contingently are included in the material.
Prompting	
—Errorless responding:	Instructional prompts are sequenced so that learner errors are kept to a minimum.
—Fading:	Are prompts sequenced so ultimately the learner can perform under the conditions of the objective?
— *No prompts provided:*	The learner simply practices the objective under the conditions of ultimate performance.
Amount of adaptation required:	The amount of adaptation is related most directly to the instructional characteristics of the materials. If one of these is lacking or inappropriate, it means that the teacher will have to do something about it. Simply write in the numbers of the instructional characteristic areas where it seems that some adaptation may be necessary.

The final section of the Materials Review Form pertains to an assessment of field-test information. Both informal and formal types of field-test information are included in the checklist. Of particular note is the difference between field testing that does and that which does not include measures of learner performance. A detailed account of these differences is included in Chapter 8. Less than 1 percent of the available materials report field-test information. Teachers' manuals, brochures, and catalogues are the likely sources of this information.

Self-Check 2-3 provides practice regarding the back side of the Materials Review Form (Figure 2-5).

PUTTING THEM TOGETHER

Using the Materials Inventory Form (Figure 2-3) and the Materials Review Form (Figures 2-4 and 2-5) consistently will result in a file of analyzed material that can easily be referred to when you need the information. The Materials-Analysis File will serve as a continuing reference. It can be built upon as you acquire new materials. Each new acquisition should be placed on the inventory and analyzed to determine its potential utility.

WHAT MATERIALS ARE NEEDED?

Completion of analyses on available materials will help to complete the Materials Inventory Form (Figure 2-3). The final two columns are "Analysis Showed Them Useful?" and "Material Pinpoint Need?" A simple yes or no for each column is all that is needed. The results will help to narrow down the range in the search for new materials. If you have no available materials that were shown to be useful, there most likely is a material need for that skill. Not only has the skill been identified but the review form should help to specify what kind of instruction program is needed. For instance, in handwriting, the SRA Lunch Box program by Science Research Associates provides drill and practice materials. If pupils are not writing at all, an initial or remedial instruction program, and not a massed drill and practice program, is called for.

PRELIMINARY SELECTION

With materials needs identified, it may be expedient to select materials at this point, particularly if there is an immediate instructional need and if the materials are inexpensive. The most direct means of selecting materials are from publisher catalogues and brochures and printed materials summaries from information retrieval systems. Other sources include publications such as the Educational Products Information Exchange releases (e.g., Indepth Report #48, 1973) and reviews of products by publications such as the *Journal of Special Education Technology*. These materials information retrieval sources are described in detail in Chapter 3.

Selecting materials based on these preliminary information sources may prove to be risky. Brochures, advertisements, and catalogues highlight the more appealing features of materials and may not clearly represent all of their characteristics. Information retrieval systems generally provide brief descriptions of materials, which seldom suffice in place of a complete review of the materials. Although some selections can be made at this point, it is generally wise to regard these information sources as an initial step.

OBTAIN, REVIEW AND ANALYZE NEW MATERIALS

Before making a total commitment, the better and surprisingly easy alternative is to review and critique the actual materials. Materials can be obtained on a limited time basis from several sources. Publisher representatives will often loan demonstration or sampler sets of materials to a teacher for a week or more. Many publishers also send materials on a trial or review basis (10 days to 1 month). Others will supply materials on a 15- to 30-day approval basis. Other sources include local and regional centers that loan materials, teachers in your school who have the materials, and curriculum developers from local colleges and universities. Again, procedures for capitalizing on these sources are detailed in Chapter 3.

The same Materials Review Form (Figures 2-4 and 2-5) shown for assessing available materials is quite appropriate to help determine whether new materials will be useful. The form is filled out in the same manner as described and then scanned to help determine if new materials are to be purchased or retained. If at this point doubts about materials still remain, and the skill that needs to be taught is important enough, a child-based materials evaluation, as described in Chapter 8, may be useful.

INDIVIDUAL PRESCRIPTION SELECTION

When a particular student has specific instructional needs identified, say, as is on a written, individualized education plan, teachers are interested in analyzing more than just the materials. Characteristics of the student must somehow be aligned with appropriate materials characteristics to select materials for an individual prescription. Some published diagnostic-prescriptive programs are designed to match one or more student variables with available materials (see Chapter 3). The materials-management system described in Chapter 5 can also assist in matching materials with learners.

The outline shown below lists major steps that should be considered in matching materials to individual student needs.

Individual prescription materials selection

1. Develop an instructional specification for a student.
    a. From an individualized plan
    b. From test information
2. Develop a child profile including,

Self-Check 2-3

Instructions

Use the brochure shown here to fill out the Instructional characteristics portion of the Materials Review Form. If you can find nothing on the brochure pertaining to an item, place a question mark and skip that item. Remember, you need to do some guessing or estimating because the information will not simply jump out at you.

SPEECH AND LANGUAGE 9

NON-SLIP KIT

NON-SPEECH LANGUAGE INITIATION PROGRAM

by

JOSEPH K. CARRIER, JR. and TIMOTHY PEAK

NON-SLIP

A PLASTIC SYMBOL SYSTEM FOR DEVELOPING COMMUNICATION IN SEVERELY HANDICAPPED PERSONS

1975, $238.00
ISBN 0-89079-019-1,
H & H Catalog No. 19

Speech involves motor responses that require an ability to talk which is absent or very limited in most low-level retarded children. Non-SLIP provides a set of symbols that are used to teach the child language rules. These symbols are geometric forms that represent words. The child chooses the correct form, which is a behavior similar to actually saying the correct word, except that it involves a simpler motor response, and that response is the same for "saying" each word. A child can say "tree" by picking up the symbol for tree and placing it on the tray. He or she says other words in the same manner. But rather than being forced to engage in the complex process of speech production, the child performs the same motor response (picking up and placing a symbol) for each word used.

Each form is a different shape so the child has no trouble telling one word from another. All nouns are marked with one color cue. All verbs are marked with another color, articles with another, and so forth. The handicapped child works on a one-to-one basis with an instructor (who need not be a college, or even high-school graduate) who shows the child a picture stimulus card and asks the child to construct a sentence describing the picture. For example, the card may show a baby sitting on the grass, or a cat standing on the floor. Using visual as well as spoken cues, demonstrations, and positive reinforcement techniques, the trainer or instructor helps the child learn to discriminate symbols and place them on the tray.

The sub-programs within the overall Non-SLIP program are step-by-step procedures for teaching linguistic rules without requiring the child to emit spoken responses. Children learn to use the symbols as words and morphemes, and to select appropriate forms and to arrange those forms on the response tray as if they are writing sentences. For example, if the target response is a sentence "The boy is sitting on the floor," the child would select a form for "the" and place it in the tray. The child would then select the form for "boy" and place it in the tray to the right of "the." The child would then select the symbol for the verb "is" and place it to the right of "boy" and so on until the sentence is complete. Both tangible reinforcement (toys, food) and social reinforcement (praise, attention, contact) are used to strengthen correct responses.

The children first learn to recognize and discriminate the different symbols. They then learn to match similar symbols and to construct sentences in a rote fashion. The various segments of the program then train the child to select appropriate "words" and to sequence the "words" (symbols) according to grammatical rules, to combine selection and sequencing activities into a variety of different types of sentences, and to use available vocabulary and rules to generate new responses.

Although instructors who use Non-SLIP to train developmentally disabled persons need no special academic background, they should know how (or be willing to learn) to use behavior management techniques (reinforcement).

Non-SLIP is not intended to teach any child all he or she needs to know about any aspect of the communication process. But, properly implemented, the instructor can expect children in this program to progress to the point where they are ready to move into more traditional communications programs designed for less severely handicapped children.

The Non-SLIP Components

The Non-SLIP kit contains 59 symbols that represent words in the English language. Also included is a tray divided into marked sections. The children learn to construct sentences by placing the word symbols on the tray.

There is an accompanying manual which discusses the rationale behind the program, the population with which it was developed, the basis of this work and other research with symbolic languages, and the procedures of the Non-SLIP programs. The manual includes instructions for solving problems, and tables that give the expected times required for children to master various sub-parts of the Non-SLIP program.

The kit also includes a set of visual stimuli cards, and a set of step-by-step instructions for the trainer to use in administering the program.

Purpose

The purpose of Non-SLIP is to give severely handicapped children (and some adults, including aphasics) some form of basic communication skill. For some children this skill will be limited to communication with symbols. For others, the training will extend into the use of signs and gestures for communication. And for other children, speech therapy may follow or be integrated into the Non-SLIP program to train the child to emit speech.

Not all children will learn to speak. And it takes from three months to a year for children to complete the Non-SLIP program. Non-SLIP is a language initiation program, whether that language in the end becomes gestures, writing (or symbol arrangement) or actual speech. Non-SLIP is designed to start severely handicapped children along the road to acquiring some form of communication skill.

Response

Planning

1. Objectives: specific___ general___ not stated___
   Comment ______________________________
   (Do the stated or implied objectives match your intent for the materials?)

2. Sequence: complete___ gaps___ not determinable___
   Comment ______________________________
   (Is the sequence thorough and in logical order?)

3. Redirection: can recycle___ can vary instruction___ no redirection specified___
   Comment ______________________________

Measurement

4. Initial assessment: placement___ pretest___ no initial assessment___
   Comment ______________________________

5. Progress assessment: daily___ weekly___ summary chart or graph___ none specified___
   Comment ______________________________

6. Mastery assessment: same as initial assessment ___
   same as progress assessment___
   new assessment ___
   no mastery assessment ___
   Comment ______________________________
   (Are you going to have to supply another assessment?)

Direct Teaching

7. Appropriate practice: all pupil work is appropriate ___
   some pupil work is appropriate___
   no pupil work is appropriate ___
   Comment ______________________________

8. Reinforcement: general instructions ___
   specific instructions___
   none specified ___
   Comment ______________________________
   (Are you going to have to design and implement your own reinforcement?)

9. Prompting: errorless responding possible___
   fading of prompts ___
   no prompts provided ___
   Comment ______________________________

10. Amount of adaptation required (number of characteristics)___

Compare your response to the sample response in Appendix A.

Source: Reprinted from *H & H Enterprises Catalogue* with permission of the publisher. Copyright 1979, H & H Enterprise Inc.

a. The objective(s) to be acquired
b. The pertinent entry skills of the student
c. The most preferable instruction formats the student can work in (see Table 2-1)
d. Any sensory or motor impairments
e. What response mode the student can use (e.g., motor, oral, written)
f. Known types of reinforcement
g. Preferred teaching mode for that student
h. Time at work task
i. Other ______________________

3. Select one or more materials and compare their analyses to the child profile.
   a. Complete analysis using the Materials Review Form
   b. List child profile and material characteristics side by side
   c. Note where a match is not evident

Instructional Specification

An *instructional specification* is a statement of skills or tasks to be taught to a student, the time line involved, and the means of assessing whether these skills or tasks have been taught. This can be taken from the short-term objectives and time line of an individualized education program (IEP) or from results of a recent test.

Child Profile

The *child profile* includes learning conditions you are aware of about a particular student that should reflect corresponding conditions in instructional materials if they are appropriate. This information is usually drawn from school records, an IEP, tests, and daily classroom experience. We have selected what we consider to be the most salient child features. You may have several others to add to the list.

Objectives: What the child needs to learn can be drawn from the instructional specifications.

Entry skills: The entry skills are those skills the child has that are necessary to begin work toward acquiring the objectives.

Instruction format: These are the types of classroom conditions (group, individual, and so on) that the child can be expected to work under. The amount of supervision required is the critical element here.

Sensory or motor impairments: Note any impairment that may limit the selection of stimulus presentation alternatives; a hearing impairment may require the elimination or altered use of a program that includes audiotapes. A motor impairment may limit a wheelchair-bound person's access to a media carrel. A vision impairment may mean that print materials must be audiotaped or read to the learner.

Response mode: What type of response can the learner perform? Can he or she write, circle, or place an "X" on paper? Can he or she perform a motor response such as pointing to an object or pushing a button? Or must the type of response be oral or limited to a head nod? Most materials require either written or motor responses so a permanent result is available.

Reinforcement: What type of reinforcement has worked in the past? Is *progress* through the material reinforcing? Social praise? Edibles? Tokens or points earned toward something else? All of these things, and often none of them, are reflected in different forms of materials.

Preferred teaching mode: What are the modes of teaching (presenting a stimulus, obtaining a response, and providing a consequent event) that have been successful in the past? What types of practice, prompting, and error correction have been successful?

Time at task: How long does the child usually work at a given task? How far can this time be extended with appropriate reinforcers?

Table 2-1 shows a sample listing of child characteristics, a corresponding column for checking off matching materials characteristics, and a notation for what part of the Materials Review Form may provide the needed information about materials.

MATCH MATERIALS ANALYSES WITH BUDGET INFORMATION

Although analyses of materials may have shown them to be useful, most teachers will have to justify the purchase of these materials against a limited

TABLE 2-1 Child Profile — Materials Characteristics Match List

Child Profile		*Match*	*Nonmatch*	*Materials Review Form Parts*
a. Objectives to be acquired		______	______	Objectives, purpose, scope
____________________	comments	____________	____________	
____________________		____________	____________	
b. Pertinent entry skills		______	______	Prerequisites required
____________________	comments	____________	____________	
____________________		____________	____________	
c. Preferred instruction formats		______	______	Format
____________________	comments	____________	____________	
____________________		____________	____________	
d. Sensory-motor impairments		______	______	Sensory-mode required; safety; student ability to use media-equipment
____________________	comments	____________	____________	
____________________		____________	____________	
e. Response modes used		______	______	Response(s) required in the material
____________________	comments	____________	____________	
____________________		____________	____________	

f. Types of reinforcement		______	______	Reinforcement
______________	comments ______________			
g. Preferred teaching mode		______	______	Preparation; physical characteristics
______________	comments ______________			Appropriate practice
				Prompting
h. Time at task		______	______	Time involved
______________	comments ______________			
i. Other		______	______	
______________	comments ______________			

budget and other materials needs. A three-way judgment is necessary between the costs of materials, their potential usefulness, and their importance as compared to other materials that may have to be budgeted. Penny pinching is the rule of thumb in current and future materials budgets. Chapter 4 provides a handy schema to help teachers compare the costs and benefits of materials against an entire budget. The decision may be to purchase materials, to store the critique and budgetary information for later use, or to reject materials even if they are highly useful but possibly not worth the cost expenditure.

It has probably become apparent after reading this chapter that what we have dealt with in the materials-selection process is only the tip of an iceberg. To go about materials selection in some sort of organized fashion teachers must be aware that there is more to it than simply perusing through a catalogue or thumbing through the pages of an instructional material. The processes of selection are highly dependent upon teachers' knowledge of materials retrieval systems, budgetary decisions, and exactly what can and should be taught in the classroom. Teachers are also going to have to know when they should rely upon the ultimate decision maker for selecting instructional materials—the performance of the learner. It is ultimately the handicapped child who will determine whether the selection of a particular material was a good one.

CHAPTER 3

Retrieving Instructional Materials

Objectives

1. Identify and use sources of information about materials.
   - What are the national materials-information sources and how can teachers use them?
   - What are the state and local materials-information sources and how can teachers use them?
   - What information about materials can teachers expect from publishers?

2. Identify and use sources of instructional materials.
   - How can teachers obtain materials from instructional materials centers?
   - What options are there in obtaining instructional materials from publishers?

3. Locate and obtain materials from within the school district.
   - How can I obtain cooperation from school district personnel to obtain appropriate materials?
   - What options are there available within my own school?

Information sources on how to locate and obtain instructional materials have changed dramatically over the last ten years and are currently in a state of flux. Some results of these changes are encouraging and some are disturbing.

Materials-information sources are numerous. Many of these sources are directly accessible only by a select few. Some sources are directly accessible by teachers, but most are not. The focus of this chapter is on identifying which sources are directly accessible and which are not.

A BRIEF HISTORY OF SPECIAL EDUCATION MATERIALS RESOURCES

Before 1968 there was no concerted national effort to provide materials or materials information for teachers of the handicapped. In 1968 a national network of Special Education Instructional Materials Centers (SEIMCs) and Regional Media Centers (RMCs) was developed and funded through the Bureau of Education for the Handicapped (Erickson, no date). This network included nine regional materials centers, state centers, and, later, numerous satellite centers based primarily on college and university campuses. The regional centers served to collect and catalogue materials, distribute materials on loan, provide training and technical assistance, and develop and evaluate materials. The state centers aided in these functions.

In 1974 funding of the SEIMC-RMC network was discontinued for a number of reasons; chief among them was the criticism that the centers, being campus based, were expensive, served colleges and universities, and provided little service to practicing teachers.

In 1974 a system of Regional Resource Centers (RRCs) and Area Learning Resource Centers (ALRCs) was established as an alternative to the SEIMCs. The Regional Resource Centers assumed training and technical assistance responsibilities. Development of Area Learning Resource Centers was the responsibility of individual states, and these centers were to assist in the location and distribution of special education instructional materials. This network was backed up by the National Center on Education Media and Materials for the Handicapped (NCEMMH). This center catalogued, evaluated, and developed instructional materials. It also sought dissemination avenues for materials. The chief accomplishment of NCEMMH was the development of NIMIS I, a computer information and cataloguing system on special education materials. Specialized national centers were also established.

For several reasons the RRC-ALRC network did not fully develop. With the exception of selected RRCs, the system was disbanded in 1977.

Of five specialized national media and materials centers funded to serve selected functions, four are currently operating. In addition, the National Center on Media and Materials for the Handicapped and the National Information Center on Special Education Materials (NICSEM), an information cataloguing and dissemination center based in Los Angeles, California, are providing services. Individual state agencies and local education agencies vary a great deal in materials services ranging from no formal services provided to sophisticated instructional materials distribution networks.

NATIONAL INFORMATION CENTERS

In preparation for the writing of this chapter a direct survey by phone and by mail was carried out with all known national materials-information sources. The picture drawn from this survey is ambiguous to say the least. There seems to be an "official line" from each of the national information sources, coupled with "off-the-record" feedback that is often conflicting. Since the extent of direct impact these sources have on the classroom teacher is uncertain, our treatment is reserved to brief descriptions and our impressions of what can be used by teachers.

NCEMMH

Organization Name

National Center for Education Media and Materials for the Handicapped (NCEMMH).

Stated Goal

The goal of NCEMMH is to assist and support personnel working with the handicapped in choosing and locating educational materials and media.

What It Is

It is a national center to help regions, states, and localities provide media, materials, and educational technologies. The center consists of four parts: (1)

Media, Materials, and Technology (MMT), which facilitates the distribution of instructional and training materials; (2) Information Services (IS), which deals in information retrieval (see separate section on NIMIS); (3) Coordination Services (CS), which sees that all parts operate together; and (4) Administration and Central Technical Services (ACTS), which administers to the whole.

Who Can Use It

It is available to handicapped learners, teachers (public and private), parents, school administrators, librarians, media specialists, resource center personnel, medical center staff, rehabilitation center staff, researchers, and preservice teachers in special education programs.

How to Use It

Order materials and media in the NCEMMH catalogue directly from the manufacturer. Call Information Services (IS) for information not covered in the catalogue. Order other catalogues and in-house publications from the Ohio State University Press.

Costs

Catalogue and services are free; publications are available at a modest price.

Where to Order

Catalogue: c/o NCEMMH Information Services, The Ohio State University, 356 Arps Hall, 1945 North High Street, Columbus, OH 43210, (614) 422-7596 or 422-8787. Publications: c/o Ohio State University Press, 2070 Neil Avenue, Columbus, OH 43210. For information, contact the associate director.

NIMIS I

Organization Name

National Instructional Materials Information System (NIMIS I). NIMIS I is a subcomponent of NCEMMH.

Function

The function is to provide abstracts of materials and media from a data base. These abstracts are designed to aid in a search for appropriate materials when designing individualized education programs (IEPs).

Form

Thirty-seven thousand abstracts are accessible through 41 hard-bound bibliographies divided into seven areas: Learning Disabilities, Early Childhood, Mildly Handicapped, Trainable Mentally Handicapped. Severely Mentally Handicapped, Hearing Impaired, and other topics. A computer printout may also be ordered.

Additional Publications

NIMIS Data Preparation Manual (approximately $6), Instructional Materials Thesaurus for Special Education (approximately $7). Note: New Service—Special Materials Analysis and Review by Teachers (SMART). Teachers provide information on materials they have used for possible entry into NIMIS I.

Prices

Individual abstracts (approximately $3-$5; entire set of abstracts (approximately $162); computer services (prices vary according to services).

Contact

Publications Sales Divisions, Ohio State University Press, 2070 Neil Avenue, Columbus, OH 43210.

NICSEM

Organization Name

National Information Center for Special Education Materials.

Function

The function of NICSEM is to aid in the search for appropriate materials by collecting abstracts from a data base along parameters defined by key words.

Forms

Numerous indexes are offered for sale (see NICSEM for a complete list). A computer search is also available through NICSEM. There is an on-line interface with Lockheed (DIALOG) and BRS systems. Over 80,000 abstracts are available.

Prices

Index prices are quoted under NICSEM section. On-line computer-service prices vary with the type of service.

NOTE: NICSEM is currently working to assist state education agencies in preparing and utilizing NICSEM products and services in their respective states.

Where to Order Indexes

University of Southern California, NICSEM, University (RAN) 2nd Floor, Los Angeles, CA 90007, Information Officer (213) 741-5899.

HLMDC

Organization Name

Handicapped Learner Materials Distribution Center (HLMDC).

Stated Goals

The goals of the HLMDC are to serve as a backup source in the event that materials are otherwise unavailable for loan. Materials may be used for evaluation for possible purchase or for actual use.

What It Is

It is a storehouse of materials for use with handicapped learners. Materials are accessible through catalogue orders for short-term loans.

Who Can Use It

Any organization, institution, or agency working with the handicapped or training workers with the handicapped can use it. Also, it can be used by parents of a handicapped child.

How to Use It

(1) Determine the materials desired; the materials must be unavailable through local loan services. (2) Order them by mail, phone, or in person (a three-week notice is preferred). (3) Use the materials for one to seven days (longer loans are available on request). (4) Return the materials to HLMDS (the user is responsible for return postage).

Cost

There is no charge for loans. A catalogue is available upon request. NOTE: The user does accept responsibility for the condition of the material as returned to the HLMDC. Extensive guidelines are listed in the catalogue and the newsletter (vol. 1, no. 1, 1979) available from HLMDC.

How to Order Materials

(1) Obtain a catalogue from Handicapped Learner Materials Distribution Center, Indiana University, Audio-Visual Center, Bloomington, Indiana 47405, (812) 337-1511 — Circulation Department. (2) Obtain a HLMDC account number at the same address and phone number. (3) Order needed materials three weeks in advance (some orders may be handled faster if phoned). (4) Return materials to HLMDC (the user pays return postage).

Severely Handicapped

Organization Name

The National Media/Materials Center for Severely Handicapped Persons.

Stated Goals

The goals of the center are to (1) locate, retrieve, and review all available instructional media-materials for the severely handicapped; (2) locate gaps where needed materials do not exist; (3) develop or adapt materials to fill gaps; (4) conduct a yearly symposium for professionals to discuss new needs and trends; (5) deliver information to the private consumer.

What It Is

It is a project to assess available instructional media, discover unmet needs, develop and disseminate information and materials.

Who Can Use It

It can be used by teachers, paraprofessionals, media specialists, students, religious organizations—anyone with a need for information on instructional media and materials for the severely handicapped.

How to Use It

To use it, one needs to call or write for information regarding (1) materials lists (in-house publications) that are available; (2) quarterly newsletters available upon request (have your name placed on the mailing list); (3) Media Center-conducted evaluations of local services that are available upon request.

Cost

Services of the Media Center, materials list, and newsletter are free. Products under commercial production are priced by the producer.

How to Order Services or Materials

Call or write Coordinator of Public Information, National Media Materials Center for Severely Handicapped Persons, George Peabody College for Teachers, Box 318, Nashville, TN 37203, (615) 327-8280. The proceedings of the first two symposia were published in the *Journal of Special Education Technology*.

Hearing Impaired

Organization Name

Media Development Project for the Hearing Impaired.

Stated Goal

The goal of the project is to serve the educational technology needs of the deaf by identifying, developing, adapting, and evaluating the effectiveness of instructional materials.

What It Is

It is an instructional design and development project for the hearing impaired.

Who Can Use It

There is no direct contact with the public other than through a mailing list. Teachers' access to information on the materials is through NIMIS II.

How to Order Services or Materials

An annual symposium is published yearly: American Annals of the Deaf, "Higher Conference Proceedings," 5034 Wisconsin Avenue, NW, Washington, DC 20016.

Where to Write to Get on Mailing List

MDPHI, 318 Barklay Memorial Center, University of Nebraska, Lincoln, Lincoln, Nebraska 68583, (402) 472-2141 (2145).

ERIC

Organization Name

Educational Resources Information Center (ERIC) (Clearinghouse on Handicapped and Gifted Children).

Stated Goal

The goal of ERIC is to collect information in the field of special education for the handicapped and gifted; to screen, index, abstract, and file the information in the master ERIC System for specialized retrieval.

What It Is

Educational Resources Information Center (ERIC) is a network of sixteen clearinghouses. CEC serves as one of the sixteen (the ERIC Clearinghouse on Handicapped and Gifted Children). ERIC as a whole is concerned with all education, this clearinghouse with the special educational portion.

Who Can Use It

Anyone interested in education can use it.

How to Use It

(1) The microfiche files of any one of over 800 subscribers—usually colleges and universities—are available; (2) computer searches through Lockheed or BRS interface are also provided; (3) computer tapes for local computer systems may be purchased; (4) call or write to one of the Clearinghouses.

Cost

The cost varies with the service.

Contact

ERIC Clearinghouse on Handicapped and Gifted Children, Council for Exceptional Children, 1920 Association Drive, Reston, VA, 22091 (703) 620-3660.

ECER

Organization Name

Exceptional Child Education Resources (ECER) is a collection of information.

Stated Goal

The purpose of ECER is to serve as a comprehensive literature depository for the area of education—to screen, index, abstract, and disseminate information on English language materials.

What It Is

An ECER catalogue abstracts and indexes this literature for storage in a machine-readable data base, and for publication in a quarterly journal that offers access to printed materials, dissertations, theses, and professional media are also available.

Who Can Use It

Anyone interested in education can use it.

How to Use It

It is used by (1) manually searching the journal (in libraries); (2) a computer interface with Lockheed (DIALOG) or BRS; (3) subscription to the journal.

Cost

The computer search varies in cost according to the type of search.
ECER Journal: Institutions: $55.00 per year
(S) CEC member: $25.00 per year
private individual: $35.00 per year
Contact: Information Services Council for Exceptional Children, 1920 Association Drive, Reston, VA, 22091. (703) 620-3660.

Visually Impaired

Organization Name

American Printing House for the Blind.

What It Is

A publisher, printer, and manufacturer of materials for the blind.

Who Can Use It

Anyone can use it, but certain materials are restricted solely to use by the legally blind. There are some copyright restrictions on the use of certain products.

How to Use It

Use the service by (1) ordering the catalogue and, in turn, ordering necessary materials from it; (2) under the Federal Quota System you may be entitled to certain materials free—to determine eligibility, check with a representative from the State Board of Education.

Cost

The catalogue is free. Prices on the products range from $1 to $495 (approximate figure).

Where to Order

American Printing House for the Blind, P.O. Box 6085, Louisville, KY 40206, (502) 895-2405 (no collect calls are accepted).

State and Local Information Sources

State Agencies

A request for information on materials was sent to 56 education agences. Information was obtained from 31. Table 3-1 depicts the types of materials resources indicated by each state. A list of names and addresses of contact persons for each state respondant is also included.

Table 3-1 should help to provide a picture of the state education agencies' relationships to materials-information and dissemination activities in a teacher's particular state. Even though for some states the table does not depict an extensive relationship between materials and state education agencies (SEAs), the next step, writing a letter of inquiry, is still advised.

Local materials centers that have established contacts with materials resources on the state level may be available to teachers. Also, the school librarian can be of great assistance in helping teachers locate materials resources. Often, however, teachers find that they must be self-reliant in identifying such resources.

Classroom teachers seldom have direct contact with education officials. In some cases protocol requires that teachers go through channels. In many cases, teachers do not feel they can or should seek help from state agencies. Actually, they would be pleasantly surprised at the responsiveness of state officials to

Table 3-1 Types of Materials Resource Services Identified by Responding States and Protectorates

States and Territories	*Contact Person(s)*	*Regional Center*	*Statewide Services*	*Local Services*	*Other*
Alabama (responded)	Fred R. Wells Supervisor Learning Resource Services Department of Education State Office Building Montgomery, AL 36130 (205) 832-5824	X (12 regional centers)			
Alaska	John M. Stamm Administrator Division of Instructional Services State Department of Education Pouch F Juneau, AK 99801 (907) 465-2970				
American Samoa	Beth Scott Division of Special Education State Department of Education Pago, Pago, American Samoa 96799 (Dial 9-0) 271-3183				
Arizona	Charles Essings State Department of Education 1535 West Jefferson Phoenix, AZ 85007 (602) 371-2161				

Arkansas (responded)	Diane E. Sydoriak Area Supervisor Special Education Section Department of Education State Education Building Little Rock, AR 72201 (501) 371-1461				No formally organized services
California (responded)	Carl Murray Coordinator of Staff Development Special Education Support Unit State Department of Education 721 Capitol Mall Sacramento, CA 95814 (916) 445-4036	X (6 regional special education resource centers—staff development)		X (58 intermediate education units with materials resources)	
Colorado (responded)	Constance Rose Consultant Colorado Department of Education State Office Building 201 East Colfax Denver, CO 80203 (303) 839-2282)		X (visually handicapped)	X (either developed resource centers or contracted services)	
Connecticut	Dr. Tom Gillung, Bureau Chief Bureau of Pupil Personnel and Special Educational Services State Department of Education P.O. Box 2219 Hartford, CT 06115 (203) 566-4383				

Table 3-1 (continued)

States and Territories	*Contact Person(s)*	*Regional Center*	*Statewide Services*	*Local Services*	*Other*
Delaware (responded)	Steven Godowsky State Supervisor Exceptional Children Programs Department of Public Instruction The Townsend Building Dover, DE 19901 (302) 678-5471	X (4 learning resource centers)			
District of Columbia	Dr. Doris A. Woodson Division of Special Education 415 12th Street, N.W. Washington, D.C. 20004 (202) 724-4018				
Florida	Dr. Landis M. Steeler Bureau of Education for Exceptional Students State Department of Education 319 Knott Building Tallahassee, FL 32304 (904) 488-1570 or 3205				
Georgia	Dr. Allan Gurley Director Division of Early Childhood and Special Education State Department of Education State Office Building Atlanta, GA 30334 (404) 656-2678				

Guam	Ms. Victoria Harper Associate Superintendent Department of Education P.O. Box DE Agana, Guam 96910 (Dial 9-0) 772-8300			
Hawaii (responded)	Miles S. Kawatachi Special Needs Branch State Department of Education Box 2360 Honolulu, HI 96804 (808) 548-6923	X (Library for the Blind and Visually Handicapped)		X (new materials reviewed by SEA consultants)
Idaho (responded)	Linda Gibbs Regional Special Education Consultant 1910 University Drive Boise State University Boise, ID 83725 (208) 385-3687	X (four regional learning resource centers)		
Illinois (responded)	Dr. Joe Fisher Assistant Superintendent Department of Special Educational Services State Department of Education 100 North First Street Springfield, IL 62777 (217) 782-6601	X (Illinois Resource and Dissemination network)		
Indiana (responded)	Paul Ash Coordinator Instructional Materials Center for Handicapped Children and Youth Box 100, Butler University Indianapolis, IN 46208 (317) 927-0219	X (Instructional Resource Center)	X (Instructional Materials and Resource Center for Handicapped Children and Youth)	X (7 university minicenters)

Table 3-1 (continued)

States and Territories	*Contact Person(s)*	*Regional Center*	*Statewide Services*	*Local Services*	*Other*
Iowa (responded)	Gail Sullivan Fleig Division of Special Education State Department of Public Instruction Grimes State Office Building Des Moines, IA 50319 (515) 281-3176	X (15 area education agencies with media sections, special education media specialists)	X (commission for statewide library services, Iowa Braille and Sight Saving School; Iowa School for the Deaf)		
Kansas	James E. Marshall Division of Special Education State Department of Education 120 East Tenth Street Topeka, KS 66612 (913) 296-3866				
Kentucky (responded)	Billie R. Downing Bureau of Education for Exceptional Children State Department of Education West Frankfort Complex 19th Floor Capital Plaza Tower Frankfort, KY 40601 (502) 564-4970	X (Regional Resource Center, Lexington, Kentucky)			
Louisiana	Dr. Henry Smith Special Educational Services State Department of Education Capitol Station P. O. Box 44064				

	Baton Rouge, LA 70804 (504) 342-3641		
Maine (responded)	John T. Kierstead Division of Special Education State Department of Education and Cultural Services Augusta, ME 04330 (207) 289-3451	X (Northeast Regional Center)	
Maryland (responded)	Consuelo Anderson Curriculum and Instructional Materials Specialist Division of Special Education Maryland State Department of Education P.O. Box 8717, BWI Airport Baltimore, MD 21240 (301) 796-8300		X (information network using NICSEM data base)
Massachusetts	Dr. Roger Brown Associate Commissioner and Director Division of Special Education State Department of Education 31 St. James Avenue Boston, MA 02116 (617) 727-6217		
Michigan (responded)	Theodore R. Beck Supervisor Development & Training Program Special Education Services Department of Education Lansing, MI 48909 (517) 373-1695		X (Information Dissemination Service Center)

Table 3-1 (continued)

States and Territories	*Contact Person(s)*	*Regional Center*	*Statewide Services*	*Local Services*	*Other*
	Alida Geppert Manager Information Dissemination Service Center P.O. Box 30007 Lansing, MI 48909 (517) 374-9637				
	Carolyn M. Benscoter Curriculum Resource Specialist Saginaw Intermediate School District 6235 Gratiot Road Saginaw, MI 48603 (517) 793-3760	X (22 regional educational media centers)			
Minnesota	John C. Groos Special Education Section State Department of Education Capitol Square 550 Cedar Street St. Paul, MN 55101 (612) 296-4163				
Mississippi (responded)	Bob H. Moore Coordinator Mississippi Learning Resources System Division of Instruction Department of Education Box 771 Jackson, MS 39205 (601) 354-6950	X (10 learning resource centers)	X		

Missouri	Dr. Roland J. Werner, Jr. Division of Special Education Department of Elementary and Secondary Education P.O. Box 480 Jefferson City, MO 65101 (314) 751-2965		
Montana (responded)	Shirley Miller Special Education Office of the Superintendent of Public Instruction State Capitol Helena, MT 59601 (406) 449-5660	X (Access Library—computer access to national systems)	X (20 cooperative service areas)
Nebraska (responded)	Gary Sherman Special Educational Section State Department of Education 223 South 10th Street Lincoln, NE 68508 (402) 471-2471	X (Nebraska Diagnostic Resource Center, Nebraska School for the Deaf, Nebraska School for the Visually Handicapped	X (17 education service units—all have media-materials centers)
Nevada	Frank South, Director Division of Special Education State Department of Education 400 W. King Street, Capitol Complex Carson City, NV 89701 (702) 885-5700 x 214		

Table 3-1 (continued)

States and Territories	*Contact Person(s)*	*Regional Center*	*Statewide Services*	*Local Services*	*Other*
New Hampshire (responded)	Mary V. Osgood Consultant Special Education Section Department of Education 410 State House Annex Concord, NH 03301 (603) 271-3144	X (18 regional centers with materials resources)	X		
New Jersey	Paul B. Winkler Deputy Associate Commissioner, PPS State Department of Education 225 W. State Street Trenton, NJ 08625 (609) 292-7602				
New Mexico (responded)	Elie S. Gutierrez Division of Special Education State Department of Education State Educational Building 300 Don Gaspar Avenue Santa Fe, NM 87503 (505) 827-2793		X (general education library)	X (materials centers in some of the larger school districts)	
New York (responded)	Lawrence C. Gloeckler Bureau Chief Bureau of Program Development Room 1061 EBA State Education Department Albany, NY 12234 (518) 474-2251	X (Bureau of Program Development)	X (50 materials resource centers)		

North Carolina (responded)	Mark Sumner Coordinator Technical Assistance Services Division for Exceptional Children Department of Public Instruction Raleigh, NC, 27611 (919) 733-3921	X (8 regional centers with instructional resource specialists)	X (all local school systems receive support funds applicable to materials)
North Dakota	Roger Miller Special Education State Department of Public Instruction State Capitol Bismarck, ND 58501 (701) 224-2277		
Ohio	S.J. Bonham, Jr. Division of Special Education State Department of Education 933 High Street Worthington, OH 43085 (614) 466-2650	X (NCEMMH—see this chapter)	
Oklahoma (responded)	Dr. Merlin J. Taylor State Administrative Officer Oklahoma Regional Education Service Centers 2500 North Lincoln Boulevard Oklahoma City, OK 73105 (405) 521-3351	X (20 regional education service centers)	X
Oregon	Dr. Mason D. McQuiston Division of Special Education State Department of Education 942 Lancaster Drive, N.E. Salem, OR 97310 (503) 378-3598		

Table 3-1 (continued)

States and Territories	*Contact Person(s)*	*Regional Center*	*Statewide Services*	*Local Services*	*Other*
Pennsylvania (responded)	Camilla C. Grigsby Associate Director National Learning Resource Center of Pennsylvania 500 Valley Forge Plaza 1150 First Avenue King of Prussia, PA 19406 (215) 265-3706	X	X (National Learning Resource Center of Pennsylvania)		
Puerto Rico	Gloria Bermudez de Miranda Special Education Program for Handicapped Children Department of Education Box 759 Hato Rey, PR 00919 (809) 764-1255				
Rhode Island	Charles Harrington Division of Special Education State Department of Education 235 Promenade Street Providence, RI 02908 (401) 277-3505				
South Carolina	Robert S. Black Office of Programs for the Handicapped State Department of Education Room 309, Rutledge Building Columbia, SC 29201 (803) 758-7432				

South Dakota	Dr. George Levin Section for Special Education Division of Elementary & Secondary Education New State Office Building Pierre, SD 57501 (605) 741-2851			
Mariana Islands	Elsa Thomas Special Education Coordinator Department of Education Saipan, Mariana Islands 96950			
Tennessee (responded)	Vernon L. Johnson Education for the Handicapped State Department of Education 103 Cordell Hull Building Nashville, TN 37219 (615) 741-2851	X (9 district offices—reference centers)	X (Media Center Library for visually limited and physically handicapped)	X (each local school must have a materials center by law)
Texas (responded)	Ken Crow Department of Special Education Texas Education Agency 201 East 11th Street Austin, TX 78701 (512) 475-3501	X (20 education service centers with special education instructional materials centers)	X (Special Education Information Center)	X (Special Education Resource Systems for most LEAs, districts, or co-ops)
Utah (responded)	Joanne Gilles Specialist, Special Education Instructional Media Utah Learning Resource Center 4984 South 300 West Murray, UT 84107 (801) 533-5982	X (13 associate learning resource centers)	X (Utah Learning Resource Center)	

Table 3-1 (continued)

States and Territories	*Contact Person(s)*	*Regional Center*	*Statewide Services*	*Local Services*	*Other*
Vermont	Jean S. Garvin Special Education and Pupil Personnel Services State Department of Education Montpelier, VT 05602 (802) 828-3141				
Virgin Islands	Lorrene Logzdon Division of Special Education Department of Education P.O. Box 630, Charlotte Amalie St. Thomas, Virgin Islands 00801 (809) 774-0100 x 213				
Virginia (responded)	James T. Micklem Division of Special Education State Department of Education 322 East Grace Richmond, VA 23216 (804) 786-2673				
Washington (responded)	William Hulten Special Services Section State Department of Public Instruction Old Capitol Building Olympia, WA 98504 (206) 753-2563	X (18 education service districts with materials centers)			

West Virginia	Keith Smith Division of Special Education Student Support System State Department of Education Capitol Complex, Room B-057 Charleston, WV 25305 (304) 348-2034			
Wisconsin (responded)	Kenneth McMahon Department of Public Instruction Division for Handicapped Children 126 Langdon Street Madison, WI 53702 (608) 266-1649	X (14 special education instructional materials centers)	X (Wisconsin School for Visually Handicapped)	X (3 city special education instructional centers)
Wyoming (responded)	Beth Early Curriculum Coordinator/Handicapped Cheyenne, WY 82002 (307) 777-7411	X (12 educational resource centers)		

their inquiries. At the very least, a brief inquiry to the special education division of the state department of education would help rule out some sources and help direct teachers to more appropriate local materials sources. The sample letter shown in Figure 3-1 is suggested as a preliminary inquiry. We also suggest that teachers first obtain approval of this inquiry from their immediate supervisors.

Local materials resources vary in what is available. Many large metropolitan school systems have teacher centers where a collection of materials can be found. Most often the district office will have a collection of films. Information about these resources can usually be obtained through the special education supervisor in the school system.

Publishers as Information Sources

Publishers are also important sources of information about materials, but they are primarily sources of information about their own materials. At times, when talking with publisher representatives or perusing a publisher's brochure, it may seem that the only materials worth looking at are their own. Three sources of information from publishers are (1) brochures, advertisements (Boland, 1976), and catalogues; (2) demonstrations by publisher representatives; and (3) convention exhibits.

Of these three sources, brochures, advertisements, and catalogues characteristically provide the least information as is evident in the Chapter 2 Self-Checks. Brochures and advertisements usually focus on one or a few products and are more descriptive than are catalogues. Some brochures provide "good sounding" information about a product and tell the reader almost nothing about its instructional capabilities. Others are honest attempts to provide the clearest picture possible within the available space regarding what the product is, what it can do, and what it cannot do. Figure 3-2 shows a collection of excerpts from two advertisements. Notice the difference in clarity of information between the two. Brochures, advertisements, and catalogues are helpful at the initial inquiry stage. Be extremely careful about purchasing products with little more information than that provided by brochures or catalogues. Teachers often receive a flood of brochures but these are selective mailings. It is advisable to write to certain publishers who produce materials in pertinent subject areas and request to have your name placed on the mailing list. If you are on a publisher's mailing list, catalogues as well as a full array of brochures and advertisements will be sent to you regularly.

Contact with representatives of large publishers can be made to obtain more detailed information on a product. Many publishers will forward requests for a demonstration or explanation to local representatives. These representatives cover rural as well as urban areas in their travels. However, you should not request a special demonstration unless you are seriously considering making a

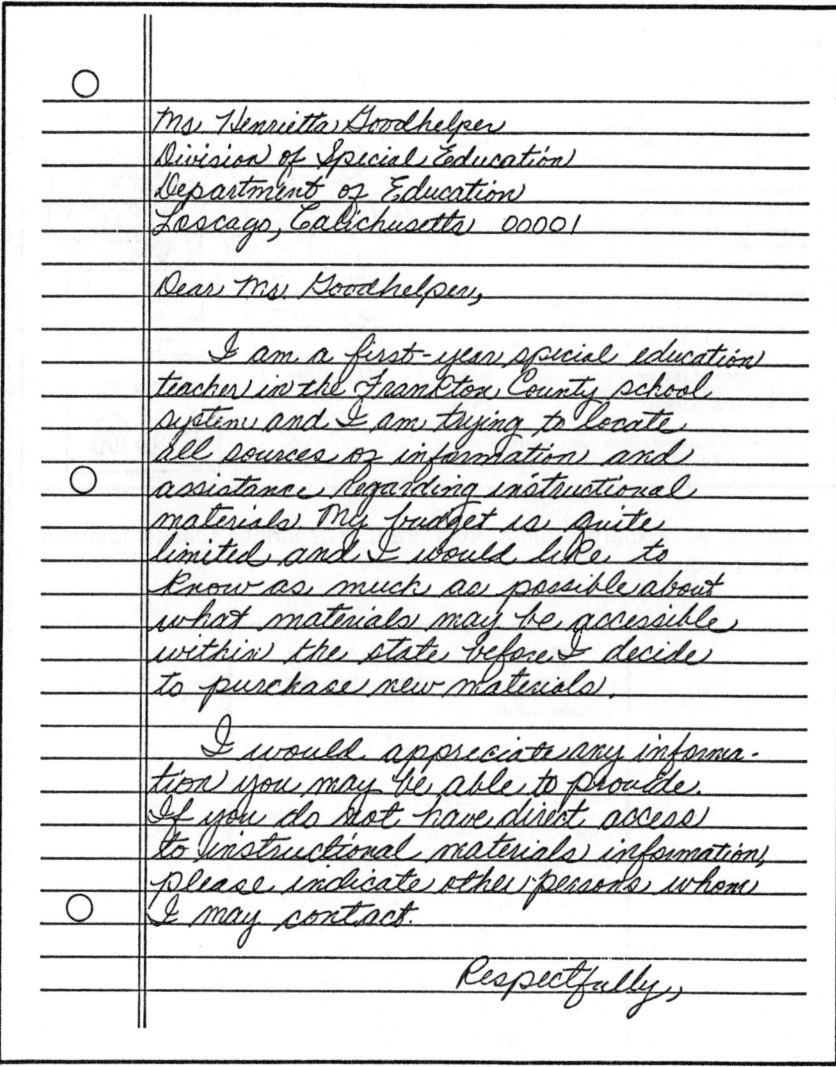

Ms. Henrietta Goodhelper
Division of Special Education
Department of Education
Loscago, Calichusetts 00001

Dear Ms. Goodhelper,

I am a first-year special education teacher in the Frankton County school system and I am trying to locate all sources of information and assistance regarding instructional materials. My budget is quite limited and I would like to know as much as possible about what materials may be accessible within the state before I decide to purchase new materials.

I would appreciate any information you may be able to provide. If you do not have direct access to instructional materials information, please indicate other persons whom I may contact.

Respectfully,

Figure 3-1. *Sample Letter of Inquiry Regarding State and Local Materials Resources*

purchase. Some representatives also make routine visits to schools without specific requests.

Often, the amount of information a teacher may obtain is dependent upon the knowledge of the product that the representative brings along. Few representatives are educators. All are salespersons. The amount of training varies with the publisher. The most extensive training will include information on the

Ready-Go Alphabet

AN INDIVIDUALIZED PRE-READING PROGRAM — Grades K-1, ESL

By Eunice Insel, M.S. and Ann Edson, M.Ed.

Components . . .

- 26 individualized self-directing, self-correcting lessons, one for each letter of the alphabet. Each lesson contains about 10 minutes of recorded time plus activity time. The unique, beautifully illustrated activity book contains three pages for each lesson which include experiences in identifying, tracing, visual discrimination using motivating game and puzzle activities, fun symbols, appealing animals, children, and everyday objects
- Pretest for diagnosis and placement.
- Post-test for review or recycling.
- Diagnostic evaluation sheets so that individual prescription and ongoing evaluation records can be maintained for each child.
- Teacher's Guide with specific behavioral objectives.

An exciting MULTISENSORY way for children to learn identification, naming, and forming the letters of the alphabet.

Children learn by doing things that have results. Each sequential step in READY-GO ALPHABET provides an immediate check and reinforcement of skills. Success is built-in!

AR 16 – 7 LP RECORDS, 10 ACTIVITY BOOKS, Guide	$64.90
AC 16 – 7 CASSETTES, 10 ACTIVITY BOOKS, Guide	$64.90
Extra ACTIVITY BOOKS	$ 1.79

Dittos available in place of Activity Books—Please specify.
Extra Set of Dittos — $17.90

Example A: Excerpt from a brochure that describes specific features of the product.

Ready-Set-Read-Along

A Reading Readiness Program for Pre K-1

By Eunice Insel, M.S.

A tested, exciting, unique learning series that introduces alphabet letters, both capital and small; shapes; numbers and numerals by means of cartoons, silly situations, puzzles, stories and games.

BOOK 1 — DO YOU SEE SILLIES?
Introduction to alphabet letters, both capital and small.

BOOK 2 — DO YOU SEE SHAPES?
Circle, square, triangle and rectangle are presented in various sizes, positions and hidden in things a child would find in his normal environment.

BOOK 3 — 1, 2, 3 . . . DO YOU SEE NUMBERS AND NUMERALS?
A delightfully entertaining story that involves the listener in the visual discrimination of the numbers 0-9 and relates the numeral to its quantity (number).

AR 17 — 3 BOOKS, 3 RECORDS, Activity Cards	$10.75
AC 17 — 3 BOOKS, 3 CASSETTES, Activity Cards	$18.75
ARS 17 — Set of 18 BOOKS (6 of each), 3 RECORDS, Activity Cards	$27.95
ACS 17 — Set of 18 BOOKS (6 of each), 3 CASSETTES, Activity Cards	$34.95
Set of 3 BOOKS only	$ 3.95

EACH LESSON INDEPENDENT, SELF-CORRECTING FOR INDIVIDUAL, SMALL OR LARGE GROUP INSTRUCTION

Example B: Excerpt from a brochure that vaguely describes a product.

Figure 3-2. *Example of Varying Types of Information Found in Advertisements for Procedures*

Source: Reprinted from *Educational Activities Catalogue* with permission of the publisher. Copyright 1979 by Educational Activities Inc.

product, the service provided by the publisher (if any), the field testing done (if any), and particularly how to sell the product. The least extensive training will focus purely on how to sell the product.

Some representatives are prepared to demonstrate the use of their product with students. Others are willing to assist the teacher in getting a program started. In Self-Check 3-1 you have a chance to develop a list of questions that the publisher should be prepared to answer. You will recognize the categories since they are related to the major categories of the Materials Review Form discussed in Chapter 2.

Many publisher representatives will leave a program or a sample unit or lesson with teachers so they may use it on a trial basis. The trial basis provides an excellent opportunity to conduct a child-based materials evaluation (Chapter 10).

As travel is becoming more restricted by a conserving economy, attendance at education association conventions and meetings is also becoming more difficult for teachers. However, these conventions can be a gold mine for the materials-conscious teacher. We restrict our discussion in this section to what information can be obtained on materials. The section How to Rob from Publishers and Make Them Love You for It, below, examines the role convention exhibits play in obtaining materials for teachers.

Unlike a brochure, a convention exhibit has the real thing. Teachers can comparatively examine, firsthand, a variety of materials that pertain to any given subject or skill to be taught. Questions can be answered by publisher representatives and immediate follow-up on materials of interest can occur. In addition, teachers can directly confront publisher representatives with problems that materials purchased previously have caused them. Satisfactory solutions to these problems are often arrived at. It is not unheard of to have over 200 publishers represented under one roof at a national convention. Teachers literally have them cornered.

Published Materials Information

There are several published sources of information regarding materials. These sources range from materials reviews to computer-based diagnostic prescriptive programs. The list that follows is by no means exhaustive but represents major published materials information sources. Many of these publications would be useful to local or school materials centers.

Educational Products Information Exchange (EPIE)

The purpose of EPIE is to gather and disseminate descriptive and analytical information about instructional materials, systems, and equipment. Its services

Self-Check 3-1

Instructions

Assume that you are a teacher who will be meeting a publisher representative to examine a remedial reading program. Develop a list of questions to ask the representative about the program—concerning the following areas:

Response

1. Instructional characteristics

   Question(s) ______________________________

   ____

2. Validity (field testing)

   Question(s) ______________________________

   ____

3. Service provided

   Question(s) ______________________________

   ____

4. Cost

   Question(s) ______________________________

   ____

5. Media-materials

   Question(s) ______________________________

   ____

Sample responses can be found in Appendix A.

are designed to help the consumer make informed decisions concerning instructional materials and equipment. Their analyses of materials and equipment are candid and objective.

EPIE is a nonprofit organization supported by grants, memberships, subscriptions, or individual publication orders; (1) a *comprehensive member* receives 8 EPIE Reports yearly plus 36 EPIEgram newsletters (two mailings per month, October through June), (2) a *materials member* receives 4 reports plus 18 materials newsletters, (3) an *equipment member* receives 4 equipment reports plus 18 equipment newsletters, (4) a *comprehensive subscriber* receives 36 EPIEgrams, (5) an *EPIE material subscriber* receives 18 materials newsletters, and (6) an *EPIE equipment subscriber* receives 18 equipment newsletters. A free publications list is available on request. Costs for membership or subscriptions range from $24 to $100 per school year. To place your order, contact EPIE Institute, P.O. Box 620, Stony Brook, NY 11790, (516) 751-1457.

Technical Applications Project (TAP)

Most members of the teaching profession do not have access to voluminous amounts of useful instructional materials, because of the difficulty of getting materials published. TAP is designed to identify and catalogue some of the "less visible (but educationally rich) instructional systems." These instructional systems include adult training packages as well as instructional materials for use with children. TAP includes a catalogue of brief descriptions (over 2,000) that can lead to individually ordered Instructional System Technical Descriptions (ISTDs), which in turn can lead to an individually ordered sample of the actual instructional material. Figure 3-3 depicts examples of catalogue entries.

Notable featuers of this system are that (a) emphasis is placed on the inclusion of systematic self-contained instructional packages and modules, (b) a priority is placed on field-tested materials, (c) the system leads selectively to more detailed information on materials in a particular interest area, and (d) unpublished materials, often provided at the cost of duplication, are available. A minicatalogue of materials is available on request. Costs include ISTDs—up to $1.25; sample lessons—up to $4.00; catalogues—a variety of combinations—up to $245.80 (approximate figure). Order from Technical Applications Project, 10455 Pomerado Road, San Diego, CA 92131.

Prescriptive Materials Retrieval System (PMRS)

The complete PMRS system is a self-contained manual search and retrieval system for instructional materials. It is not included in the next section of this chapter on diagnostic-prescriptive programs because it is often used as an information source by instructional materials centers. The Basic Educational

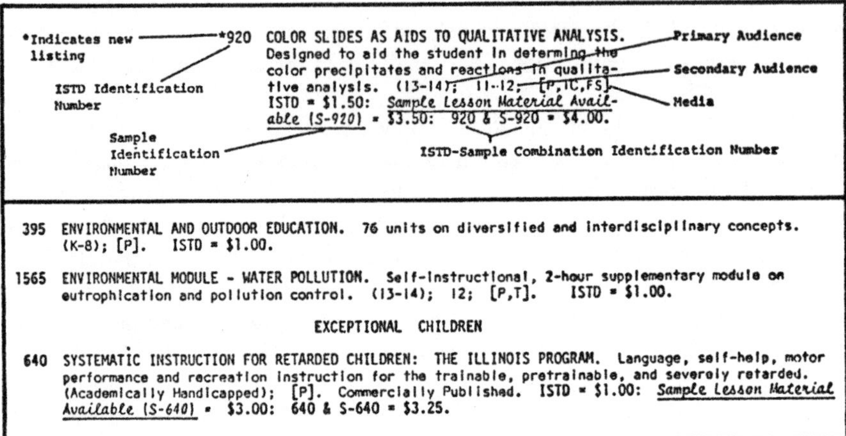

*920 COLOR SLIDES AS AIDS TO QUALITATIVE ANALYSIS. Designed to aid the student in determing the color precipitates and reactions in qualitative analysis. (13-14); 11-12; [P,IC,FS]. ISTD = $1.50: *Sample Lesson Material Available (S-920)* = $3.50: 920 & S-920 = $4.00.

395 ENVIRONMENTAL AND OUTDOOR EDUCATION. 76 units on diversified and interdisciplinary concepts. (K-8); [P]. ISTD = $1.00.

1565 ENVIRONMENTAL MODULE - WATER POLLUTION. Self-instructional, 2-hour supplementary module on eutrophication and pollution control. (13-14); 12; [P,T]. ISTD = $1.00.

EXCEPTIONAL CHILDREN

640 SYSTEMATIC INSTRUCTION FOR RETARDED CHILDREN: THE ILLINOIS PROGRAM. Language, self-help, motor performance and recreation instruction for the trainable, pretrainable, and severely retarded. (Academically Handicapped); [P]. Commercially Published. ISTD = $1.00: *Sample Lesson Material Available (S-640)* = $3.00: 640 & S-640 = $3.25.

Figure 3-3. *Sample TAP Catalogue Entries*

Source: Reprinted from *Technological Applications Project: Mini-Catalogue of Instructional Systems and Materials* with permission of the publisher. Copyright 1975, Technological Applications Project.

Skills Inventories (Adamson, Shrago, & Van Etten, 1972) for reading and mathematics, are assistive but not necessary to use the retrieval system. They do, however, allow the user to zero in on specific student skill deficits.

This system permits users to match specific child descriptions (418) to a selection of over 10,000 education materials. It also provides an index of some 200 publishers. The system can be updated (latest update-1979) and is compatible with almost any instructional materials service. Localization of the PMRs to fit specific holdings is possible.

The expense of PMRs (over $3,500) relegates its use largely to instructional materials centers serving entire school systems. Its materials descriptions (Descriptive Analysis Sheets) range from one to four pages and should be considered a preliminary step in locating materials. The descriptions should not be expected to replace teacher inspection of the actual materials, but do allow teachers to narrow the range of potentially useful materials or to more selectively choose materials they may wish to purchase. Order from B.L. Winch and Associates, 45 Hitching Post Drive, Building 2, Rolling Hills Estates, CA 90274.

Diagnostic-Prescriptive Programs

The criterion-referenced instruction movement has promoted the development of a variety of new approaches toward materials. Mastery tests are now routinely imbedded in basal materials and standardized achievement tests are often accompanied by a means of correlating test results with instructional objectives.

Another important development is the diagnostic-prescriptive program. These materials are published under a number of different titles and come with a variety of trappings. Their common feature is that instructional objectives are correlated with published (exception, IBAS correlates test results with clusters of objectives only) educational programs, often right down to the page number. They can assist not only in the selection of materials, but in the daily management of progress. A brief sample list of diagnostic programs is shown below:

Fundamental Operations Resources Environment (FORE or System FORE)

Function: Correlates teacher-made and commercial materials to skill sequences (strands) in language, reading, and mathematics at 36 (birth to 16 years of age) developmental levels; provides informal inventories, a standard materials list of publishers, and other information.

Components: The System FORE manual consists of sequences of objectives, informal inventories for each objective, materials information lists, and instructions for use.

Advantages: Teachers may add to or update the materials lists (published or teacher-made). The inclusion of language and the detailed sequencing of skills increase the utility of this program for the handicapped. It is affordable by single-classroom teachers.

Potential Drawbacks: System FORE is primarily prescriptive to materials that teachers may or may not have. Complete assessment is time consuming if not broken into sessions between units of instruction. There may often be a lack of correspondence between the sequence of objectives and the sequence of a child's current development.

Source: One of several versions may be obtained from FORE TRAIN, Box 237-A, Gainesboro, TN 38562.

Instruction Based Appraisal System (IBAS)

Function: IBAS is a planning and management system designed specifically for handicapped learners. Emphasis is placed on providing assistance in the development and management of individualized educational plans (IEPs).

Components: IBAS includes an introductory manual, a diagnostician's manual, a teacher's guide, six objective cluster banks, and a series of management forms.

Advantages: IBAS can be afforded and used by a single-classroom teacher. A variety of teacher-selected assessments may be used with the system. It is designed for diagnosticians as well as teachers. Objectives are clustered into goal banks.

Drawbacks: IBAS is not prescriptive about what instructional materials may be appropriate. Teacher variance in self-selection or preparation of reassessment systems is possible; general goals are mixed with specific objectives.

Source: Edmark Associates, P.O. Box 3903, Bellevue, WA 98009, (800) 426-0856.

Fountain Valley Teacher Support System in Reading (FVTSS-R) and *Fountain Valley Teacher Support System in Mathematics (FVTSS-M)*

Function: The Fountain Valley Teacher Support Systems in Reading and Mathematics were designed to provide classroom management systems including criterion-referenced tests based upon behavioral objectives and prescriptions for over 320 basals, programs, kits, workbooks, and audiovisual materials.

Components: A complete series of individual modules, color coded by grade level, grades K-8. Kits include a teacher's manual, cassette-taped test instructions or test-administration manuals, self-score or hand-score tests, teaching-alternatives supplements by grade level or packaged with individual tests (which provide prescriptions by page number, test number, film strip number or card number for over 320 commonly used materials available in the schools), and matching behavioral objectives on a one-to-one basis.

Advantages: The modules can be used within a single-teacher classroom or by a group of teachers and provide prescriptions for materials already used in the schools.

Drawbacks: It does not accommodate teacher-made materials or rarely used published materials.

Source: Richard L. Zweig Associates, Inc., 20800 Beach Boulevard, Huntington Beach, CA 92648.

Diagnosis: An Instructional Aid—Reading

Function: This program includes a detailed system of criterion tests that permit a teacher or diagnostician to match instructional objectives with basal reading programs and materials.

Advantages: "*Diagnosis:. . . .*" can be feasibly used within a single classroom if the teacher can afford the initial expense. Kit organization of probes permits easy access and reuse.

Drawbacks: The program is prescriptive only to a selected set of basal programs. Test materials are consumable duplicator pages. The program is fairly expensive considering a single teacher's budget (over $300). It is limited to the tests designed for the program.

Source: Science Research Associates, 155 North Wacker Drive, Chicago, IL 60606.

These are but a few of an inexpensive array of diagnostic-prescriptive materials that are available. Because they employ systematic measurement procedures and carefully sequenced objectives, they are of particular value for the instruction of handicapped children. Their potential for assisting in the transfer of handicapped children from special to regular classes is also a plus.

Some drawbacks are evident in the use of many diagnostic-prescriptive programs currently published. One problem arises when teachers attempt to use these programs as they may use other materials, picking and choosing some items or procedures. These teachers often become dismayed at the results and consider the program defective. The use of a diagnostic-prescriptive program is an all-or-nothing affair. The entire system, its procedure, its materials, and the materials it prescribes must be followed religiously. Otherwise the probability of success with the program is diminished. This requirement puts a tremendous burden on the program to demonstrate sufficient flexibility to be appropriate for a variety of classroom situations and materials currently in those classrooms. This is where the difficulty often lies with the selection of a single diagnostic-prescriptive program.

Another problem with many diagnostic-prescriptive materials is their limited use for a single-classroom teacher who decides to embark upon such programming alone. A few programs are designed for use within a single classroom (e.g., IBAS, Reading Diagnosis), but the costs of even these programs often exceed the entire materials budget for a single year ($125 and up). Since the programs are usually comprehensive, covering the entire primary range of a skill, finding other teachers who are willing to invest the time and cooperatively use a program is difficult (exception, System FORE). Several of the published diagnostic-prescriptive programs require the cooperation of an entire school (e.g., *High Intensity Reading*, Random House, 1974) or school system (e.g., *Individually Prescribed Instruction*, Research for Better Schools) as well as supportive clerical staff (now try Self-Check 3-2).

Because the concept of diagnostic-prescriptive programming is critical to the successful use of materials with handicapped children, teachers must be persuaded to adopt the principles as regular classroom routine. They must develop skills as diagnostic-prescriptive managers of instruction. That is the focus of Section II of this book: to help teachers manage materials in a systematic fashion. This management position is critical, whether it be through the use of a published diagnostic-prescriptive program or through a teacher-developed management system as described in Chapter 5.

Self-Check 3-2

FORMAT............ Programmed Paper

DOCUMENT NUMBER 367

READING LEVEL..

SHELF NUMBER

COST................

DESCRIPTIVE ANALYSIS SHEET

TITLE: Handwriting with Write and See Book 2 Manuscript-Cursive

AUTHOR: B. F. Skinner and Sue-Ann Krakower

PUBLISHER: Lyons and Carnahan

COPYRIGHT: 1968

NARRATIVE: Handwriting with Write and See, Book 2, Manuscript-Cursive, is designed for children who have mastered manuscript satisfactorily and are ready to learn cursive writing. The first 6 sections review the manuscript alphabet and numbers one through nine, and teach the child to recognize a uniform letter size, to estimate distance, to correct poorly-formed sections and teaches the formation of cursive lowercase and capital letters and cursive numerals. The author states that the book permits the student to work by himself much of the time, with the teacher functioning more as an advisor. The material can be adapted to any size group because each student may proceed at his own rate. The author suggests that students may be able to work for longer periods of time, having fewer periods per week. The paper is chemically treated to bring about a certain reaction when used with the special pen. There is a complete Teacher Edition for each text. In the teacher edition the correct letters and words are shaded in gray. In the pupil's book these areas are printed in invisible ink. The area shows how much a child may depart from the prescribed standard and still be considered correct. The teacher edition has an explanation for each section with comments about the exercises. Also included are suggested activities which offer supplementary experiences.

Instructions

A Descriptive Analysis Sheet (DAS) from the Prescriptive Materials Retrieval System is shown above. This self-check allows you to assess the materials information provided on the DAS regarding how informative it is on describing instructional characteristics. Use the portion of the Materials Review Form reproduced below to determine what information is provided.

Response

Direct Teaching

7. Appropriate practice: all pupil work is appropriate ___
some pupil work is appropriate ___
no pupil work is appropriate ___

Comment ______________________________

____

8. Reinforcement: general instructions ___
specific instructions ___
none specified ___

Comment ______________________________

____

(Are you going to have to design and implement your own reinforcement?)

9. Prompting: errorless responding possible ___
fading of prompts ___
no prompts provided ___

Comment ______________________________

____

10. Amount of adaptation required (number of characteristics) ___

Instructional Characteristics:

Format

	Self Instruction	One to One Tutoral	Small Group	Group
Initial Instruction	___	___	___	___
Drill and Practice	___	___	___	___
Enrichment	___	___	___	___

Comment ______________________________

____

Compare your response to the sample response in Appendix A.

How to Rob from Publishers and Make Them Love You for It

This heading may sound larcenous, but it sets the tone for this section. Teachers, particularly self-contained classroom and resource special education teachers, can be viable aides in disseminating information locally about a publisher's products. As the emphasis on accountable field-tested materials increases, publishers are going to find that they must establish a closer relationship with school personnel who may influence potential buyers. The teacher who is in a position to try out materials then can potentially benefit both publishers and other teachers.

The procedures outlined below are for obtaining materials preceding their purchase, or for experimental purposes. These procedures should not be employed under false pretenses. Teachers must make an honest attempt to do what they tell publisher representatives they are going to do with materials.

What may be offered to publishers in exchange for materials:*

1. You will thoroughly review the materials and inform other teachers for whom the materials may be appropriate.
2. If you are involved in curriculum committee decisions, you may offer to introduce the materials for consideration by the committee.
3. You may offer to try out and evaluate the materials in your classroom and thereby provide a locally based proving ground for materials that may assist in the transfer of educational progress from special to regular classrooms. Resource-room teachers are in an ideal position to offer and carry out this option since they usually have a variety of students receiving instruction on a wide range of skills.

Some points to aid you in establishing an alliance with publisher representatives include the following:

1. Large, established publishing companies are not as eager to give their products local visibility and may not be as willing to provide materials.
2. Publishing companies will be more interested in the local exposure of their materials but may not have sufficient resources to permit material give-aways.
3. Moderate-sized publishing companies that have been in business for a few years may be the most receptive to your offers of local assistance.

Procedures for obtaining assistance from publisher respresentatives exhibiting at education conventions are:

---

*The assistance of Kathy Reynolds is greatly appreciated.

1. Throughout the convention, spend some time simply talking to representatives at exhibits of interest. At the least, you will gain information and friendly interchange.
2. Do not hesitate to request a catalogue or to have your name placed on a mailing list.
3. To obtain materials that you will use, you must be able to explain precisely how you will be able to gain exposure for the materials among teachers "back home."
4. If you are unable to obtain the materials as an outright gift, request the materials on loan for a specified time.
5. One procedure for obtaining materials inexpensively is to wait until the last day of the convention when publisher represenatives are packing to leave. Many representatives would prefer to sell at half price or even give you some materials than to pack and transport large amounts of materials.

These same procedures are also helpful when a local representative visits your school or in written requests to publishers. In addition:

1. Ask specific, not general, questions about the materials and their use. If you are vague about what you want or how you will use materials, publishers may assume that you are on a fishing expedition and they may put you off.
2. Again, if free materials or sample units cannot be obtained request materials for a free examination period (see Figure 3-4).

Above all, be shrewd, but be honest in your dealings with publishers. Do not offer to do something with the materials you obtain unless you fully intend to follow through on your offer.

Free and Inexpensive Materials

You can obtain materials in a number of ways at no cost or at least inexpensively. The following list is a limited example of the sources that the ingenious teacher can conjure up.

1. *A Guide to Free and Inexpensive Materials* (*Free and Inexpensive Learning Materials,* 1975). This publication provides a wealth of alternatives that range from national to local sources.
2. *Federally supported research and development.* The Bureau of Education for the Handicapped supports a number of projects that are developing and field testing instructional materials. You may write to the var-

Figure 3-4. Sample Free-Examination Materials Request

ious divisions such as Media and Captioned Films or Field Initiated Research and obtain a list of their currently funded projects. From this list, appropriate projects may be selected for further correspondence. Materials can often be obtained from these projects for the cost of duplication.

3. *The school library.* You may obtain useful supplementary reading materials from books that are to be discarded at the end of the year or duplicate copies of current material. The school librarian can be a helpful "scout" on media and materials if you give him or her a list at the start of the year of the types of materials you are looking for.
4. *Private schools.* Materials that differ from those adopted by the public school system may be obtained from private schools. They often have unused materials and they may be willing to trade for some of your materials. Make sure that you have the approval of your immediate supervisor before you release public school property.
5. *Local merchants.* Materials for young or severely handicapped learners may be things obtained from hardware stores instead of publishers. Often local merchants will be interested in and receptive to helping a class of handicapped learners, particularly if it is for nonstandard school materials. Some sources and types of materials obtainable are listed below.

Source	*Type of Material*
Hardware stores	Home utensils, vocationally related items
Lumber yards	Shelving
Furniture stores	Carpet remnants, repairable furniture
Department stores	A broad variety
Grocery stores	Edibles for use as reinforcers, empty egg cartons, cut boxes for setting up a model store, and so on
Printers and business supplies	Paper, office supplies
Meat packing houses	Butcher paper
Crafts supply outlets	Manipulatives

SUMMARY AND CHALLENGE

There are a number of materials-information sources, as well as sources of materials at the national, state, and local levels, that teachers may take advantage of. It is also apparent that teachers are going to have to become increasingly self-reliant in their acquisition of materials information.

At the beginning of this chapter it was mentioned that there are some disturbing aspects of the materials-retrieval picture. It seems, through our informal surveys, that many materials-retrieval functions have become diverted to purposes other than direct assistance to teachers. We have no doubt that these other purposes can be supported by their potential for indirect or ultimate benefit to teachers. They may direct teachers toward appropriate publishers; they may seek publishers for worthy materials; they may develop new materials. The result may be that these are the best avenues for materials-support expenditures. We know that direct materials support for teachers on a national basis (e.g., the former SEIMC/RMC network) was an expensive endeavor. We also know that some direct support systems at the state and local levels were highly successful (e.g., Texas Education Agency, Franklin Pierce School System, Tacoma, WA).

Our point is that the indirect materials-support services now funded, taken as a whole, provide an unclear picture of exactly how much support the classroom teacher is actually receiving (Martin, 1974).

It seems that this condition has arisen from two sources: (1) instructional materials specialists' lack of agreement regarding the directions that materials-support services should take and (2) the apparent apathy of special and regular educators about expecting and getting materials support for handicapped children. Federal funding sources are simply responding to the advice and proposals of specialists in the field. State education agencies cannot be expected to place a high priority on materials support when their local constituents do not, and the local school system is going to have to cut the materials budget ("frills") first in its current fiscal plight.

Yet we are at a point where direct materials support for handicapped children is most critical and that support is at its lowest ebb. The demands of P.L. 94-142 and individualized education plans (IEPs) are ultimately the demands for appropriate instructional materials and their use, for few short-term objectives can be successfully fulfilled without materials. When the mainstreaming and normalization trends imposed significant changes in the classroom composition of regular-class teachers, as well as public school special education teachers, was there a concomitant shift in materials and other support? Many educators say no. Our current economic condition provides probably the strongest argument for a reexamination of indirect and direct materials support. School systems and teachers can afford to buy less from publishers; yet indirect materials support is often channeled through the publisher (more information about published materials, more materials published, new materials developed for publishers). It just may be that teachers need materials support at points where they *cannot* afford simply to purchase materials from publishers.

It appears that it is time to take a closer look at the ways in which materials support should be directed—and to consider returning to a "grass-roots" movement in the manner of more direct support for teachers. This does not mean the reestablishment of a national network, such as the SEIMC/RMC, is

Self-Check 3-3

OPEN ENDED

Complete one of the following:

A. Request information from one of the centers listed in this chapter.
B. Locate and order information from one state or local source.
C. Send a letter of inquiry to a publisher.

Since this self-check is open ended, there is no sample response.

needed, but a concerted effort to examine other direct support alternatives should be seriously considered. There have been numerous attempts to establish workable and cost-efficient, direct materials-support systems. Many have been less than successful but some local attempts have provided exemplary models. Enough have been developed to encourage further investigation. Sponsorship of further investigation into the development of local, direct materials-support systems seems to be one worthy alternative expenditure of the materials retrieval dollar.

The final self-check of this chapter (Self-Check 3-3) provides the reader with an opportunity to apply the materials-retrieval information of this chapter. Consider completing this self-check after you have finished the entire book.

CHAPTER 4

The Materials Budget: An Investment or an Expenditure?

Objectives

1. List the primary factors a teacher must consider when setting up a *new* classroom and determining what instructional materials to purchase.
   - Why is it important for the teacher to get an overview of the total classroom needs and all potential resources?
   - Why must student needs, teacher needs, and the physical setting be assured?
   - Is it wise to commit a substantial portion of your budget to diagnostic tests?
   - Should a teacher commit the majority of the budget to instructional materials, practice and drill materials, tests, games, or other motivational activities?

2. Describe the steps a teacher would take to determine which materials to purchase for an *ongoing* classroom.
   - Why is it important for this teacher to consider replacement items?
   - How can the teacher make a relatively judicious expenditure if the students to be served are not known?
   - Should a teacher ever arrange to make collaborative purchases with another teacher?

3. State three alternatives that teachers have to purchasing instructional materials.
   - What materials resources are available at the national or state level?
   - How can teachers join together to create instructional materials centers?
   - What can teachers do to influence the buying patterns of the people who are responsible for selecting materials at the local and state levels? To help the "buyers" understand teacher needs? To advocate for more control of the budget?
   - Why could "selling yourself" be considered a teaching competency?

To the teacher confronted with a severely restricted budget and seemingly unlimited needs, simply coping may seem virtuous. Such a teacher might ask (not too pleasantly), "What purchasing advice can be meaningful to me? I'm setting up a new classroom (or buying instructional materials for next year's class) with a meager $150. Is that not like asking someone who needs winter boots to be careful how he spends his 75¢ *and* be sure to get the best buy?"

At first glance, the budgetary constraints placed on most teachers look so tight as to border on the ridiculous. After further consideration and the realization that it is unlikely that this austere condition will improve in the near future, a number of ways to reduce the potential negative impact of this situation becomes apparent. First, the teacher must realize that there are wasteful ways and intelligent ways that even limited funds may be spent. Teachers can do more than just cope with a bad situation. They must realize that their purchasing decisions will either lead to improved student performance or detract from student learning. They must also recognize that they have the power of influencing higher level decision makers in productive ways.

For the teacher with a limited budget, effective and meaningful expenditure of funds begins with the understanding that purchasing materials is but one component of the larger task of matching total classroom needs to available resources. Ingenuity is required. The teacher willing to invest time and energy initially in the process of making budgetary decisions will find that thoughtful planning pays off in improved student performance. In all, wise budgetary decisions will necessitate assessment of all resources and total needs and matching them to each other. When teachers decide to purchase instructional materials, they are not simply deciding to *spend*. The decision to buy is a decision to *invest*. As with any investment, the teacher selects material A, B, or C because of expected short- and long-range advantages. The teacher's interest is to maximize profits and minimize losses.

The purpose of this chapter is to provide the teacher with guidelines for making sound investments in the instructional-materials market. The guidelines are intended to help the teacher minimize losses (pupils' wasted time) and maximize gains (student performance outcomes). Of course, priorities and actual investments will vary across teachers and student populations, but basic investment rules and procedures apply to all. The basic difference between materials investments and the stock market is that the profit to be gained is measured by changes in student performance rather than in dollars.

The most essential fact for teachers to keep in mind when selecting instructional materials is that publishers have designed and marketed materials to appeal to teachers. They are trying to sell you. They are experts. They know how to sell. In fact, they probably already know what you like. Publishers are aware of the latest jargon, special education trends and what will "turn you on." They use this information systematically. Publishers often create jargon, too, trying at once to be "with" and *slightly* ahead of the times. The teacher's task is to penetrate the smoke screen of fancy packaging, sophisticated titles, and promising testimonials. As one publisher has noted, the most expensive materials you will ever buy are those that do not work. Finding materials that do work is the teacher's charge. Materials that work but sit on the shelf because they are very narrow in scope or application or are only used occasionally are equally expensive.

WHAT TEACHERS ARE UP AGAINST

The marketplace is flooded with highly attractive, potentially usable, and oftentimes highly entertaining materials. Common materials are frequently given fancy titles, elaborately illustrated and sold at inflated prices (Hickman & Anderson, 1979). Publisher claims are appealing. Salespersons present convincing arguments for their products. Many materials claim to be designed for just the type of student found in the teacher's classroom, that is, the learning disabled, hyperactive, poor attender, and so on. Many of these materials look promising (see Chapters 2, 5, and 10 for more information on evaluating materials), but data on their effectiveness is often limited (Hickman & Anderson, 1979). The teacher must not be an impulse buyer (Bleil, 1975). The teacher must not purchase any material unless it is on a list of carefully selected materials previously chosen based on student needs. The teacher must not be tempted by "reasonable" prices or fancy displays.

The Teacher's Shopping List

The teacher uses basically four kinds of materials in the classroom. By knowing the kind of material that generally is most productive and identifying into which category chosen materials fall, teachers will be able to make wiser use of their limited funds. The four categories of materials are:

1. Instructional or core materials
2. Drill and practice materials
3. Test materials
4. Free-time activities materials (Bleil, 1975)

This is also the order in which purchasing priorities should be established. The bulk of money should be invested in instructional materials. Money is better expended on instructional materials than the other three options for several reasons:

1. It is critical to have sound core curriculum programs. These programs are the backbone of successful teaching, and every effort should be made to have such programs in all classrooms.

2. Well-sequenced, validated instructional materials take a tremendous amount of time and money to develop and test (Armstrong, 1971). Teachers can not prepare nor should they be expected to prepare wide-ranging instructional materials. Teachers should not "save" by planning to construct these materials themselves.

3. The educational goals that teachers and parents set forth in any given child's individual education plan (IEP) will most likely be related to improving performance and attaining forward progress across a sequence of skills in one or several of the major curricular areas. Instructional materials that provide for teaching the scope of priority curricular areas are vital to successful implementation of IEPs. The teacher's aim should be to build a pool of instructional materials that will allow for systematic teaching in all the basic curricular areas.

4. Drill and practice materials are not priority expenditure areas since these kinds of materials are often already available if the teacher takes the time to investigate. They may be found in storage rooms or central supply offices and borrowed from other teachers. Drill and practice materials and free-time activity materials are also simple and easy to construct. Similarly, if the curriculum does not contain placement and posttest materials, it is easy to construct criterion-referenced measures from core instructional material. This is not to imply that drill and practice is not important. For handicapped persons, it is often the most productive instructional and remedial approach if used appropriately. Emphasis should be more on teaching procedures than on the materials when drill and practice is considered (see Chapter 9).

5. Spending money for diagnostic tests not only reduces the amount available for purchasing instructional materials, but generally means that the teacher will be spending an intensive, extended period testing students before instruction. Given that scores from many standardized tests do not relate directly to

instruction, it seems that more direct instructional planning activities would be of greater benefit to students than long teacher-administered diagnostic batteries. Moreover, if extensive diagnostic testing seems warranted, it is probably more beneficial and cost effective to have the school's educational psychologist or diagnostic team conduct that testing.

In all, it is recommended that teachers expend the limited funds they have available to them on instructional materials. Most other materials needs can be satisfied by other means (see Tapping All Resources, below). For instance, drill and practice materials and free-time activity materials may be constructed in cooperative teacher work pools, by volunteers, aides, or the students. Why purchase materials that are easy to construct with minimal cost? The goals of instruction, it must be remembered, will not be met by filling the school day with a myriad of one-shot activities. A variety of experiences with different materials are beneficial, but they are not sufficient for achieving the gains that are possible using well-sequenced, integrated learning activities. Avoid spending money on frills and entertainment. Aim for spending money on materials that will promote student growth and skill development in guaranteed predictable ways!

Beware of the Kit!

Given that teachers know they should spend the majority of their budget on core instructional materials, they must be reminded that Madison Avenue tactics are often involved in instructional materials dissemination. They are silently but imposingly rendered in carefully worded advertisements; and the aftereffects of these tactics may be stacked three feet deep and six feet high in school supply and storage rooms.

Convenience is so valued in modern-day living that it may become a primary criterion for purchasing. Few would eat at a fast-food hamburger chain if they were required to wait for service similar to that in a fine restaurant. Fast food is convenient. We make our purchase quickly and fill an immediate hunger need. Quality and long-range benefits sometimes are not our concern. Similarly, kits are convenient. They are convenient to transport and store, but remember, if their content is in any way inappropriate, incomplete, or poorly sequenced, the price is dear. The more specially packaged and polished the materials, the more expensive they will be. Occasionally, components of a kit may cost substantially more than similar materials bought separately. On the other hand, kits are convenient and teacher time is at a premium. Generally, everything the teacher will need for a given lesson is there and readily accessible. Furthermore, the likelihood of accidental loss or breakage of material is reduced since the kit is a self-contained, well-organized, protective storehouse.

SETTING UP A NEW CLASSROOM

Setting up a new classroom is an exciting and challenging adventure. Often it occurs when special education programs are being expanded or moved to a new location. In the flurry of activity that typically accompanies such a situation, it is particularly critical for the teacher to take a long, concentrated look at the overall educational needs of students and at available resources. An overview of what will be required during the coming school year is an essential prerequisite to wise use of yearly funds. How well the teacher assesses the overall needs and resources will be reflected in:

1. The purchase of instructional materials that will enhance learning and facilitate classroom management
2. The purchase of materials that prove to be of little practical worth and force the teacher to back up and compensate for this year's mistakes with next year's funds

Needs Assessment

When teachers make an overall assessment of classroom needs, they consider three primary needs: the student's instructional needs, teacher needs and equipment, and space needs of the classroom itself (Boland, 1976). This overall assessment, although general in nature, should be made as specific as possible. Student needs, for example, may be assessed as in the following hypothetical case.

Suppose a teacher is preparing a needs assessment for a new class to be comprised of eight adolescent, moderately and severely mentally retarded students she has never met. Based on the teacher's knowledge of similar classrooms in the school system, she should have some notion of the kinds of skills and concepts that will need to be taught. The teacher is relatively safe in assuming that communication, functional academics, daily living, safety, and prevocational skill training will be high priorities (Bender & Valletutti, 1976). Integrating the students into school and community activities will also be a priority. It is likely that several students may have physical disabilities or sensory impairments. Seating and classroom arrangement must be considered. Several students may present behavior management problems, so a classroom-management system may be required. For all students the primary goals will be to move them to the highest level of independent functioning in the shortest time possible. Individualized instruction will be required—small-group teaching formats as well as one-to-one and independent work formats will be appropriate.

After having delineated the probable characteristics and needs of the student population, the teacher needs to consider her own needs. Is she prepared to teach in these priority areas? Which teaching formats are most effective for this teacher? It is likely that behavior management will be an issue with some students. The teacher prepares for this by taking into consideration classroom arrangement, instructional materials, and teaching procedures. The issue of how aides and volunteers can most effectively be employed must be addressed. How much training will be required to make these other people positive contributors to the classroom program? How will the selection of instructional materials affect these questions?

Finally, the teacher must analyze what is needed to make classroom space most useful. Are modifications needed with regard to the available open space? Is basic equipment missing? Are sinks, closet space, cooking areas, and so on available? Do partitions, tables, or other furniture need to be constructed? In short, a general inventory of the needs of the students, teacher, and classroom must be made. Only then will the teacher be prepared to make an initial determination of whether available instructional materials and equipment are adequate to her needs. By listing needs and potential resources, the teacher can identify the most pressing concerns. In the example below, the teacher has listed needs and resources on a sheet of paper. Based on a list such as this, a teacher will be better able to determine the kinds of instructional materials that will be most important to purchase (see Figure 4-1). Next, the teacher attempts to ascertain how many of these needs can be met without spending any of the allocated funds. After checking all the resources listed (and discovering some new ones), the teacher determines that she is mainly in need of an instructional package that teaches communication skills, in particular, expressive language. It is at this point that the teacher begins to review materials catalogues and assess the relative merits of different programs.

Specific Budgetary Considerations

Having identified an area of instructional materials need, the teacher is ready to assess the materials on the market and relate their price and potential effectiveness to available funds. Comparing the costs of instructional materials is highly advised (Brown, 1975). To make this assessment the teacher must consider a number of specific questions pertaining to the instructional materials of interest. After the teacher answers the questions on the Materials Review Form (see Chapter 2), she can compare dollar amounts of different materials to each other and to his/her needs statement. For instance, it may be that a full curriculum or instructional package is not needed or cannot be purchased because of limited funds. In that case the teacher will want to determine which components are essential and which elements might be eliminated, constructed, or replaced with materials already in the classroom. For example, many programs

Student Needs	Resources
communication training	-($300 total budget) speech/lang. therapist parts to Peabody kits available
functional academics	-curric available (need drill & practice)
daily living	-sequence available (need materials for toothbrushing and personal hygiene)
prevocal final	-several local businesses, shop & other school work areas
Teacher Needs	
varying teaching formats	-have self-paced materials
communication training competency	-speech, language, therapist for staff dev't
Physical Setting	
partitions, cubicles	-volunteers, donated materials
audio-visual equipment	-loan, school and public libraries
Other	
petty cash	-church, business and other clubs, parents, rotary
raw materials	

Figure 4-1. *Teacher Notes on Needs and Resources*

have audio-tutorial components that provide students with an introduction, rehearsal, or review of skills and concepts. In instances where the audio-tutorial materials are purely supplementary, a regular education teacher may choose to forego purchasing them. On the other hand, if the materials are designed to enhance and further extend a program being used by the regular classroom teacher, a resource teacher may select to purchase them. Materials that are inexpensive but allow for repeated use and appropriate practice, for example, sequenced worksheets, may be wise to buy in situations where audio-tutorial or other material requiring hardware have not been selected. The Materials Review Form, an initial form completed by the teacher, will be a helpful guide for determining which materials to purchase. After completing a material review of two or three instructional materials, the teacher should place the reviews side by side and compare the utility and benefits of each material.

Several sections of the Materials Review Form contain information that is particularly relevant for the teacher who is about to compare materials to make a purchasing decision. Figure 4-2 presents a sample of the general information section on that form. This general information is critical when screening materials initially for purchase. On the line next to "Subject," the teacher has written "Reading." "Self-care," "Language," or any other label might be entered, depending on the instructional materials being reviewed. The date the materials were reviewed is recorded next to the topic area. Materials being reviewed may relate to a particular level—grade level or functional level—and this is noted. Next, information on the "Scope" of the materials is checked. This information is very important to the teacher during the initial screening of potential instructional materials. Before comparing any material further, the teacher needs to determine that all reviewed materials focus on the skills or concepts that are intended to be taught. The scope of the materials, whether it is a comprehensive program, across-skill kit, or a single-skill kit, is indicated with a check mark. If the teacher is interested in a comprehensive reading program, single-skill kits will be eliminated from further analysis at this time. Only comprehensive curriculum materials and across-skills kits that seem particularly appropriate will be given closer inspection.

After reviewing all materials review forms in the reading file, the teacher will select two to three materials that appear to have potential. The teacher will then look at the section of the Materials Review Form entitled "Costs."

Figure 4-3 shows the actual price of the program should the teacher initially purchase the entire package. The costs of replacing parts of the program is also shown. The teacher should look to see what portion of the program needs to be replaced regularly. In this example, 20 percent of the material is consumable and would have to be regularly replaced. Replacement costs are practical considerations since decisions made this year could determine how the teacher

MATERIALS REVIEW FORM

Subject **Reading** Date Reviewed **9-12-79**

Level **K-6** Scope: Comprehensive **X**

Across Skills ____

Single Skill ____

Costs: (See Chapter 4)

Initial cost **$325.00** Comment (Are the cost factors within reason?)
cost per student **$36.00**

Replacement cost **$43.00** ____
portion consumable (%) **20%** ____
portion reusable (%) **80%** ____

Initial cost low? **X** ____

Replacement cost low? **X** ____

Hidden costs? **none** ____

Physical Characteristics:

(A) Media/hardware required..... ____
available................ **no**
obtainable............... **yes**
non-obtainable........... ____
alternatives?............ ____
service warranty?........ **yes**
local service?........... **yes**
can get on loan?......... ____
requires special training? ____

(B) Duplication required........ **X**
mimeo.................... **X**
xerox.................... ____

(C) Extra materials required.... **X**
locate................... ____
make..................... ____

(D) Sensory mode required
visual................... **X**
auditory................. **X**
tactual.................. ____
olfactory/gustatory...... ____

(E) Safety
toxic.................... ____
non-toxic................ **X**

(F) Durability of manipulatives
durable.................. **X**
non-durable..............

Figure 4-2. *Relationships between Information on Side One of the Materials Review Form and Budgetary Considerations*

Time Involved:

(A) Time to complete in program (estimated)
weeks 52 days 8/unit

(B) Daily time required
of teacher 20min. of learner 40min.
Comment Students maintain own records

Planning

1. Objectives: specific ✓ general ___ not stated ___
Comment ___
(Do the stated or implied objectives match your intent for the materials?)

2. Sequence: complete ___ gaps ___ not determinable ✓
Comment it appears to be complete, particularly lower level skills
(Is the sequence thorough and in logical order?)

3. Redirection: can recycle ___ can vary instruction ✓
no redirection specified ___
Comment not programmed for recycling at every level; intermittent recycling

Measurement

4. Initial assessment: placement ✓ pretest ✓
no initial assessment ___
Comment ___

5. Progress assessment: daily ___ weekly ___
summary chart or graph ✓ none specified ___
Comment ___

6. Mastery assessment: same as initial assessment ✓
same as progress assessment ___
new assessment ___
no mastery assessment ___
Comment ___
(Are you going to have to supply another assessment?)

Direct Teaching

7. Appropriate practice: all pupil work is appropriate ✓
some pupil work is appropriate ___
no pupil work is appropriate ___
Comment ___

8. Reinforcement: general instructions ✓
specific instructions ___
none specified ___
Comment Answer sheets could be constructed easily; children can do their own graphing
(Are you going to have to design and implement your own reinforcement?)

9. Prompting: errorless responding possible ✓ (in some activities)
fading of prompts ___
no prompts provided ___
Comment ___

10. Amount of adaptation required (number of characteristics) minimal

Figure 4-3. *Relationships between Information on Side Two of the Materials Review Form and Budgetary Considerations*

spends next year's money. Cost per pupil is figured. How many children will use the program and what it will cost for each student are important variables. Next, the teacher who reviewed the material will indicate whether these costs are low enough to be feasible purchases within the current and projected budget. Any material that is 80 percent reusable, as in this example, will have much appeal. The teacher also will have noted whether the program has any hidden costs, costs that might become apparent only after the initial purchase is made and the program is in use. For instance, a large number of batteries might be required or transparencies that are not included in the price of the program may be necessary for group presentation. A service warranty that does not state that an initial $10 charge is made on all service or that materials must be rented while the teacher's equipment is being fixed are hidden costs.

After the actual dollar amounts are reviewed, the teacher will look at the "Physical Characteristics" section of the Materials Review Form. There are several questions in this section that are pertinent to purchasing materials. First, the teacher will see if the instructional materials require the use of special hardware, media, or other equipment. If so, is that equipment already available to the teacher? Whether the equipment has a warranty and whether service can be procured locally are important budgetary considerations. Can materials be made available on loan during the time repairs are being made? Is special training required to use the materials? All of these factors are conditions that may potentially preclude use of an instructional material. As has been mentioned, any materials that are not being used, whatever the reason, are the most expensive materials the teacher will ever purchase. Materials that require special training to use, maintain, and repair are also potentially more costly in the long run. In addition, the teacher should check to see if the materials are durable. Durable materials are very desirable. Children are not going to handle materials gently. For some populations, especially durable materials may be required. Durable materials, although initially expensive, will eventually save money. The example material costed out in Figure 4-4 is attractive in regard to all of these factors.

Having compared instructional materials along these dimensions, the teacher should then examine the sections of the Materials Review Form pertaining to "Time Involved" and "Instructional Characteristics" (see Figure 4-3). Materials that seem most amenable to the classroom schedule and children's needs should be given higher consideration for purchasing than materials that do not provide satisfactory coverage in terms of daily instructional time or total length of the program. The teacher also needs to consider the time required each day interacting with the materials or with the students and the materials. In the "Instructional Characteristics" section, the teacher will pay particular heed to the comments and questions regarding adaptation. If substantial adaptation is

Budget - $150.00

1. Instructional Materials	Cost
Reading Program	$325.00 - $200.00 (from shared buying with Mrs. D & Ms. W) leaves $125.00 - $25 (donation from Rotary)
	$100.00
2. Drill & Practice Materials	use current supply center
	$15.00 - copy & adaptation
3. Test Materials	N.A.
4. Free Time Materials	$10.00 - rental fee
5. Other Costs	
Reinforcers, Field Trips, etc.	$30.00
	$155.00
	- 5.00 (get donation or reduce free time costs)
	150.00

$115/150 ≈ 5/6 of budget for instructional purposes)

Figure 4-4. Example of a Teacher's Budget Summary

required, albeit in designing measurement systems or modifying the core instructional materials themselves, it may not be economical for the teacher to consider purchasing the materials. Materials such as those in Figure 4-3 will provide 40 minutes of instruction to the learner for an entire year. This again seems to be a positive attribute. Twenty minutes of daily teacher time may or may not be an advantage, depending on the teacher's overall classroom schedule and materials-management plan.

After comparing as many completed Materials Review Forms as needed, the teacher is ready to make a final instructional materials selection. The teacher should write down all the materials purchased on a sheet of paper to summarize the expenditures. Other costs besides instructional are also entered on the summary sheet. This sheet will serve as a record of all items included in the budget in any given year. It will allow the teacher to evaluate the overall budget and to review previous budgets so unnecessary costs are avoided in the future. The teacher should note the *kinds* of expenditures planned. The summary notes of the teacher can be kept in the Materials Analysis File in its own folder.

A teacher setting up a new classroom should expect to spend 75 to 80 percent of the total budget on instructional materials, about 15 to 20 percent on other materials, and the remainder on miscellaneous costs. If the percentage of expenditures breaks out grossly different from these figures, the teacher should be able to justify the deviation.

Before proceeding further in the chapter, complete Self-Check 4-1, which consists of questions related to spending limited funds for instructional materials.

THE CONTINUATION BUDGET

After several years of serving special learners, most teachers will have gathered a relatively comprehensive range of curricular materials. Although these teachers may no longer be in need of purchasing core instructional materials, the task of spending money wisely, to supplement or enrich their core materials, is still difficult. Since materials are usually purchased in the spring, teachers may buy materials that will not be useful in their fall classes. Often teachers do work with children whose learning characteristics are similar from year to year; however, a number of next year's children will likely have considerably different instructional needs.

For a starting point, the teacher budgeting for next year's class will need to completely inventory all materials. Those materials that are battered and have important pieces or components missing should be set aside from the other materials. An effort should be made to determine if these materials can be salvaged. If so, a plan should be made to repair or replace such materials. In

Self-Check 4-1

Answer the following questions.

1. Name the four categories into which materials can be placed.

 ____

 ____

2. Which materials should receive higher purchasing priority, test materials or instructional materials?

 ____

3. State two reasons why the purchase of diagnostic tests may be ill-advised, particularly if the teacher's budget is limited.

 ____

 ____

4. Name the three major needs that a teacher must assess to determine overall needs before setting up a new classroom and spending allocated funds.

 ____

 ____

Please answer true or false

1. Materials that are well sequenced, comprehensive, and have numerous pre-posttests are inordinately expensive if they remain on a shelf.
 True *False*
2. Drill and practice materials often can be borrowed from other teachers or constructed relatively cheaply.
 True *False*
3. Kits should never be purchased unless the teacher has an unlimited budget.
 True *False*
4. The Materials Review Form contains a section on "Physical Characteristics" of materials. The amount of hardware, service warranties, durability, and hidden costs are assessed. These items are all relevant to the teacher making purchasing decision.
 True *False*
5. Materials that require extensive adaptation might be "expensive" even if the original cost per student is low.
 True *False*

other cases the damaged or incomplete materials may need to be tossed out and new ones purchased. Boland (1976) suggested that teachers should not throw away all the components of materials that are being replaced. Rather, remaining parts should be saved and used as replacements. When purchasing replacements is necessary, the teacher will need to determine precisely which components are needed and how many units of each to order. If a major instructional program is in poor condition, this may be the time to consider purchasing an entirely new product.

Since teachers often are required to order instructional materials for the coming year in the spring, they will in fact be trying to predict learner needs. In spite of the likelihood that teachers can accurately predict learner needs most of the time, it is possible that teacher's expectations will not match student needs. In instances when the teacher finds that materials ordered are inappropriate, he or she should consider returning the materials and selecting more appropriate instructional materials to order. It is unlikely that a teacher will have difficulty receiving credit for returned materials. The major disadvantage of reordering in the fall might be having to wait for the new materials to arrive. On the other hand, postponing some instructional activities may be less expensive in the long run than spending time and money to adapt inappropriate materials.

When considering the purchase of instructional materials for the coming year, it is helpful for the teacher to evaluate student needs in each area in which more materials may be required. Figure 4-5 shows how one teacher determined his instructional materials need in reading. First, the subject area of reading is divided into five major subskill areas. The materials currently available to the teacher are noted next to each subskill and a check mark is used to indicate whether the materials are adequate to meeting learner needs. When "No" is checked, the teacher has found another material. Its price is also noted. In this example the teacher required additional material in primary vocabulary building and comprehension. Materials totaling under $50 were located and ordered. (See Chapter 2 for more on conducting an inventory of available materials.)

One habit well worth forming is to continue searching for instructional materials throughout the entire year. The best preparation teachers can make to provide for next year's instructional material needs is to increase their knowledge of available materials in a consistent, systematic manner. Surveying materials and then further analyzing one to three instructional materials each month should keep any teacher generally knowledgeable of what the marketplace has to offer. These activities will also help teachers make objective decisions regarding which materials are most likely to yield the greatest gains. Nurturing relationships with company representatives by frequent telephone contacts or inviting them into your classroom also has benefits. Besides making

Subject		Adequate? yes	no	New Materials
Reading	Sounder, Distar			
Sound-Symbol	" "	✓		
Word Attack	" "	✓		
Sight Words			✓	Pathways to Reading Prim. Vocab. Skills
Oral Reading			✓	\$9.00
Comprehension			✓	Corrective Reading Levels A, B, C \$10.00; 22.50; about 10.00

COMMENTS: a total of about \$50.00 will be required, possibly more. I need to check new price and listing.

Figure 4-5. *Evaluating Costs of Materials for a Continuation Budget*

the teacher aware of the latest educational products, many representatives can serve as consultants, advising teachers on how to use given materials and describihg the means by which other teachers have employed the materials successfully. Across the years such persons may become one of the teacher's primary resources. Similarly, with each additional year teachers will become more familiar with other teachers in their school and their ability mutually to capitalize on ideas and materials resources should increase.

COPYING AND COPYRIGHT

Since conservation and wise expenditures will serve teacher and children well in the short and long run, teachers should always be looking for ways to save. One common practice is to copy materials from various programs and use them as needed in supplementary, drill, or testing functions. Although this is relatively economical, often it is illegal. Some publishers give permission to copy components of their materials printed in the materials themselves; others seldom provide blanket permission. To avoid a potential copyright suit, the teacher might just as easily seek permission from the author or publisher to reproduce parts of their program. In many cases the author and/or publisher will gladly grant their permission. To ask permission to copy materials, send a brief letter explaining who you are, why you want to copy the materials, and how they will be used. Most publishers and authors reply to such requests promptly. It might be wise, however, to submit permission letters during the summer, if you can anticipate which materials you will be using. Figure 4-6 is a sample of a letter a teacher might use to seek permission to reproduce components of an instructional program. The teacher in this example states her purposes clearly and suggests that the publisher will benefit by granting her permission to copy materials. (Please take time to complete Self-Check 4-2. It should be enjoyable.)

TAPPING ALL RESOURCES

The money available for teachers to purchase instructional materials is indeed minimal and usually insufficient for its intended use. The most feasible alternative for teachers is to seek means of meeting the needs of the students, teachers, and the setting without spending precious funds.

Surprisingly, a relatively unlimited number of optional revenue and materials resources are available. Many and varied means are also available by which instructional materials and other materials needs can be met with minimal or no expense. Suggestions for meeting instructional needs or cautions for avoiding unnecessary or unwise expenditures are presented below:

1. Collaborate with other teachers in the purchase of core instructional materials. It may be that other teachers in your school are also in need of similar instructional materials. By combining funds, the desired materials may be able to be purchased to the mutual satisfaction of all participating teachers. Teachers must be sure they agree upon the manner in which the materials will be dispersed or shared once they arrive.

2. Do not attempt to hold your money over from one year to the next. It may seem beneficial not to spend all of the budgeted money because more positive outcomes could be achieved if money combined from two years was used to buy one major program. However, such planning seldom works out to the advantage of the teacher. Usually money held over between fiscal years is returned to a general fund and not reassigned to the thrifty teacher the following year.

3. If you have a choice when to buy materials, select a time of the year when you can anticipate your needs at least six to twelve weeks in advance. This will help ensure that your materials order is processed and the materials delivered by the time you need them. Also, buy when you will have enough time *adequately* to assess materials effectiveness and compare costs.

4. Joint construction and use of materials is also very productive for most teachers. Cooperative plans among teachers can save time and money. General rules and responsibilities should be established with regard to the manner in

BURNSTOWN UNIFIED SCHOOL DISTRICT
BURNSTOWN, PENNSYLVANIA

Superintendent
A. Henry Henry

Assistant Superintendent
Grace Glace

September 29, 1979

Dear Sir or Madame:

I have been a special education teacher at Woodworth Elementary School in Burnstown, Pennsylvania for five years. During that time I used the Rebus Reading Program very successfully as my initial reading program for children with moderate to severe learning handicaps. Recently, I was promoted to special education supervisor for the county. I would like permission to duplicate pages from the Rebus Workbooks so that my teachers might make overheads and conduct group lessons with the children. I have found such adaptations to be quite helpful in the past with other programs, feel it would promote learning across the classrooms that I will be supervising, and thereby increase teacher receptivity to the program.

Thank you very much for considering this request for permission to duplicate.

Very truly yours,

Samuel Reelyneedy
Special Education Supervisor

Figure 4-6. Sample Letter to a Publisher Requesting Permission to Duplicate

Self-Check 4-2

Please read the following sample letters and state three reasons why each is or is not a letter that is likely to receive a positive response from the publisher.

A. My school is not giving me enough money to do half of what I need to do to see that my children get a good education this year. For one thing, I have to order all my materials early in the spring for the next year. This year when I got to school I did not get the class I thought I would be teaching. Now I need to teach arithmetic. I do not have any more money to spend and there are no materials for teaching arithmetic. May I copy your workbook materials to use with my students?

____

____

B. I am teaching in a special school for children with learning disabilities. We are a private, nonprofit organization that has just opened for the first year of school. If our program is successful we will be expanding to two new locations in Idaho next fall and three out-of-state locations. At this time, however, we have not determined which materials will be used in our reading program. We have several programs that we will be trying out this year. Your program, Open Highways, will be used in four classrooms. I would like to request permission to copy components of the readers so we can give special, frequent individual tests to our students. If the program works well, we will adapt it next year and use it throughout all of our schools.

____

____

C. I am giving workshops to different groups of teachers throughout the state of Wisconsin on improving the spelling performance of their students. Typically, 300 to 500 teachers will participate in these workshops. I would like to introduce them to Michigan Learning Modules, Programmed Spelling, by J. Smith, C. Farrell, J. Wolter, and D. Smith. I am unable to purchase these materials because of the cost that would be incurred since all of my teachers will be participating in simulations that require actual responding in the material. Therefore, I would like permission to make photocopies of sections of the Programmed Spelling Modules so I will be able to use your materials in these workshops.

____

____

Compare your response to the sample response in Appendix A.

which individual teachers will contribute to and benefit from cooperative ventures. Another idea is to convert extra school space into a central storage, retrieval, and work area. Workbenches, ditto and copy machines, raw construction materials, and other equipment can be kept in that room and teachers or volunteers will have a single, central location to construct and file materials.

5. A number of companies or projects provide samples or prototype versions of materials free or inexpensively. Teachers should watch for advertisements in catalogues, professional journals, and even local newspapers.

6. Ordering in bulk will be a long-term savings; however, if the materials ordered are not appropriate for the children, they will end up in storage. Try to anticipate your true needs for various materials. Order only materials you have tried out or reviewed. Otherwise order materials for a trial period before purchasing.

7. Avoid buying most representational objects, for example, toy brooms, chairs, and so on; use real objects instead. Often "real" materials will prove to be less expensive!

8. Rather than purchase commercial manipulatives for mathematics programs, for example, use familiar, common objects. Have a local carpenter (who is volunteering) make your counting rods with materials donated from a local lumber company. Students in the classroom and older students can also be very helpful in gathering raw materials and constructing many things. Be sure to use good raw materials to ensure their durability. An arrangement with the art teacher for the construction of specified items is always a probability.

9. Project or year endings are good times for teachers. Many materials of educational worth are often given or thrown away by other teachers at the end of the school year, at the termination of a state or federal project, or at "going out of business" sales. Be there. Get your share.

10. Most companies are willing to provide sample materials and materials on a tryout basis. See that your name is placed on all lists for receiving samples. Local sales representatives are often a good source for materials and can put your name on such lists. (See Chapter 3 for further information on retrieval of materials.)

11. At conventions and professional conferences, many publishing companies display their products. This is a good time to get to know the exhibitors and gather samples. The teacher can also ask about company policy with regard to donating or loaning materials. Teachers might even volunteer to participate in the field testing of company products.

12. Be sure to talk with someone who is familiar with instructional materials that you have not tried. Ask for expert help in interpreting any validation data the publisher may supply.

13. Often there are lending libraries within your local or state school system. Find out how to gain access to these. Do not purchase materials you can bor-

row or that will only be used for short periods. Other teachers often have a personal library of instructional materials. They may have something perfectly suited to another teacher's needs. It is important for teachers to ask around. Colleges and universities often have materials lending libraries that are available to be used by teachers. (See Chapter 3 for further information.)

14. Because many services and materials may be obtained through local citizen groups, churches, and businesses, it is very important for teachers to learn to present their "situation" effectively. Diplomatic but straightforward requests for money, reduced costs, services or opportunity to use facilities, and so forth should be stated to make the giver feel that he or she is contributing to something meaningful and important (and/or something that will be of direct benefit to the benefactor, for example, a tax deduction, good publicity). Teachers should not be afraid to ask for assistance on repeated occasions, even if they were not granted their initial request. Often there are new people in decision-making roles at a later date or the person will now be more amenable to your idea. Of course, never forget to provide a personalized, and preferably public, thank you. Recently a resource room teacher commented that she felt like a "con artist" in her many attempts to gain free materials and services. She then went on to tell of the great progress her students were making, smiling broadly, knowing that her style of asking had reaped many positive returns for her students. We are sure that her uneasy feelings are ill-warranted, since her students' progress was remarkable and her "beneficiaries" continue to respond positively to her requests.

15. If it appears that no federal- or state-funded educational programs are located in the area, look for related programs that might have a surplus of materials. Programs for senior citizens, for instance, often have a wealth of raw construction material available. Furthermore, the participants in such programs are often skilled in a number of areas and able to help teacher and students in many additional ways. Look for other such programs.

16. Remember to use each succeeding year to build the basic curriculum areas. Keep long-range goals in mind with regard to all purchases or commitments of time and energy.

17. Audiovisual hardware and software are often very expensive. It is advisable to chart out the possibility of requisitioning these on loan or rental before considering purchasing them.

SPECIAL PROBLEMS?

Too Much Money

Could it be possible that some teachers find themselves in the position of having more money than they know how to spend? Yes, although very few teachers actually do have too much money. Teachers in such a "dilemma" are often in special settings and projects that receive funding from a variety of sources. In some respects their task is as formidable as the teacher with limited funds. "Rich" teachers must be careful not to succumb to the temptation to buy everything in sight. If they are not cautious their shelves might become stacked with materials, many in duplicate, while their students' learning environments may be no more conducive to learning than relatively Spartan classrooms.

The responsibility of spending excessive funds in an accountable fashion is equally serious, if not more serious, than spending small dollar amounts. As with other teachers, "rich" teachers should set priorities—first, purchasing instructional materials that will build a strong, valid core curriculum. Another reasonable expenditure is to buy consumable instructional materials that children are allowed to keep and that will afford continued use. For instance, paperback readers might be purchased and replaced instead of using hardback. Clearly it is more valuable to have materials distributed and being used than on a shelf.

Teachers with too much money should keep a cumulative list of products they believe will be wise purchases. Each time the teacher discovers and reviews a product that would make a worthwhile purchase, it should be added to his or her list. This list should then be used in the purchase of all materials. Such a list should control impulse buying and strengthen the teacher's materials reserve. Teachers with excessive funds may decide to place a greater amount of money in drill and practice materials than teachers with limited funds who need to construct their own drill and practice materials. This is a legitimate expenditure. To further extend the benefits derived by students through the use of materials, teachers with a generous budget may create their own lending library. Other teachers could then borrow materials that are not currently being used.

No Money

If you are receiving absolutely no money for purchasing instructional materials and covering other miscellaneous costs, it is advisable for you to make inquiries at higher administrative levels. Money has probably been allocated for your classroom but is being dispensed in other ways because no one has voiced a need. The teacher will need to claim the money or claim the right to say how it should be spent.

Another way that teachers can extend their instructional materials supply in a "no-money" situation is evident when parents volunteer to contribute directly to the preparation or purchase of materials for use *at home*. In such instances, the teacher materials are for *their* child only. During parent conferences or in writing, the teacher should inform interested parents of the possible benefits of materials used at home with small additional costs to the family. Teachers should identify inexpensive items that would help their son or daughter improve his or her skills if they are used in the home. It should also be stressed to parents that they spend no more than two or three dollars a month purchasing instructional materials or educational games. Teachers should keep parents informed about their son or daughter by sending a short note home once or twice a month. On the note the teacher could list materials that would be particularly helpful for their child to use at home. For instance, they might suggest that flash cards be prepared or bought for practicing simple arithmetic computations. The teacher should also provide suggestions on how the materials might be used (e.g., how long each evening practice session should be, what kinds of things the parent can do to help the child if they are working with him or her, and so on). The teacher should also ask parents to report occasionally to the school. This would give the teacher input on how sessions at home are going and when new suggestions are needed. By setting up a system whereby parents buy materials for their own children and are given instructions on how to help their child, teachers will effectively increase the amount of time that each student interacts constructively with materials.

Infiltrating the Decision Makers to Make Friends and Advocates for Your Students.

Many decisions are made, ostensibly for the welfare of all students, but seem to reflect little concern for individual or special students. For example, the only instructional reading material available to teachers of learning disabled children, 8 to 12 years of age, in one system was a choice of one grade level in a state-adopted basal series. Unfortunately for the students and the teacher, the reading competencies of the students ranged from two total nonreaders to one child reading at the 7th grade level. A supply of 15 third-grade readers was hardly sufficient to meet the educational needs of these students and to allow the teacher to design an efficient learning environment.

If teachers are ever to overcome such situations they will need to infiltrate the decision makers and have an impact on the decision-making process. The questions to ask are simple. Why are things the way they are? How can they be changed to accommodate needs A, B, and C? If teachers are ever to have their instructional needs met, they will need to begin advocating for themselves and their students. Such advocacy should begin the first day of school and continue throughout the year. Waiting until it is time for next year's budget to be drawn up is usually too late. Policies and procedures with regard to delivering educational services to exceptional learners should be discussed with anyone who will listen and with decision makers in particular. Principals, administra-

Self-Check 4-3

OPEN ENDED

Instructions

Complete the following assignment. You will need to gather two to three instructional materials to finish this assignment.

You are teaching in a resource room for children in a middle school. You need to purchase a basic curricular program for teaching reading.

Use the Materials Review Form to evaluate two available instructional materials that appear to be able to meet your needs.

Which program would you select? Why?
What are the features of the instructional materials that are most central to meeting your particular needs?

Which program would you select or what elements would you purchase if your budget were limited to $250?

Since this self-check is open-ended, there is no sample response.

tors, school board members, and parents should be invited to classrooms and thoroughly informed about what is needed and why. It may be that teachers are not allocated sufficient funds, for example, simply because no one has been informed about teacher needs precisely enough to advocate for them when budgets are prepared. Continuous advocacy work on the part of individuals and groups of teachers is likely to be required before policies for purchasing and distributing materials are improved. Although the law technically supports the position that better instructional materials and closer attention to individual learner needs must be matched, often more than legislative action is necessary to ensure change. By advocating for the special learners in your classroom and persisting in the demand for improved policies with regard to spending money for exceptional children, teachers and learners will reap increased benefits. In short, the role of advocating for sufficient funds to purchase needed instructional materials is part of each teacher's personal, professional, and ethical responsibility. (At this time proceed to Self-Check 4-3.)

II
Materials Management

CHAPTER 5

Managing Progress Through Materials

Objectives

1. Describe how to transfer individual education programs (IEPs) into daily plans and skill sequences presented through materials.
   - What is a standard reference point for comparing all aspects of instruction?
   - How can I manage my planning so IEP implementation is an integral part of instruction?
   - How can I relate materials to the implementation of IEPs?

2. Prepare and implement a materials-management system.
   - What is involved in selecting and supplementing skill sequences?
   - Which tests can I match with the skill sequence?
   - How can I manage materials using this section?
   - How does this system help the IEP reporting process?
   - How can I report results using the IEP?

3. Adapt tests and other materials for management purposes.
   - Can I adapt tests to make materials prescription more feasible?
   - How can I adapt instructional materials for testing purposes?

IEPS, DAILY PLANS, AND DAILY INSTRUCTION

Teachers are in the process of assuming a different role. Instead of acting as direct interveners, they are rapidly becoming managers of instruction (Brown, 1975). The need to individualize instruction, particularly with handicapped learners, has made it necessary for teachers to seek ways other than direct minute-by-minute teacher contact to provide adequate instruction. Materials are increasingly relied upon to assist teachers. Consequently, the demands upon teachers to improve their organization and management skills has also increased.

As we have repeatedly intimated throughout this book, the effective use of instructional materials is highly dependent upon how closely the teacher can relate materials to critical elements of instruction. This is a management concern.

Written individualized education programs (IEPs) are required for all handicapped persons enrolled in school. Implementation and reporting of progress made and goals met are also required. The means by which IEPs are implemented, including the specification of materials to be used, is also required.

The implementation of IEPs is currently viewed by many teachers and school administrators as a pain in the neck. The extra paper work, meetings, and information reporting are thought to be getting in the way of teaching. This condition will continue as long as the writing, implementing, and evaluating of IEPs is carried on outside of regular instructional activities. However, there is another alternative. What if these IEP functions were merely a by-product of normal instructional activities? What if teachers used a classroom-management system that allowed them simply to transfer what they are doing on a day-to-day basis in their classroom over to an IEP reporting form? If this could be done, it would drastically reduce the extra work brought on by IEPs.

This chapter presents critical elements in materials management that are being successfully employed by teachers who have handicapped children in their classrooms. IEP writing, implementation, and evaluation are part of routine activities in these classrooms. Of course, some of the other IEP functions that are external to the classroom still require additional time and effort.

For review, here is an abbreviated list of the components of an IEP:

1. A statement of present levels of educational performance
2. A statement of short-term objectives to be attained
3. A listing of the annual goals to be attained
4. Objective criteria, evaluation procedures, and a schedule of checkpoints for when short-term objectives are to be attained
5. A list of person(s) responsible for the attainment of these goals and objectives
6. A statement of the educational and special services to be performed, including (a) the services and (b) a physical description
7. The date begun and the length of time involved
8. The extent of participation in regular education programs
9. A justification for the type of placement

Although a separate IEP form and progress report will always have to be maintained for each student, the main problem arises when teachers must dig into a variety of past and present records to come up with the appropriate information necessary to fill out the forms. If this information were available in a centralized source that was used on a routine basis, the transfer of information to IEP reporting forms would be a simple process. The management system described in this chapter is intended to make IEP reporting a routine process. It would provide information contributing toward (1) identifying present levels of educational performance, (2) specifying short-term objectives, (3) formulating annual goals, (4) specifying criteria and evaluation procedures, (5) designating the special services performed, particularly the materials involved, and (6) noting pertinent dates for the start and end of instruction on given objectives. These points are discussed further following a rationale for and a description of the management system.

A Standard Reference Point

One of the most notable features of an IEP is that it helps to reduce major educational decisions to a standard reference point: the educational performance of the handicapped learner. This reference point is most clearly represented by an objective.

An objective, particularly a behaviorally stated objective, has utility far beyond how it is frequently used. It is often something that may be prepared at the start of instruction and then left in a planning folder until instruction is completed, or it may be used to compare against results at the end of instruction in May, when it is too late to do anything about it. Actually, it is directly related to all aspects of instruction and is the gauge against which these aspects of instruction may be compared. The basic question to be asked then is: "Does what the learner does (his or her response) in (a) tests, (b) materials, and (c) direct instruction match the response stated in the behavioral objective?"

All other judgments about the quality of instruction, short of the learner's resultant performance, are minor compared to this most crucial question.

To reiterate:

- A test should sample the behavior specified in the objectives.
- A set of materials should allow the learner to practice the behavior specified in the objectives.
- As a teacher involved in direct interaction with learners, you should allow them to engage in the responses specified in your objectives.

The third point seems utterly obvious, and yet it is either the most commonly violated or the most difficult principle of instruction to attain (Smith, Neisworth, & Greer, 1978). Children are often seen practicing five or six different responses on a work sheet when the objective specifies one response. A teacher will often spend an inordinate amount of time explaining, prompting, directing, questioning, and so on, while the learner rarely has an opportunity to engage in responding other than listening. A test often assesses a general skill area while providing little information on specific objectives of interest.

If there is anything we know about what affects learning, it is time—the time a learner has to work at a task. A management system must help match learners with materials so the greatest amount of time is spent practicing the responses specified by the objectives.

Mastery Criteria

How do we decide the exact point at which instruction on an objective should start, stop, or change? No single point is right for all tasks and all children; yet floating criteria can also produce a substantial amount of wasted teacher-learner time. "I'll move Jimmy on when I feel confident that he has sufficiently internalized the concept of borrowing in subtraction" is an objective and criterion that could keep Jimmy sitting for days or even weeks on a task that he could have moved up from. Conversely, many handicapped children are moved too rapidly up a curriculum ladder before they have a firm grasp on the lower rungs. Floating criteria at both the lower and more advanced levels will often prevent the teacher from detecting difficulty early enough.

Fixed and quantifiable criteria are essential to effective materials management. These criteria may have to be arbitrarily set at first, but they can be adjusted later as experience shows whether they are too lenient or too strict. The point is that an exact level must be set and used to decide precisely when instruction on an objective can start, stop, or change. Below are listed some rules of thumb for setting mastery criteria. Notice that these criteria may be needed for different stages of instruction, initial instruction, or maintenance following instruction.

Rules of Thumb for Setting Mastery Criteria

Accuracy:	Important in initial instruction on a task in particular and at all levels in general
Speed:	Important when the task must be employed repeatedly, rapidly (at an "automatic" level), and in high numbers in the performance of higher level tasks; not so critical during initial acquisition of task
Consistency:	Important when tasks may be acquired and lost without repeated performance in consecutive teaching sessions
Review: (Retention)	Important when a skill that has been acquired may be used only periodically
Error Allowance:	Helpful when a task is just being acquired, when students cannot handle numerous trials on the same task, and when the task is not critical to the performance of a skill
No Errors: (High Rate)	When a task is a critical prerequisite to more complex (higher level) tasks

Now check your application of the rules by completing Self-Check 5-1.

DESIGN A MATERIALS-MANAGEMENT SYSTEM

Why a Management System?

Crisis intervention is a common way of operating in public schools. Many different things arise that must be dealt with immediately. However, this method of functioning gets old when it is the standard means of solving problems. Responding to each daily problem with a new solution "on-the-spot" involves a high-effort expenditure. Many of those problems, particularly the instructional problems, can be planned for. This planning requires that a manageable system for handling day-to-day activities be included.

Teachers usually expend their greatest planning efforts in the first two or

Self-Check 5-1

Instructions

Select one box of the grid to the right of each student performance description to indicate what types of criteria are *most* crucial to focus on at that student's point in the instruction sequence; also select a criterion level and place your (✓) mark in that space.

Response

		Criterion Level: No Errors	Criterion Level: Some Error Allowance
Johnny is just beginning to sound out vowel digraphs correctly; instruction is in its second day.	Accuracy	_____	_____
	Speed	_____	_____
	Consistency	_____	_____
	Review	_____	_____
Jason will work multiplcation problems correctly and rapidly (with carrying) for five to ten days in a row; have him drop them and come back to them four weeks later when he is back to carrying instead of borrowing.	Accuracy	_____	_____
	Speed	_____	_____
	Consistency	_____	_____
	Review	_____	_____
If you give Gessell an hour and let her take off her shoes and socks so she can count on her toes, she will get most of the addition facts right	Accuracy	_____	_____
	Speed	_____	_____
	Consistency	_____	_____
	Review	_____	_____

but it doesn't do her much good on two and three place addition problems when it takes so long to finish a problem.			
Beverly will call back sight words correctly and at a very rapid rate by the end of a teaching session, but by Monday she will have forgotten half of the words.	Accuracy Speed Consistency Review	_____ _____ _____ _____	_____ _____ _____ _____
Julie has just begun to work on identifying which is the front and which is the back of various coins because it is the first lesson in the workbook (*Money Makes Sense*). Mrs. Jones doesn't feel that this is a prerequisite skill.	Accuracy Speed Consistency Review	_____ _____ _____ _____	_____ _____ _____ _____
Robin can say the correct vowel sound in rhyming syllable exercises 83 percent of the time and quite rapidly. When she tries to sound *out vowels in words, her error level skyrockets.*	Accuracy Speed Consistency Review	_____ _____ _____ _____	_____ _____ _____ _____

Sample responses can be found in Appendix A.

three years of teaching. From that point on, planning usually involves building upon what was done previously and it is extremely difficult to make drastic changes. It behooves the teacher to design a useful, dynamic management system right from the beginning.

Management System

Management of instruction involves (a) coordinating *what* is taught and (b) directing *how* and *when* teaching is carried out. The remainder of this chapter focuses on describing a management system for controlling *what* is taught. Chapter 8 includes information on managing how and when instruction is conducted.

Teachers must complete many time-consuming types of paperwork, both instructional and noninstructional, during the school year. Noninstructional paperwork has a single coordinating device—the student file. When teachers do not have a single coordinating device for instructional paperwork, they often have difficulty getting organized. A brief sample of this paperwork may include the following:

- Achievement test papers and results
- Weekly or daily test results
- Scoring work sheets, drill pages, or practice exercises
- Records of students' performance in oral exercises
- Records of students' performance in self-instructional programs (i.e., System 80, self-tutoring program)
- Graphs or charts

All of these records have something to do with instruction. Do they all merely float by themselves with no relationship to one another? Definitely not. At least they should be related. It is our conviction that the objective is the most salient coordinating element. So a materials-management system naturally should have objectives as the focal point for the rest of the system (Crutcher & Hofmeister, 1975). The system should correlate objectives with test materials, instructional materials, teaching procedures, and student performance on each. These are the basic information elements of a materials-management system. The steps involved in setting up the system require a large initial effort and expenditure, but following this initial setup, it is merely a matter of adding new information regarding materials or tests to the system as the teacher makes new acquisitions. An example of a materials-management system that has been successfully implemented by teachers of exceptional children is illustrated in Figure 5-1.

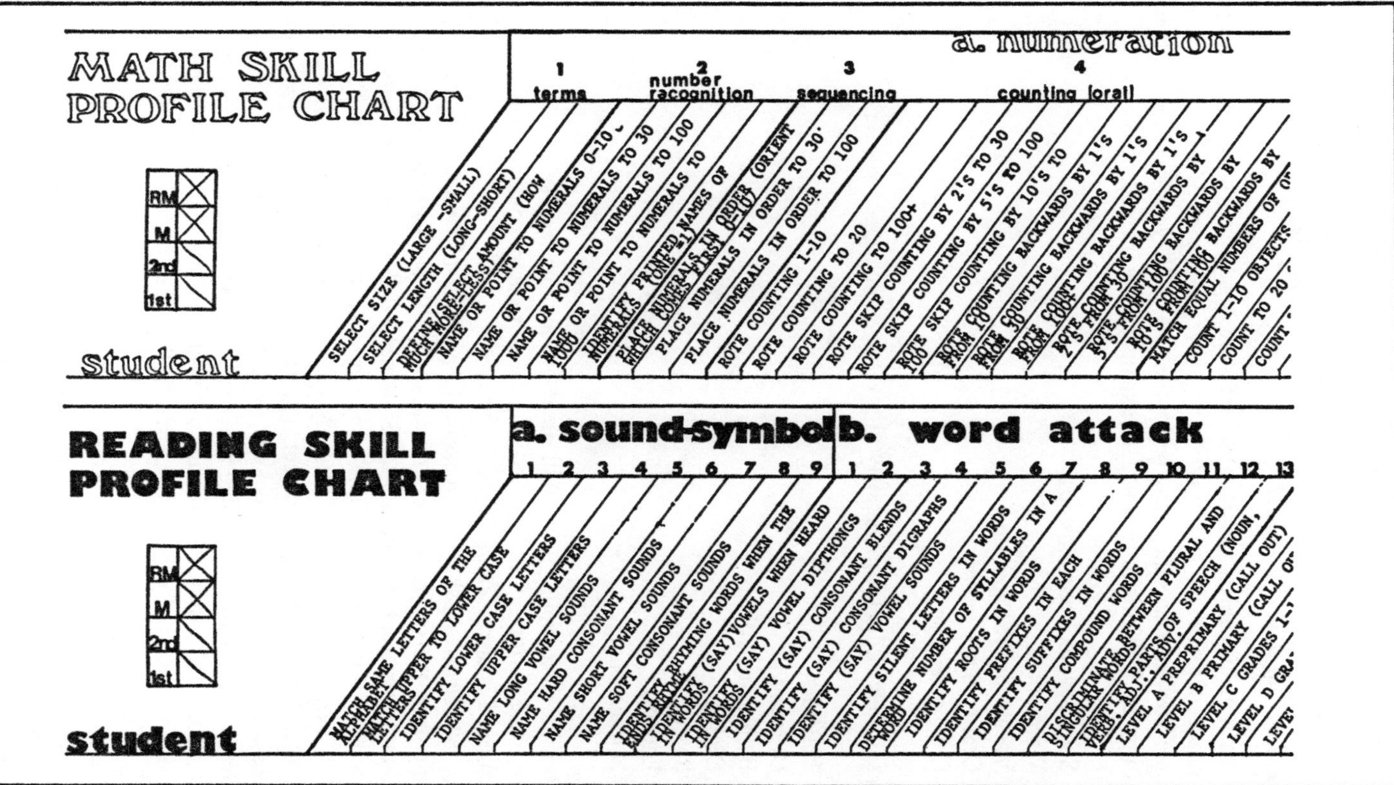

Figure 5-1. *Sample Subskill Groupings*

Source: Reprinted from *Skill Profile Charts* by Joseph J. Stowitschek with permission of the author. Copyright 1978 by Joseph J. Stowitschek.

Step 1: Lay Out a Skill Sequence

For each major subject that is taught (reading, mathematics, spelling, and so on), a sequence of skills and subskills that cover the range of where your students are now to where they may be by the end of the year must be set down in writing. Major skills in reading, for example, may include:

1. Sound-symbol relationships
2. Word attack
3. Vocabulary recognition
4. Oral reading
5. Comprehension

Or in self-help skills for moderately to severely handicapped learners:

1. Toileting
2. Dressing
3. Bathroom skills
4. Dining
5. Safety
6. Laundry
7. Housekeeping

Subskills listed under these skill areas are abbreviated objectives. The response to be performed is specified and the curriculum content upon which it is performed is also identified (see Figure 5-1).

The number of subskills for a particular subject, of course, will vary, depending upon the subject matter and the range of your students. However, to maintain a manageable system, we recommend that subskills be restricted to somewhere between 60 and 100. Numerous instructional programs have prescriptive systems designed into them. Many of these programs list as many as 2,000 objectives for a single subject. Programs such as Science Research Associates' "Diagnosis: . . ." Random House's "High Intensity Reading," and "System FORE" provide detailed tracking of subskills, when detail is needed. It is apparent from numerous discussions with teachers that this strength may also be a weakness. Teachers often repeat that they lose sight of the forest, having to deal with so many trees. These programs seem to succeed on the analysis side, breaking a skill down into minute subskills, but often fail on the synthesis side, combining subskills to ensure that the parts add up to the skill to be acquired. "Sally has excellent phonic and structural analysis skills, but I'm still uncertain that her reading has improved."

A materials-management system based upon objectives must be detailed enough so significant subskills and trouble spots in a skill can be pinpointed. It must also permit the teacher to keep an overview or "big picture" of how students are progressing. When more precise detail is needed, the teacher can resort to a more detailed sequence of a single program, without being committed solely to the use of that program for all students. Examples of subskill sequences that have been used by numerous teachers to manage materials can be found in Appendix C.

Another option open to the teacher who develops his or her own management system is that certain skills can be as detailed or as simple as desired, depending upon what is taught by that particular teacher. In designing his or her system, a teacher is not hampered by selecting a single program where all skills are treated in intricate detail. The self-designed system will allow the teacher to pick and choose the best from these programs.

Step 2: Match Materials with Skills and Subskills

The main intent of this management system is to permit the teacher to make rapid decisions regarding the choice of appropriate materials he or she has available for an objective the student needs to attain. The system must be a quick reference source for this purpose. This does require that the teacher know what is in these available materials. An analysis of available materials, such as that described in Chapter 2, will help provide this information. The analysis focuses solely on estimating how much opportunity the material will give the learner to practice the behavior specified by the skill or subskill. Since this is only an estimate, it can be expressed as the pertinent sections of a program (e.g., Unit I, Part A), the number of pages in a book (e.g., pp. 11, 12, 15-24), the percentage of work on a page (e.g., pp. B-1, B-2, B-3—60%), or by some other method that is logical to the teacher. Since only the pertinent material will be matched, a cursory inspection will eliminate much of what is available in many materials, yet may not provide practice that is directly appropriate. The Materials Inventory Form described in Chapter 2 (Figure 2-3) will be of much assistance here.

Materials may be matched at two levels: (1) by skill area and (2) by subskills. Many materials overlap across subskills and provide practice on several subskills at once. Consequently, these materials can be matched only by general skill area. Figure 5-2 shows a sample of materials matched by skill area to program parts or sections.

Matching materials by subskills involves a more intense analysis. It also requires that student practice in the materials can be separated according to the subskills. This match will produce more specific prescriptions, which offsets the greater time expenditure. Matching at this level usually involves designating not only parts or sections of programs but pages and rows or columns on

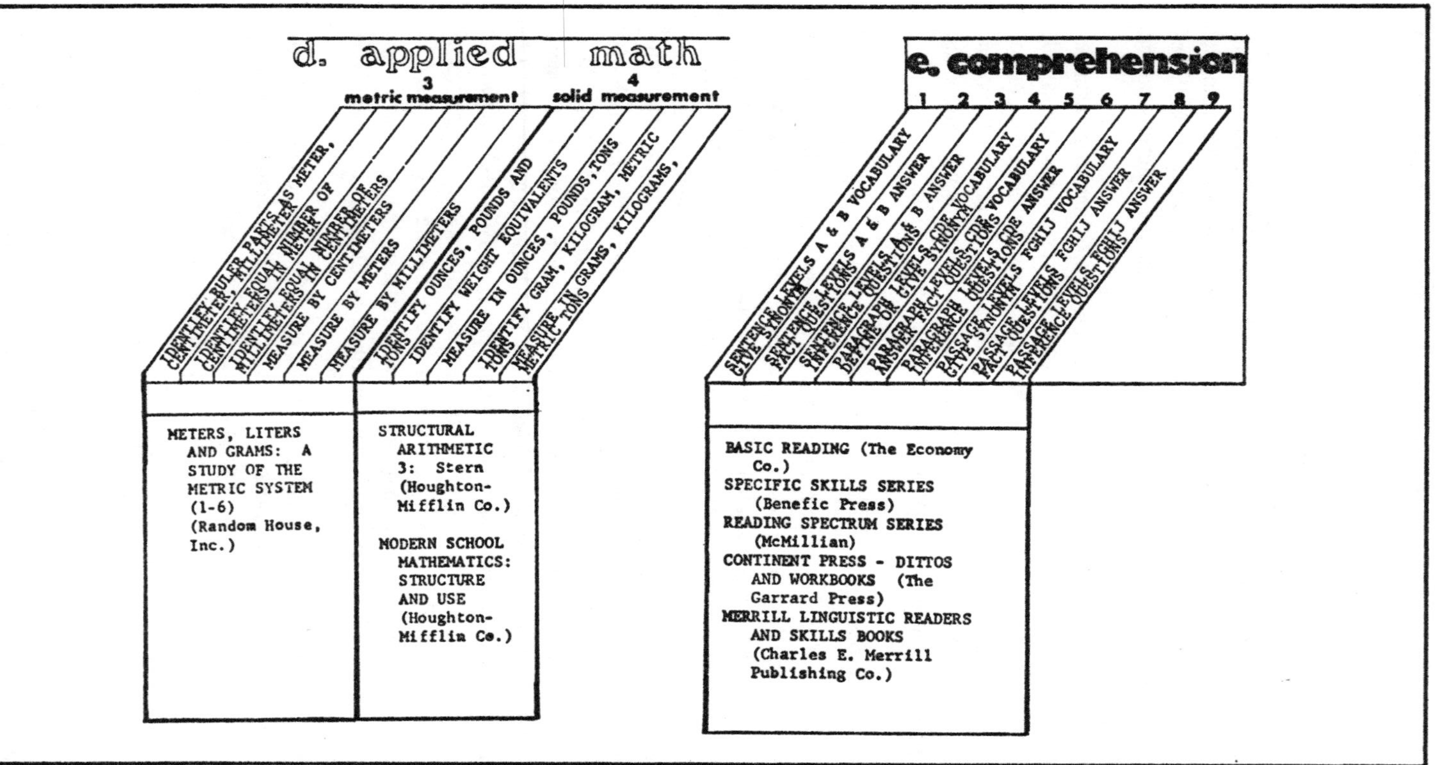

Figure 5-2. *Sample Match between Skill Areas and Available Materials*

Source: Reprinted from *Skill Profile Charts* by Joseph J. Stowitschek with permission of the author. Copyright 1978 by Joseph J. Stowitschek.

those pages. An example of how this information could help daily instruction prescriptions is described below (Figure 5-3).

1. Ms. Denigal scans the recorded summary of the previous days student results and works down the student roster.
2. When she reaches Sally Q's name, she scans the list of subtasks and notices that Sally reached criterion on adding fractions with a common denominator. She decides to start her on subtracting fractions with a common denominator—because of her previous trouble understanding the concept of different denominators.

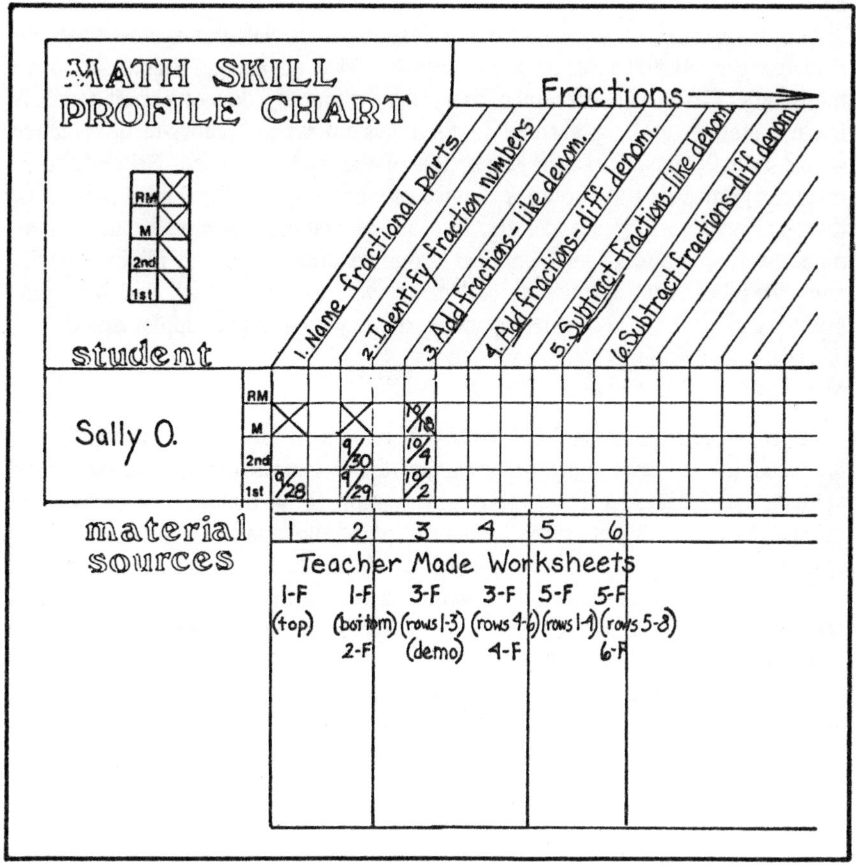

Figure 5-3. *Sample Match between Subskills and Available Materials*

Source: Reprinted from *Skill Profile Charts* by Joseph J. Stowitschek with permission of the author. Copyright 1978 by Joseph J. Stowitschek.

3. Ms. Denigal checks the materials she had listed for that subskill earlier in the year (they happened to be work sheets she had prepared the previous year!).
4. She assigns the top half of work sheet 5-F because it has demonstration items at the top.
5. Sally locates a copy of work sheet 5-F in the files and begins working at her desk.

This activity took the teacher approximately 15 seconds per student. This type of prior planning, the preparation of a material-management system, ultimately saved a lot of class time, which the teacher better spent with the students by helping them directly.

The advantages of using a teacher-designed materials-management system over using published systems are numerous. Two advantages stand out above the others. First, many commercial systems generally do not permit teacher-made materials to be presented in their system when teacher-made practice sheets actually make up a large portion of the materials used. Second, commercial systems do not allow for the use of human instructional resources when there are no appropriate materials. In place of material listings, a teacher may note "use peer tutors" or "conduct group reading circle" to fill in material gaps. Another notation may be to "make work sheet," which will help pinpoint the subskills where existing materials may have to be supplemented.

Step 3: Match Tests with Skills and Subskills

Other major instructional elements that remain to be linked with skill areas and subskills are tests and other measures that a teacher employs to determine students' performance. Tests relate information about materials at three main points: (1) when teachers initially want to place students in an instructional sequence, (2) when the teacher must decide if the student is progressing or has reached criterion (mastery) on a particular skill or subskill, and (3) when a teacher must decide whether a student has retained mastery of a skill or subskill.

For the first purpose, initial assessment, an entire test may be given at once and the results may either be separated by skill areas or by subskills. This step also involves analyzing available tests to match test parts, pages, rows on pages, or columns of test items to pertinent skill areas and subskills. Some tests may group together items that pertain to different subskills. These tests may be subdivided only by general skill areas and not by subskills.

The designation of test portions by skill area or subskill is completed in much the same manner as was described for materials. Figure 5-4 shows a sample of how test and skill matching was accomplished.

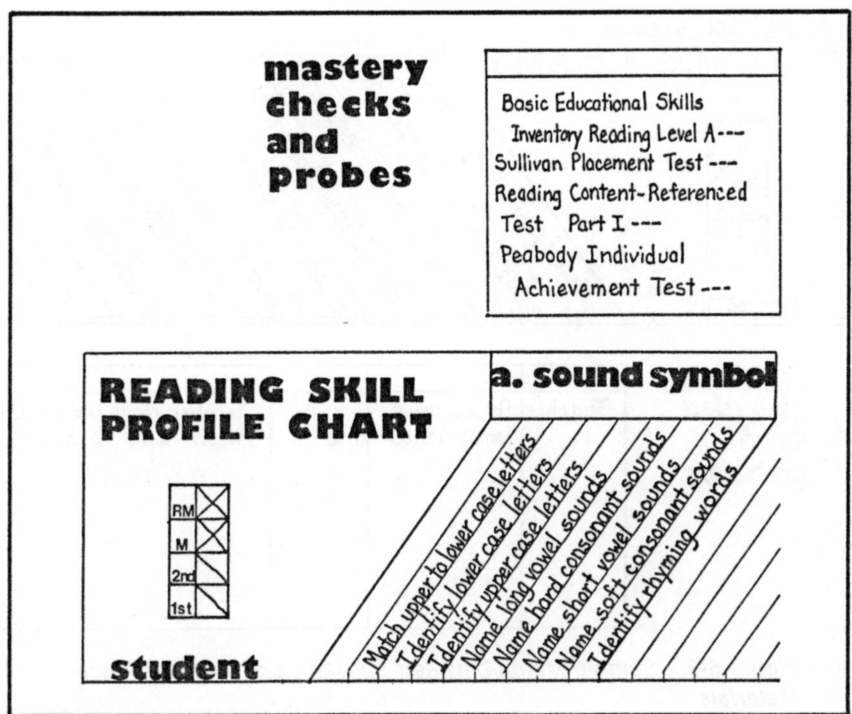

Figure 5-4. *Sample Match between Skill Areas and Available Tests*

Source: Reprinted from *Skill Profile Charts* by Joseph J. Stowitschek with permission of the author. Copyright 1978 by Joseph J. Stowitschek.

Notice that published tests were not used to match tests with subskills in Figure 5-5. This shows the flexibility of a teacher-designed materials-management system over most published systems. The teacher-designed system can be tailored to a teacher's particular resources and can pinpoint the areas for which the teacher may have to improvise and convert work-sheet materials into tests or use oral probes in place of tests as described below.

For purposes of progress and mastery assessment, the same tests can be used. In this case only the portion of the test pertaining to the subskill or skill area the student is working on at the moment is used. The trick is to be able to use only part of a test, that part which pertains to the subskill to be tested. With some tests, such as the Basic Educational Skills Inventory (Adamson, Shrago, & Van Etten, 1972) or BESI, this is possible.

The BESI has subtests that can be easily administered to determine mastery or progress in selected subskills. Other tests are not as easily used for this pur-

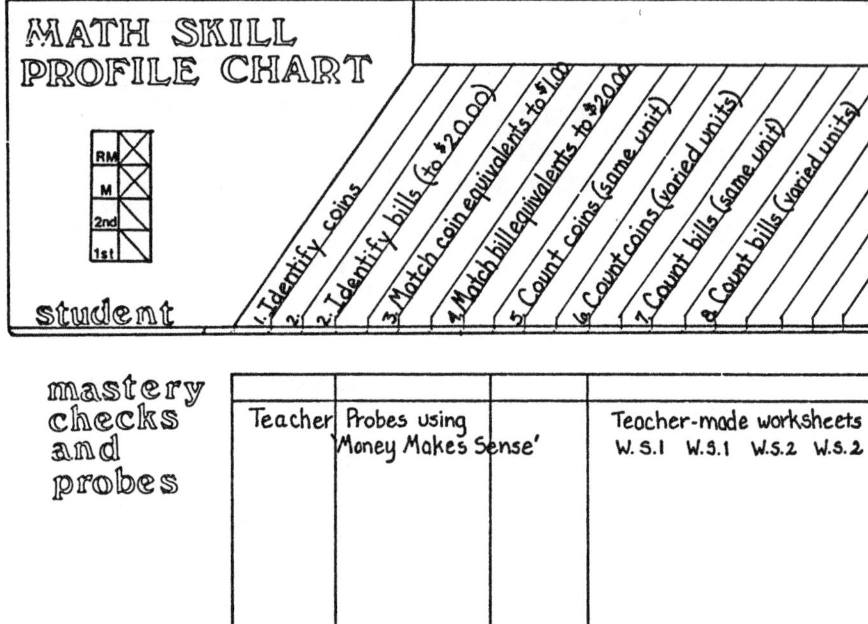

Figure 5-5. *Sample Match between Subskills and Teacher-Made Materials*

Source: Reprinted from *Skill Profile Charts* by Joseph J. Stowitschek with permission of the author. Copyright 1978 by Joseph J. Stowitschek.

pose. Many teachers find themselves using self-made materials more often for this testing purpose.

Testing retention is usually done less frequently and more skills are tested for retention at one time. The same procedures described for initial or placement assessment are recommended for the assessment of retention. The primary point to remember is that it is an extremely critical decision point in the management system—one that often is the most crucial for handicapped learners. It is these learners who require repeated relearning of a skill before it sticks. Often a "roller-coaster effect" happens (see Figure 5-6). With this effect, a child first masters a task; instruction on that task stops; the child may lose 70 percent of the skill; instruction begins again until mastery is again attained; instruction stops; the child loses only 50 percent of mastery; instruction begins again; and so on.

The crucial aspect for materials management is that this roller-coaster effect must be planned for. Children, particularly handicapped children, are going to forget what they once learned. Once this phenomenon is expected, teachers are

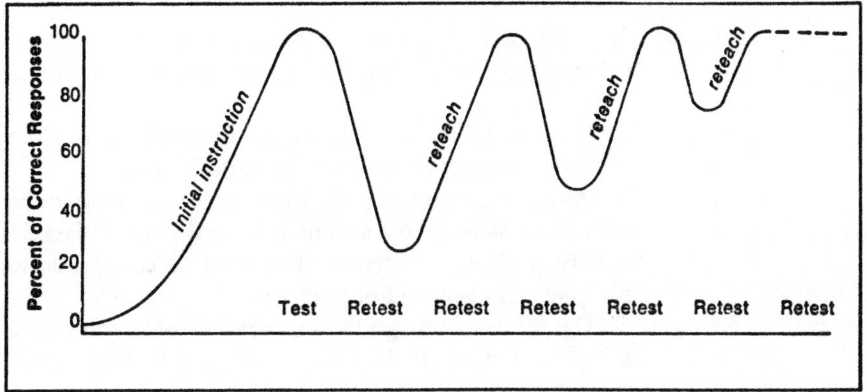

Figure 5-6. *Visual Representation of a "Roller-Coaster" Effect in Handicapped Children's Learning*

able to avoid saying, "What's wrong; she worked through those very same materials already?" Or, "I'm sure she had it down pat once. It's not my fault if she can't hold on to it!" The management system must systematically incorporate assessment for retention so the gap between mastery and "bottoming out" is reduced. Something learned once can be relearned more quickly, as long as the relearning is part of the instructional system.

Step 4: Record Student Results

For record-keeping purposes the management system can be kept either in individual student folders or as a group desk or wall chart. Advantages and disadvantages must be considered in deciding which format to use. Some of both are listed below.

Individual Student Folder System

Advantages:

1. All material on one student is kept together. The teacher can easily check the records and student work at the same time.
2. More entries can be made per subskill since only one student's results are recorded.
3. Specialized materials prescriptions can be noted for individual students.

Disadvantages: 1. A lot of duplication of records occurs since separate subskill material and test listings are needed for each student folder.
2. Much shuffling and juggling of materials takes place since they are not summarized on a single page.
3. Instructional grouping decisions are difficult to make since the results are not summarized by the entire class.
4. Visual displays of the results cannot be easily used to promote class approval of progress.
5. The teacher must go through several folders to obtain a "picture of what is going on." Quick reference is hampered.

Group Desk or Wall Chart (see Figure 5-7)

Advantages: 1. Skills, subskills, materials, and tests are written once, reducing duplication. Since most subskills and prescriptions are common to the majority of students, additional individualized entries can be added to the folder.
2. All recording is done on one chart per subject, thereby encouraging common assistance in record keeping by teacher and students.
3. A single chart provides a quick reference guide when the teacher must make rapid decisions.
4. Progress is visually displayed for ease of promoting commendations from classmates.
5. Decisions regarding grouping for instruction can be assisted by the group charts.

Disadvantages: 1. Only limited summary entries can be made (four to eight entries per subskill).
2. Individual folders must be referred to for more specific information on a student's work.
3. Large desk or wall charts are bulky and don't fit into desk drawers or folders (this may be an advantage since they tend not to get lost or forgotten).

The use of a single coordinating chart does not preclude keeping individual student folders, or vice versa. In fact, they can complement each other. We recommend using the group chart for maintaining an overview of the management system and the student folder for collecting daily work materials.

The primary records kept on the chart are (1) starting point, (2) progress checkpoints, (3) mastery point, and (4) retention. This information can be re-

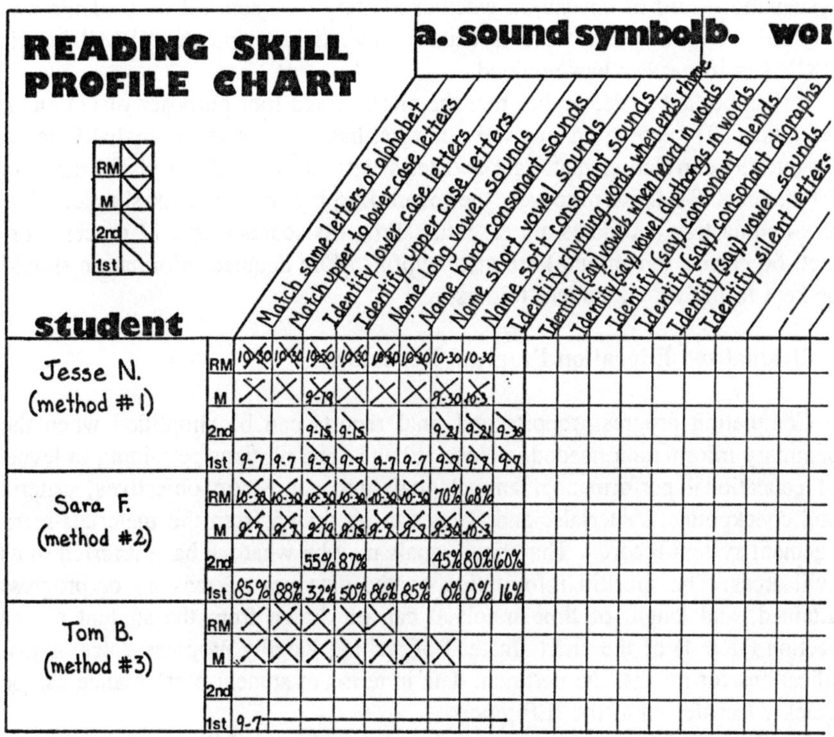

Figure 5-7. ***Three Approaches to Recording Progress and Mastery on a Skill Chart***

Source: Reprinted from *Skill Profile Charts* by Joseph J. Stowitschek with permission of the author. Copyright 1978 by Joseph J. Stowitschek.

corded in several different ways. Figure 5-7 depicts the records kept for three students.

Mastery (the box marked "M") is the most crucial entry and is "X"ed in when that subtask is mastered. On this chart "1st" denotes the pretest entry point.

The entry point may be recorded as a date, a test score, or some other designation of performance such as a + or −. If mastery occurs on the pretest or first attempt, the "M" box is also "X"ed in.

On the chart "2nd" denotes a posttest or second attempt at demonstrating mastery of the task. If mastery occurs on the second attempt, the "M" box is "X"ed in. If a third attempt is required, the results are recorded in the "M" box and it is "X"ed in if mastery occurs.

The box marked "RM" (retention of mastery) in this system allows for a systematic record of checks on whether mastery of a subskill by students was retained. A review test score is usually entered here and the "RM" box is "X"ed in if mastery was retained.

It is important to remember that the chart serves four purposes of (1) quick reference, (2) keeping an overview of what has been taught and what is to be taught, (3) correlating materials and tests with skills, and (4) visual displays for students. To these purposes, the record keeping must be kept simple. Mastery-nonmastery and dates are essential. Progress scores (e.g., 72 percent correct, 60 correct per minute) are also helpful. More detailed information should be kept in individual student folders.

Individualized Education Program Reporting

Completing progress reports and final reports can be simplified when the summary information needed is close at hand. The portions pertaining to levels of educational performance, annual goals and short-term objectives, criteria and checkpoints, materials, and dates can be drawn from the materials-management system records. The annual goals may be what we have referred to as skill areas. The subskill information on the date begun, mastery or progress attained, and length of time involved can be drawn from the student record section (step 4) of the chart. Instead of writing lengthy progress notes or justifications for results, the pertinent data in terms of student performance can be quickly transferred to the IEP report.

One last word on a chronic record-keeping problem—failing to keep the records. There seems to be a tendency to begin something new with full resolve and then lose enthusiasm for it. This is usually due to other more immediate events taking precedence and competing with record-keeping time. This problem has no easy solutions. However, it does seem that if something is regarded as important enough by teachers, they will find a way to make it work and the time to keep it up. We cannot understate the importance of developing and maintaining a standard management system. The long-term effects far outweigh the 10 or 15 minutes of daily drudgery required to maintain the system. We all must establish our priorities and the means by which we see that high priority goals get accomplished. Self-Check 5-2 pertains to IEP reporting.

Adapt Available Tests for Materials Management

If a teacher were to develop all of the tests necessary to use materials effectively, the task would be almost impossible. It is fortunate that a number of different types of testing materials are already available. But they may not be useful in their present form for making instructional decisions. However, it is possible to adapt many of these tests and materials so they can be useful. Think of the advantages. If a teacher were to develop all of the tests that he or she used, test items, test forms, administration procedures, and interpretation procedures would have to be devised. What if these same tests and materials could be used in their present forms with only a change in how the results are used? The test forms are already developed, the administration procedures are already written, and answer keys are often already provided. The only major difference is that results such as grade level, stanine scores, or standard scores are ignored and replaced with a means of interpreting results according to skill mastery. Actually, this is quite possible and teachers do have a wealth of test materials already prepared that could be easily adapted depending upon their measurement purpose. Table 5-1 shows the types of tests and materials that can be of assistance for three measurement purposes.

Standardized achievement tests have particular utility for initial assessment when teachers are interested in (a) getting an overall picture of a child's performance and (b) identifying which skills in a particular subject area may be problem areas that are in need of further testing. At the initial assessment level, achievement tests may help to narrow down and identify those skills that must be assessed in more detail. Occasionally, adapted achievement tests may be used to assist in prescribing instructional material. Some achievement tests, such as the California Achievement Test (Tiegs & Clark, 1970), supply detailed lists of objectives that are assessed by the test and render the test more useful for instructional purposes. Besides initial assessment these standardized achievement tests assist in helping the teacher periodically to evaluate students' proficiency on or maintenance of several skills. This type of test may be administered, say, every five or six weeks and should help redirect instruction.

Other standardized tests help in the diagnostic process and are useful primarily for initial assessment purposes. Again, these tests help identify skills that must be tested in more depth, say, using teacher-made or other single-skill tests.

Material-Imbedded Tests

Numerous instructional programs have tests either interspersed throughout the instructional materials or accompanying the instructional materials. These tests range from global assessments across skills to specific probes of pinpointed subskills. Their usefulness to the teacher for general purposes depends upon (a) whether they can be used independently of the material and (b) whether test items are nonspecific to the instructional material. If they meet these requirements, the tests may be used for material selection and prescription purposes that go beyond the specific program they were designed for. They can be used both for initial assessments or evaluation across skills or they can be used to provide specific, day-to-day information regarding whether a

Self-Check 5-2

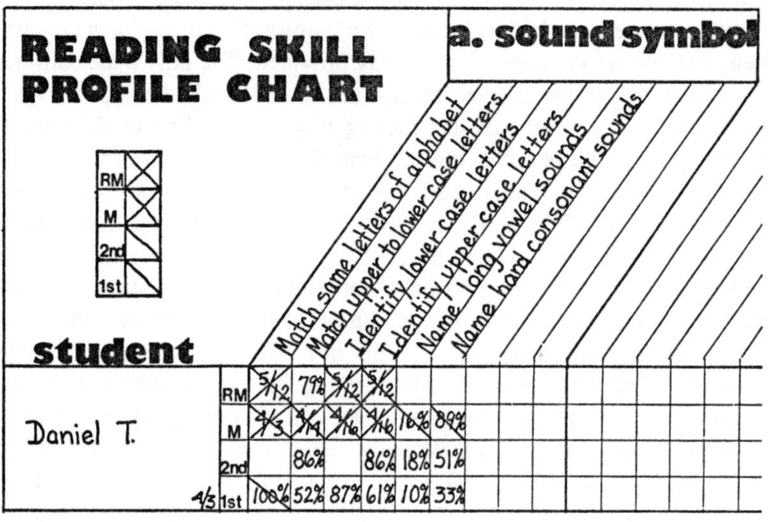

Instructions

Imagine that you are a teacher of young, mildly mentally retarded children. It is toward the end of the year and you must comply with the requirements of P.L. 94-142. Using the Reading Skill Profile Results for Daniel T., transfer this information to the Williamson County Schools, Individualized Education Program progress reporting form. All of the necessary information is on the skill chart. Comments should be focused on the data and not on general impressions.

Response

WILLIAMSON COUNTY SCHOOLS
PUBLIC SERVICES DEPARTMENT

INDIVIDUALIZED EDUCATION PROGRAM — TOTAL SERVICE PLAN

STUDENT ____________________

SKILL AREA ____________________

LONG RANGE GOAL: ____________________

INSTRUCTIONAL OBJECTIVES:

Objective	DROPPED	MORE TIME NEEDED	PROGRESS TO CONTINUE	OBJEC. MET
A. OBJECTIVE ENTRY DATE: EVAL. DATE WILL BE ABLE TO:				
	COMMENT:			
B. OBJECTIVE ENTRY DATE: EVAL. DATE WILL BE ABLE TO:				
	COMMENT:			
C. OBJECTIVE ENTRY DATE: EVAL. DATE WILL BE ABLE TO:				
	COMMENT:			
D. OBJECTIVE ENTRY DATE: EVAL. DATE WILL BE ABLE TO:				
	COMMENT:			
E. OBJECTIVE ENTRY DATE: EVAL. DATE WILL BE ABLE TO:				
	COMMENT:			

Compare your response to the sample response in Appendix A.

Source: Reprinted from Williamson County Public Schools, Public Services Department. *Individualized Education Program—Total Service Plan* with permission of the Superintendent of Schools. 1979.

Table 5-1 Types of Tests and Materials That May Be Adapted for Different Measurement Purposes

Measurement Purpose	*Standardized Achievement Tests*	*Standardized Diagnostic Tests*	*Material-Imbedded Tests*	*Teacher-Made Tests*	*Work Sheets or Drill Pages*	*Flash Cards*
Initially assess across skills	X	X	X			
Probe specific performance on a given skill			X	X	X	X
Measure progress or mastery of a single skill			X	X	X	X
Evaluate proficiency of maintenance across skills	X		X			
Evaluate proficiency of maintenance across skills	X		X			

child is making adequate progress through a set of materials. Some material-imbedded tests may be cumbersome and time consuming for a child to complete. This feature must be balanced against the information obtained.

Teacher-Made Tests

Many teachers have prepared tests on their own because of frustration with the inability of many currently published tests to provide precise instructional information. These tests usually are fairly detailed assessments of a specific skill and they are most useful for providing more detailed diagnostic information on that skill or for measuring progress and mastery of a single skill. They may require the least adaptation since most teacher-made tests are designed to yield information relevant to mastery or nonmastery of specific skills.

Work Sheets and Drill Pages

Many of the practice exercises and materials designed for instructional purposes can also be used for measurement purposes. There is a fine line between responses students make that we call instruction and responses students make that we call testing. The essential difference is in how the results of those responses are used. Work sheets and drill pages are most useful for purposes of probing, diagnosing single-skill performance, measuring progress, and assessing mastery of single skills.

Flash Cards

Written tests often leave out an important bit of information that is useful for prescribing instructional materials. They can seldom assess oral performance on a single skill and rate of performance on a single skill. Flash cards and other drill cards can be used to provide much more precise information on pinpointed areas where oral performance and/or rate of performance is critical (see Chapter 6 for probe procedures).

The key to using standardized and other tests for instructional purposes is to be able to relate what the learner does on the test to the specific skills and subskills (objectives) to be taught and, subsequently, through these subskills, to the materials that aid in teaching these skills. The changes suggested in how to use the results are to this purpose. Basically four test-adaptation steps should be followed. A fifth step is added here to illustrate how the test results can be matched with material descriptions.

Step 1: Select a Test

Some tests may be used for instructional purposes but others cannot. To be appropriate, tests must (a) sample the range of skills you want to test and

(b) contain enough items in each skill or subskill area to give you confidence that it accurately represents the child's performance on that skill. Some tests include a logical progression of skills and thoroughly sample any skill area tested; other tests emphasize some skills and leave out others (Figure 5-8). The greatest problem is finding tests that provide enough items to assess each skill or subskill. You will often find some skills with eight or more items and other skills with two, one, or zero items. The question is, how many responses (test items) do you need to have confidence that a learner can or cannot perform a task? Actually there is no set rule, but we can assume that our confidence would be limited if we had less than four items to sample a single subskill or task. In selecting a test, a balance must be made between using a test that is not too time consuming, yet will still adequately sample the subskills to be taught.

Step 2: Prepare a Skill List

A list or sequence of those skills to be assessed should be prepared or selected. This is the bridge between the test and the materials. A skill list prepared by the teacher or one that is prepared through an inspection of the test may be used. A teacher-prepared skill list would ensure that it represents subject areas that need to be taught, whereas a skill list that is drawn from the test would represent the sequence of skills that are tested. Either way, this list should allow teachers to match test items ultimately to instructional materials.

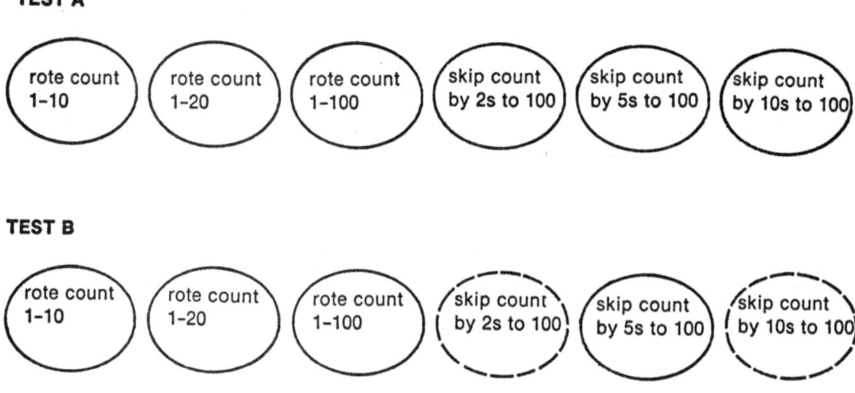

Figure 5-8. *Potential Gaps in Skills Assessment by Norm-Referenced Tests*

A sample skill list drawn from the California Achievement Test is shown in Figure 5-9. Basically, a skill list is a sequence of subskills (objectives) placed in order from those assumed to be simplest to those that are progressively more complex.

This list may also be drawn from the tèst itself if you do not have a list to start with. This is done by inspecting the administration manual and the test form—the pages the student responds to. The administration manual will provide a general overview of how the test is organized. The major skills tested can be listed from this description. The next step is to analyze the test form. This requires that the student's response to each test item or group of items be identified and translated into a task description such as "circles *-ing* endings" or "copies uppercase letters." Usually, the list will be in some sequential order corresponding tò the test sequence.

If the test is a diagnostic test, a list of possible types of errors may be a suitable option. Material descriptions can still be made from pinpointed error patterns. For instance, a list drawn from a spelling test may include "omits letters," "reverses double vowels," "substitutes vowels," "drops silent *e*." Error types can be listed across the top of the report form in the same manner as a skill list. A criterion may be set for how many errors of a certain type must occur to diagnose a pattern. This may be just as important prescriptive information as is task mastery or nonmastery.

Step 3: List Corresponding Test Parts and Set Pass Criteria

To break down the student's responses on the test according to the list of subtasks, the test items must be assigned to each subskill. In some tests, an entire test part may be devoted to one subskill. In other tests, a page or a row may test a single subskill. In still others, only one or two items may be all that pertains to a given subskill. A teacher needs to know precisely how many and exactly which test items he or she will base a decision upon about a child's performance. The pertinent information (i.e., test part I, LC. 1, items 1-14) for locating portions of the test that correspond to any given subskill are listed immediately under the subskill (see Self-Check Figure 5-3).

To set pass criteria, a minimum of four test items must be present for any given subskill in the list. There is no set standard for an acceptable criterion. This is usually determined through experience with the learners. However, an initial criterion must be set to gauge its appropriateness. As a rule of thumb, the following proportions of errors to total number of items are suggested: (a) for 3 to 5 items, all must be correct, (b) for 6 to 15 items, one error is allowed, (c) for 16 to 20 items, two errors are allowed. If more than 20 items are found under any single subskill, there is a strong possibility that the subskill should be broken down into smaller subskill units and the corresponding

Test Adaptation Results

Skill List	match same letters of Alphabet	match upper to lower case letters	identify lower case letters	identify upper case letters	name long vowel sounds	name hard consonant sounds	name short vowel sounds	name soft consonant sounds	identify rhyming endings
Test Part/Page	Part I Pg 1 Row 1 Item#	Part I Pg 1 Row 2-4 Item#	Part I Pg 2 Row Item#	Part I Pg 3 Row 1, 2 Item#	Part I Pg 3 Row Item#	Part II Pg 1 Row 1 Item# 1	Part II Pg 1 Row 2 Item#	Part II Pg 1 Row 3 Item#	Part II Pg 1 Row 4 Item#
Criterion / # Items	4 / 4	7 / 8	9 / 10	5 / 5	5 / 6	5 / 5	11 / 12	14 / 16	8 / 9
Students									

Figure 5-9. *Subskill Specifications Derived from Analyses of Norm-Referenced Test Forms*

items should be separated. The third row in Self-Check Figure 5-3 shows examples of the past criteria that have been set.

Step 4: Rescore and Summarize Test Results

If the test has already been scored, you need not rescore each item. All that needs to be done is to sum the correct responses for items pertaining to each subskill on the skill list. These scores are then summarized on the Test Adaptation Results sheet (Figure 5-9). Notice that results for an entire class of students can be summarized on this sheet. This will aid in grouping students for instruction. Generally, the correct number of responses scored is placed underneath the corresponding subskill for each student and an "X" is placed on those scores meeting or exceeding the criterion set.

Step 5: Match Results with Materials or Instructional Prescriptions

At this point the Materials Review Form and procedure described for available instructional materials in the classroom can be of help (see Chapter 2). To make appropriate prescriptions you must have an intimate knowledge of the types of responses that students will be required to make in any given set of materials. This type of analysis is discussed further in the next chapter.

Adapting available tests for instructional purposes can be an immense time saver. Imagine that you have an array of possibly 10 to 12 tests (many teachers do). If you have a summary sheet completed for each of these tests, like the Test Adaptation Results form, any time these tests are given for their normative purposes (e.g., to establish grade levels, diagnose process difficulties, determine abilities, and so on) you simply fill out this extra sheet based upon the same administration procedures and the same responses of the student. The only difference is, you have the test results broken down into a language (the skill list) that is more useful for instructional purposes. Duplication of testing effort can be decreased and further testing needed for making instructional decisions can be narrowed down to those specific skill areas that are indicated by the Test Adaptation Results form. One note of caution: once a normative test has been used for instructional purposes and the test items are taught to in that test, the same test should not be used with the same students to obtain normative results such as a grade-level score or a developmental age. Otherwise, the normative assumptions of the test will be violated.

Adapting Materials for Testing Purposes

What is the difference between testing and teaching? They are usually treated as two distinct entities by educators. Actually, with many materials, the only difference is in how the results are used. With work sheets and drill

Self-Check 5-3

Instructions

This self-check displays a portion of a graded reading test taken by a young student and a portion of the Test Adaptation Results Form. The form already has the subskills row written out. Your tasks are to (1) write in the page and row (or column) pertaining to each subskill, (2) write in the number of test items pertaining to each subskill, and (3) set and write in a mastery criterion for each subskill.

▶ Black out the letter that **begins** the word read aloud.				
A	g	j	q	z
1	b	j	p	v
2	b	d	h	w
3	c	g	k	p
4	c	g	j	k
5	b	d	k	p
6	i	o	u	y
7	a	e	i	o
8	a	e	o	u
9	a	i	o	u
10	e	i	l	o

▶ Black out the letter that **ends** the word read aloud.				
A	b	h	k	r
1	b	f	p	v
2	b	j	g	f
3	m	n	q	t
4	b	f	s	t
5	b	d	p	t
6	g	h	k	p
7	q	s	x	z
8	a	e	o	u
9	a	h	o	y
10	c	j	x	z

page 3

▶ Black out the letter that is the same letter as the first letter on the line.

	P	q	b	g	p
1	V	Z	W	Y	V
2	O	O	C	D	B
3	T	F	B	T	E
4	J	U	J	I	L
5	g	g	y	p	q
6	h	k	d	h	b
7	f	l	t	k	f
8	b	d	b	p	h
9	U	u	q	v	r
10	A	e	c	a	o
11	M	r	m	n	u
12	L	t	m	f	l
13	s	S	O	F	Z
14	y	G	Z	J	Y
15	r	V	R	N	M

page 4

▶ If two words in an item are the same word, black out the letter S.
If they are different words, black out the letter D.

A	dog	DOG	S	D
1	pal	lap	S	D
2	costume	custom	S	D
3	COMPRESS	compress	S	D
4	sign	sing	S	D
5	went	want	S	D
6	PROPERTY	PROSPERITY	S	D
7	letter	LETTER	S	D
8	PRETEND	pretend	S	D
9	ambitious	ambition	S	D
10	GRACEFUL	graceful	S	D

page 4

Response

Skill List	Identify Beginning Sounds	Identify Ending Sounds	Match Capital Letters	Match Lower Case Letters	Identify Same Words	Identify Different Words
Test Part/Page	Part___ Pg___ Row___ Item#___	Part___ Pg___ Row___ Item#___	Part___ Pg___ Row___ Item#___	Part___ Pg___ Row___ Item#___	Part___ Pg___ Row___ Item#___	Part___ Pg___ Row___ Item#___
Criterion / # Items						

Compare your response to the sample response in Appendix A.

Source: Reprinted from California Achievement Tests, Form A Level I. Reproduced by permission of the publisher. CTB/McGraw-Hill, Del Monte Research Park, Monterey, Calif. 93940.

pages, if the purpose is to provide practice on a task, we call it *instruction*. If the purpose is to determine whether a child can perform a task, we may use the same work sheets and have the child do exactly the same thing with them and call it *testing*. The only difference is that we use that practice for different purposes. With the various work sheets, drill pages, and practice exercises in materials, we have a wealth of testing resources that is rarely tapped.

The Test Adaptation Results form shown in this chapter can easily be used to adapt practice materials for testing purposes. All steps are completed in the same manner except that instead of analyzing tests, practice materials are analyzed. The skill listing remains the same. The next section on the form, labeled "Test Part/Page," is different. Instead of designating test sections that pertain to each subskill, work-sheet pages or rows are designated. Pass criteria are set in the same manner and student performance is also summarized and recorded on the form in the same way.

Relating test results to materials can be done in several ways. Two alternatives are suggested here, depending upon the number of practice pages available for any given subskill:

1. If you have one work sheet for a single subskill (10-30 items), use the top row or two rows to test and use the rest for drill and practice.
2. If you have two or more work sheets for a single subskill, use one work sheet for testing purposes (top half for pretesting, bottom half for posttesting) and use the rest for drill and practice

Both of these options assume that the portion selected for testing is representative in range and type of responses to the portion to be used for instruction. Practice materials differ considerably in how well they represent the range of responses necessary to cover a subskill and in how many subskill responses are practiced on one page. Some work sheets provide thorough practice on one skill and others may present a confusing combination of tasks for the learner to perform from one row to the next. In your decision to adapt materials for testing purposes, you will have to analyze them and select those practice materials that are clearly separable according to the subskill list. Self-Check 5-3 provides practice in completing the test parts, item designation, and criterion-setting portions of the form.

CHAPTER 6

Integrating Measurement with Materials Management

Objectives

1. Match types of educational measures and their purposes to daily materials management.
   - How do tests and other measures relate to different stages of instruction?
   - How do tests and measures relate to decisions regarding materials?
   - When are pretests and posttests useful for making decisions about materials?

2. Use daily work in materials as progress measures.
   - How can records of progress across several days of work sheets or drill pages assist in measuring retention?
   - When is a daily probe preceding work in materials a useful alternative to more formal tests?
   - What measurement supplements can help a teacher to use materials for assessment?

3. Use outcomes of measures to aid in redirecting pupils through materials.
   - Will analyzing errors on work pages indicate changes in materials to be used from one day to the next?
   - Can the analysis of oral reading help in deciding to supplement reading programs with other materials?
   - What kinds of options are there for summarizing results of pupils' daily work so better rational decisions can be made?

Effective materials management is first a matter of initial organization and second the implementation of a system for day-to-day management. Chapter 5 focused on procedures for organizing a materials-management system. The succeeding chapters in this section pertain to daily management concerns.

Daily management of materials is highly dependent upon deciding what materials are appropriate for which learner under what circumstances. Measurement of instruction is crucial to these decisions. Measurements can range from global skill assessments (that seem to have no relationship to materials) to repeated observation of a single subtask (which helps monitor progress on a specific page of materials). Some measures are more directly related to materials than others and help bring continuity to daily management decisions.

Three questions point to the content of this chapter: (1) Why measure learners' progress? (2) What types of measurement facilitate materials management? (3) How are the results of measurement related to materials? Entire books have been written on each of the several facets of measurement discussed in this section. Our purpose is to convey to the reader the importance of measurement and the particular relationship measurement has with materials management.

WHY MEASURE PROGRESS?

In recent years, special educators have shifted from attempts to identify underlying causes of children's learning problems to efforts to pinpoint specific skill strengths and deficits. Today the thorough assessment of pupil performance is widely viewed as prerequisite to the formulation of a plan of instruction and the selection of materials. Experience has shown that most traditional evaluation procedures yield little information that pertains directly to classroom instruction or to materials use. It is not unusual, for example, for there to be significant differences between grade equivalent scores obtained and measures of a student's daily classroom performance. Understandably, conventional measurement tools are being discarded in favor of procedures that result in gaining more content-specific information, information that will help to separate the useful from the useless portions of materials.

Measurement used for instructional purposes has several characteristics that distinguish it from more conventional testing. As we indicated earlier in the book, standardized testing represents a means of gathering information required for initial placement of students in a particular curricular area. At the same time, information gained through such testing seldom allows one to identify specific skill deficits. In contrast, recent developments in criterion-referenced measurement allow teachers to make sound materials-placement decisions and to assess progress and the effectiveness of remedial instruction directly and continuously. Data gathered from ongoing pupil assessment provide a ready and useful source of information for teacher and learner.

A major area of growth within the field of special education pertains to the classroom measurement of pupil progress. Many measurements designed for use in special education are infrequently administered, often indirect in what they purport to measure, and group rather than individually relevant. The use of traditional diagnostic procedures relies almost exclusively on commercially produced formal, standardized instruments. As Wallace and Larson (1978) point out, "the wide availability of formal tests, the relative ease of administering them, and the use of normative data are some of the major reasons why these tests have been used so extensively in the schools" (p.11). The most often employed assessment procedure consists of standardized achievement tests and diagnostic tests. Achievement-test batteries are usually group administered and consist of either a sample of a single content area, for example, reading, or of a number of subtests pertaining to various curricular areas, for example, reading, spelling, arithmetic (Wallace & Larson, 1978). Most standardized tests reflect a normative-based set of criteria. That is, so-called norm-referenced tests are constructed to assess pupil performance in relation to existing standards and in comparison to other learner performance. Scores obtained from administering standardized tests are used to establish a child's standing in relation to other testees. The meaning of test scores is derived from a comparison of other students' test scores. In contrast, we will be emphasizing the classroom administration of what are referred to as criterion-referenced measures, the use of which has increased dramatically in the past decade. Although more traditional instruments seek to measure pupil achievement and the utility of materials in relation to other's performance (grade level, standard scores), criterion-referenced evaluation is used to determine where a student's performance lies in relation to the goal of instruction. Performance is measured in relation to a continuum of subskill objectives that together comprise that students' long-term goal of instruction. The skill itself is directly measured instead of attempting to assess underlying causes, and measurements are employed on an ongoing or continuous basis.

Why Direct Measurement?

To the extent that test items correspond to the content of instruction, we are able to make valid judgments concerning what transpires in the classroom. Most standardized tests are global and contain too few items to permit such decisions. Only when a large enough sample of pupil behavior is obtained that is directly referenced to the conduct of daily instruction is test information useful. Three add-fact problems, one requiring carrying, do not represent the range of subskill operations that make up addition skills. Then the question is—how skilled is Billy at calculating double-digit addition problems with carrying. A test designed to measure specifically that skill must be administered.

Why Continuous Measurement?

Assessment information obtained infrequently is not useful for making educational decisions. Test scores derived at widely spaced intervals, say over a period of weeks or months, may lead to erroneous conclusions regarding the process of instruction and/or materials that aid that instruction (Lovitt, 1977). Such test data have little utility in connection with the managing of pupil progress meaningfully if teachers wish reliably to judge the worth of their performance. In short, without frequent, preferably weekly or daily, evaluation of interactions between teacher, learner, and materials, we are unable to conclude accurately whether learning experiences are having the impact desired on pupil performance.

The frequency of measurement varies with the stages of instruction. T.C. Lovitt (1971) has described three major stages of instruction, acquisition proficiency, and maintenance. These stages seem to relate to measurement decisions. In the initial stages, acquisition and proficiency, frequent measures of performance are critical. Maintenance checks can be less frequent but still must be routinely conducted.

The following is intended to aid in the selection of classroom measurement procedures, results of which are useful only to the extent that these five basic questions are taken into account.

1. Has a sequence of instruction been developed that "spells out" each subskill objective to be taught?
2. Do the items included in the test directly correspond to the objectives of instruction?
3. How often will I need to administer the test to obtain sufficient information to assess accurately the worth of my instruction and my materials?

4. Is the response required of test items directly related not only to responses during instruction but also the performance of that task after instruction has been discontinued?
5. Is the means for measuring pupil progress practical for frequent administration and scoring?

Once these issues have satisfactorily been resolved, it is possible to move on to more specific measurement questions.

A MEASUREMENT SCHEMA

The question of how to decide which form of measurement to use for which purpose is often not easily answered by many educators. Direct measurement of educational skills helps to identify the metric, but what types of measurement for what stage or phase of instruction seems to be left to individual interpretation. With the wide array of educational measurements available for an equally wide array of purposes, some means of classifying them systematically according to their instruction and materials-selection applications is needed.

The schema shown in Figure 6-1 classifies tests and measures according to the level of test sensitivity. *Sensitivity* refers to the number or duration of responses sampled (often the number of test items) per skill or subskill (task)

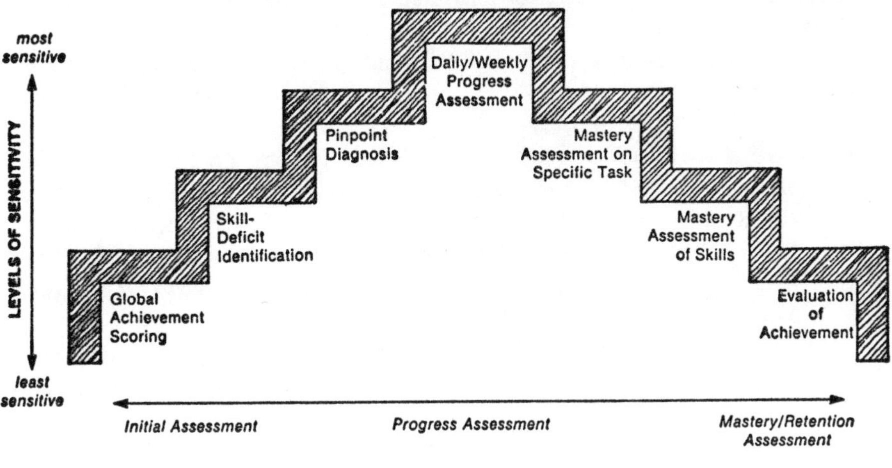

Figure 6-1. *Measurement Pyramid in an Integrated Schema for Employing Tests and Other Measures*

assessed. Generally, the more subskills assessed by a test, the less sensitive the test will be for sampling student performance on a given subskill (usually because of time constraints). The stage or purpose of instruction is somewhat arbitrary or overlapping. However, the measurement purposes preceding instruction seem to involve a different question (what to teach) than do the purposes during instruction (is teaching-learning occurring) or following initial instruction (has the skill been acquired-retained) and the information obtained is used in different ways.

Teachers must continually balance the time they can devote to measurement with the time they must devote to planning and direct teaching. The further away they are from identifying specific skills to be taught, the less they can afford to spend time doing extensive testing of a subskill (or task) picked at random. It stands to reason that the earliest assessments employed for instruction purposes should be those that will allow a teacher progressively to determine more discretely which subskills to assess in more depth. Conversely, after initial instruction has been completed, assessments of subskills relationships to skills and, in turn, those skills relationships to overall achievement should be progressively more global.

A frequent criticism of criterion-referenced instruction is that minute subskills are often taught to the exclusion of the skill itself (''Mary is really super at blending sounds but she still can't read worth a hoot!'').

This schema attempts to ensure that not only analysis (the breaking down) of subskills occurs as a result of measurement, but the synthesis (combining) of subskills to comprise the skill is also assessed.

The levels of assessment and their relationship to instructional materials are depicted as:

1. *Global achievement screening*. This is usually done through standardized achievement tests. These tests can help identify which skills in a given subject area are above, at, or below the norm and thus direct the teacher to further skill assessment. Placement in materials is usually restricted to basal programs that are sequenced by grade level. The *Iowa Test of Basic Skills* is one example.
2. *Skill-deficit identification*. Several published diagnostic tests focus specifically on identifying deficits across selected skills. Many teachers also prepare their own assessments for this purpose. Tests with this level of sensitivity may assist teachers in selecting skill kits (e.g., time telling, preschool language development, money concepts).
3. *Pinpoint diagnosis*. Often, with handicapped students, an exact specification of performance on a subskill within a skill is needed to begin instruction. Assessments at this level usually identify patterns of errors as well as subskill deficits. For example, a test of students' ability to solve

simple addition facts developed by Hofmeister (1972) can detect patterns of errors regarding the digits. If materials are available that contain practice on discrete objectives, this level of assessment can prescribe to the page and practice row.

4. *Daily-weekly progress assessment.* This is one of the most essential and often occurring levels of assessment. Pre-posttest formats as well as daily measures of pupils' performance can help govern when work in a particular section of a material should continue, when a teacher must provide additional help or when the student can move on to the next section. Selected daily-weekly progress-assessment methods are presented later in this chapter.
5. *Mastery assessment of specific tasks.* Before instruction is discontinued on a given subskill or task, assessment should be carried out on that subskill to be sure that mastery has occurred. The same type of assessment used for pinpoint diagnosis can be used for this purpose.
6. *Evaluation of achievement.* Most school systems require end-of-year evaluations of student achievement. The purposes of this level of assessment are increasingly shifting toward overall competency testing.

Before going on, you may check your understanding of this measurement schema by completing Self-Check 6-1.

MATERIALS OF CLASSROOM MEASUREMENT

Mention of pupil testing often brings to mind the occasional use of standardized tests. Doubtless, the use of these assessment instruments will continue to play a part in the evaluation of children's academic behavior. In recognition, however, of the many shortcomings of these procedures, special educators faced with making daily instructional decisions have begun to depend on a variety of alternate procedures for obtaining needed information.

The use of instructional materials as an informal type of evaluation is widespread. What is often lacking is a uniform set of administration and interpretation procedures. Skill sheets—containing addition, subtraction, multiplication, or division problems—can easily be employed not only for teaching but also for measuring systematically the impact of that instruction. Flash cards for teaching arithmetic computation, new sight vocabulary, and spelling words, and pictures for labeling in language development have for years been used for drill purposes. These materials can be incorporated into the assessment process once fixed and quantifiable criteria have been set. Workbook exercises in spelling, arithmetic, handwriting, and reading, with little time and effort, can be arranged so they become useful instruments for evaluating learner behavior.

Self-Check 6-1

Instructions

The assessment purposes listed below in the left-hand column should match with the levels of assessment in the column on the right. Your task is to realign the two columns (connecting lines will do).

Response

1. Assessing whether a program to teach coin equivalencies should be used for Sally	Global achievement
2. Assessing whether a child can hold a string at the correct distance from its end in a bead-stringing task	Skill-deficit identification
3. To determine whether the instruction for a group of pupils should focus on the phonics, linguistic word attack, oral reading, or comprehension units of a reading program	Pinpoint diagnosis
4. To assess whether students having completed spelling program A are any higher in grade equivalencies than are students who have completed spelling program B	Daily-weekly progress assessment

Compare your response to the sample response in Appendix A.

Pupil responses not as commonly associated with materials management can serve as valuable measures of the extent to which children are progressing toward mastery of a new behavior. Verbal or motor-gestural responses to materials presented by the teacher can routinely be recorded and, in turn, become a lasting measure of pupil progress. In short, a wide range of behavior exhibited *during* instruction has utility as a measure of pupil progress. In succeeding discussions we highlight the manner in which learner responses to materials can systematically be transformed into an accurate measure of the products of instruction.

PRE-POSTTEST MEASUREMENT

One tactic for obtaining direct noncontinuous performance data is to use a pre-posttest measurement system. Many programs have imbedded pretests and posttests and are to be administered periodically. Some programs are organized so daily measurement is not useful and may get in the way of rapid progress. With these materials, pre-posttesting should be used as long as learners do not encounter serious problems. When they do, more sensitive daily assessment may be necessary until progress is reestablished.

As is implied, testing is first conducted before introducing instruction. These data serve a fourfold purpose:

1. Provide information upon which to base placement decisions
2. Afford opportunity to identify subskill deficiencies and strengths
3. Stand as a yardstick against which to judge the impact of future instructional materials
4. Provide a means to assess mastery and progress toward mastery

Constructing a pretest instrument that contains items directly linked to the content of instruction allows one to pinpoint areas for remediation; at the same time, material already mastered by the learner can be dropped. When test items are referenced to instructional objectives, the pretest phase permits teachers to make decisions of both a content-specific and a child-specific nature. However, comparisons in performance can be made only when each aspect of instruction is represented in the test. A second consideration is that information obtained after concluding instruction is of little value to managing and adjusting teaching to accommodate learner needs. We should point out that the conventional wisdom of pre-posttesting —achievement tests administered at the beginning and end of the school year—poses exactly this problem. In applying the concept of pre-posttest measurement to evaluation for instructional purposes, a change in procedures is necessary.

To obtain data that are useful for ensuring that each student is working in the right place in a given material, teachers have found that increasing the number of times tests are administered renders the findings more meaningful. Then the concept of test-teach-test might be applied as "pre-, mid-, and post-assessment."

MEASUREMENT TO ENSURE RETENTION

We know that many children need repeated opportunities to interact with instructional materials before mastery is attained (Haring & Batemen, 1977). Few exceptional learners can be categorized as "one trial—he got it the first time" learners. It is less certain, however, how many trials or presentations of a lesson may be required before that skill is acquired. One tactic for assuring that students receive repeated exposure to materials is to stipulate that a child must respond correctly "x" number of times (usually in succession) before one concludes that the specified objective has been met. We have often seen teachers puzzled that a child is unable to answer a question correctly—indeed, not even evidence of a glimmer of understanding—after having demonstrated the knowledge to do so the day before. In an attempt to increase the prospect that knowledge or skills will be mastered, teachers have sometimes defined mastery not only in terms of, say, 100 percent, they have further specified that a student must demonstrate the capability to respond correctly several times. The use of daily skill sheets on which children are instructed to calculate multiplication problems repeatedly serves to illustrate our point. Unfortunately, some teachers fail to demand consistently a uniform or large enough number of correct responses; instead, they arbitrarily decide: "Jim seems to have finally gotten it." Of course, teachers may err in the other direction by demanding that children endlessly practice a task they can already perform accurately.

Establishing a set number of trials in which a student is expected to respond correctly is a useful way to compare a child's receptiveness to materials X over materials Y. To do so, a sample of academic responses in connection with a particular material is obtained, as when a phonics workbook is used for teaching a set of five new spelling words. Then a second material is tried. The effectiveness of one material over another is judged on the basis of the number of trials it takes for a student to master the new words. The material that requires fewer "trials" or teaching sessions, before mastery is attained, is used for subsequent instruction.

The criterion for mastery is usually somewhat arbitrarily established. One simply determines that "three consecutive corrects" equals the criterion. In time many teachers are able to bring greater precision to the selection of criterion levels by virtue of past learning experiences of children working to a set standard. In other instances, teachers have sought to determine "functionally" the most appropriate criterion. As many learning tasks are sequential in nature, one subskill leading to the next, teachers have stipulated that mastery at one level is demonstrated when "x" number of corrects occur. Then at the next subskill level, teachers measure if, indeed, the student is able to apply already learned skills to the acquisition of new behavior (Haring & Gentry, 1976). In yet another use of a trials-to-criterion tactic, teachers have measured the differential effects of one criterion over another. For example, by teaching spelling list A to a criterion of three corrects and spelling list B to five corrects and then administering a review test several days later, a comparison of test scores shows whether one criterion—three versus five correct trials—results in a higher score in spelling. Not only is the effectiveness of the instructional material measured, but also knowledge is gained concerning its efficiency. Fewer trials demand less instructional time; however, if fewer trials do not result in a satisfactory learning experience, then no time is saved and more trials are needed. Such a procedure is depicted on the Daily/Weekly Tally Sheet shown in Figure 6-2.

Finally, a trials-to-criterion measurement system has utility for recording a sequence of behavior that together represents a "complete response." The trials-to-criterion measure is especially useful for recording motor responses directly, as in the area of self-help training. For example, materials used in teaching the Project MORE toothbrushing program contain a series of subskill objectives. Each subskill corresponds to a discrete unit of behavior that requires mastery before a child can engage in the next behavior, until finally, the complete response is learned. Each subskill can be measured in relation to a specified criterion. Following the prescribed series of materials presentation,

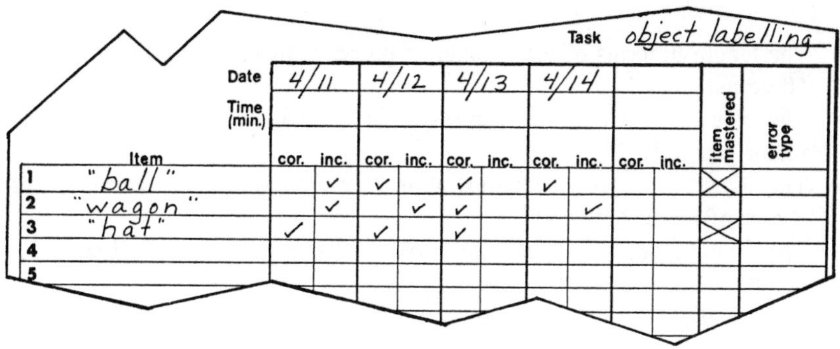

Task *object labelling*

	Date	4/11		4/12		4/13		4/14				item mastered	error type
	Time (min.)												
	Item	cor.	inc.	cor.	inc.	cor.	inc.	cor.	inc.	cor.	inc.		
1	"ball"		✓	✓		✓		✓				X	
2	"wagon"		✓		✓	✓			✓				
3	"hat"	✓		✓		✓						X	
4													
5													

Figure 6-2. *Tally Sheet Depicting Trials-to-Criterion Recording*

Source: Reprinted from *Daily/Weekly Tally Sheets* by Joseph J. Stowitschek by permission of the author. Copyright 1976 by Joseph J. Stowitchek.

learners can be "checked out" at each successive level of performance. The accompanying record form has been adapted so each element of instruction can independently be measured; together, responses lead to a child's learning to brush his or her teeth.

DAILY PROBES AS AN ALTERNATIVE TO TESTS

Daily measurement of academic responses is usually the most desirable means of assessing a particular teaching procedure and/or instructional material. Yet the time spent evaluating performance cannot be so excessive that little time is available for instruction. In place of the usual concept of testing, a probe may be a desirable alternative. Probes are based on specific objectives, usually last from one to five minutes, and are administered daily preceding or following instruction on the subskill being taught. In short, they are a quick sample of what is being instructed (Haring & Gentry, 1976). If an oral response is required, flash cards and other available materials can be used. Oral-response probes must be individually administered and the teacher must record responses. Probes requiring a permanent product, say, written responses on the top row of a work sheet, can be group administered and the teacher need not record immediately.

Probes as a measurement procedure are useful only when instruction is consistent and materials that aid in that instruction do not vary from one day to the next.

In constructing daily probes, features reported by Haring and Gentry (1976) that can be changed according to the content-specific nature of the material being tested include:

- The length in terms of the number of probe items (e.g, anywhere from 5 to 50 items)
- The way in which the learner responds to each item (e.g., oral, written, motor-gestural)
- The location of probe administration (e.g., child's desk, teacher's desk, corner of room, hallway)
- The time allotted for completing probe items (e.g., 1 second, 3 seconds, 1 minute)
- The materials used in the probe (e.g., flash cards, skill sheets, readers)
- Administration and scoring procedures (e.g., teacher-administered, self-administered, group, individual, score at end of probe, tally during probe)

Once the format for probing has been selected, it is necessary that it remain the same each day. In some cases, it is desirable not only to gain information concerning the accuracy with which learners respond but also the rate with which they answer probe items. Then the number of probe items should be adjusted so students are unable to complete all the problems in the time allotted; otherwise, progress in a student's performance cannot be measured (Haring & Gentry, 1976). For example, experience has shown that arithmetic skills are cumulative, with fluency building at one subskill level usually facilitating greater progress at more advanced stages of learning (Haring & Gentry, 1976). Teachers wishing to emphasize not only accurate computation but also attainment of a reasonable performance rate will be unable to measure improvement in rate if children are capable of completing all problems in the time allowed.

Use of Permanent Products in Probes

One probe technique relies on the use of permanent products. The term *permanent products* refers to "any tangible by-product of learner behavior," as in a written spelling test, handwriting exercise, or answers recorded on an arithmetic work sheet (Hall, 1971). Permanent products of children's academic responses are a valuable tool for analyzing performance capabilities. A notable feature is that unlike oral recitation, teachers can review written responses as often as they wish and, in turn, maintain a record of performance across time for comparison. This is important in that we cannot simply dismiss the issue of reliability because we employ a direct measurement system. Unlike observing behavior as it occurs, having a permanent procedure allows us to recheck correct and error scoring or engage others in double-checking the accuracy of scoring of children's responses. Self-Check 6-2 illustrates how daily decisions regarding the selection of materials (e.g., flash cards) can be aided by probes.

USING OUTCOMES OF MEASUREMENT

Classroom research has shown that mistakes children make in their work can often be categorized according to certain patterns that emerge over time (Cox, 1975). Daily analysis to determine these error patterns can greatly enhance efficiency in reassigning practice materials. This section of the chapter describes sample forms of error analysis that have been found effective. We must point out that caution is required in applying the procedures we discuss in that the following by no means represents the last word in terms of informal assessment. Rather, the tactics presented are a stepping stone to more thorough analysis of children's academic performance and, in turn, to increase the prospect that one is able to manage learning experiences effectively. In one form of error-pattern analysis studied by Burney and Shores (1979) as part of a precision planning procedure, errors evidenced during "multiple sampling" of pupil performance were grouped as:

Self-Check 6-2

DAILY/WEEKLY TALLY SHEET

Student: Gretchen S.

Task: spell words, 3 consecutive correct

Item	11-1 cor.	11-1 inc.	11-2 cor.	11-2 inc.	11-3 cor.	11-3 inc.	11-4 cor.	11-4 inc.	11-5 cor.	11-5 inc.	item mastered	error type
Time (min.)												
1 well		✓	✓		✓		✓		✓			one l
2 wells		✓		✓	✓			✓	✓			
3 we'll		✓	✓		✓		✓		✓			wheel
4 went	✓		✓			✓	✓		✓			wet
5 we're		✓		✓	✓		✓		✓			silent e
6 west	✓			✓	✓		✓		✓			t/s reverse
7 West		✓		✓	✓		✓			✓		cap
8 wet	✓		✓		✓		✓		✓			–
9 what		✓	✓			✓		✓	✓			
10 when		✓	✓		✓			✓		✓		wh
11 which		✓		✓		✓		✓		✓		wh/ch
12 while		✓		✓		✓		✓		✓		wh/sile
13 whine		✓		✓	✓			✓		✓		wh/sile
14 whip		✓	✓			✓		✓		✓		wh
15												
16												
17												
18												
19												
20												
21												
22												
23												
24												
25												
26												
27												
28												
29												
30												
Total												
	cor.	inc.	cor.	inc.	cor.	inc.	cor.	inc.	cor.	inc.		
Percent												
Rate												

Percent Finder on reverse side of page.
Rate Finder on reverse side of page.

Instructions

The tally sheet shown above is a record of Gretchen's spelling responses to probes, which preceded daily flash-card drill. Identify the words that pertain to the decisions listed below for the next day's lesson.

Response

1. Drop out flash cards for mastered words ______________________

____

2. Replace with __________ (number) new words.
3. Review these words ______________________________

____

in the next lesson.

4. Change instruction for words ______________________

____

Now compare your response to the sample responses in Appendix A.

- *Unknown concept*—Two-thirds or more of the learners responses were in error and the errors varied.
- *Mislearned concept*—Two-thirds or more of the learners responses were in error and the errors were the same.
- *Chance error*—One-third or fewer of the learners responses were in error.

This form of error analysis can be used while scoring practice pages or daily probes. The primary use of error analysis for instruction purposes is to help the teacher decide whether to change materials, teaching tactics, or reinforcement contingencies. The following series of examples illustrate the manner in which teachers can initiate a variety of error-analysis procedures.

Analyzing Mistakes in Arithmetic

Having reviewed several students' previous test scores in the area of arithmetic computation, Mr. L. has singled out subtraction for instruction. Teacher-made practice pages are constructed; three forms, each containing problems requiring the same subskill operation, are used during the mathematics period.

Even though some problems called for borrowing, this particular student (Figure 6-3) repeatedly subtracted the smaller from the larger number, regardless of its placement in the problem. Referring back to our definitions of error types, one can easily see that these errors can probably be attributed to a "mislearned concept." In this instance, a clear pattern of inaccurate responding exists. That is, a systematic misapplication of a borrowing procedure is evident. Once the teacher is alerted to the fact that further practice in borrowing rather than subtraction on the whole seems warranted, instruction intended to remediate this skill deficiency is possible.

In the other example in Figure 6-3, responses to addition problems suggest that the learner has some knowledge of mathematics.

A "nonpattern" of errors indicates mistakes probably are attributable to chance. A child's being distracted momentarily during the mathematics period may explain the error in the third problem in row 1 and the first and fourth problems in row 2. Given the above information, and if further work does not reveal errors otherwise explained, we might conclude that the problem is one of motivation rather than instruction. Then applying some form of contingency management procedure (discussed in Chapter 9), we might quickly correct the problem.

Analyzing Spelling Errors

Teachers have long applied various criteria for selecting new spelling words to be taught. Usually instruction simply corresponds to the words introduced in commercial spelling workbooks. At other times, teachers have grouped

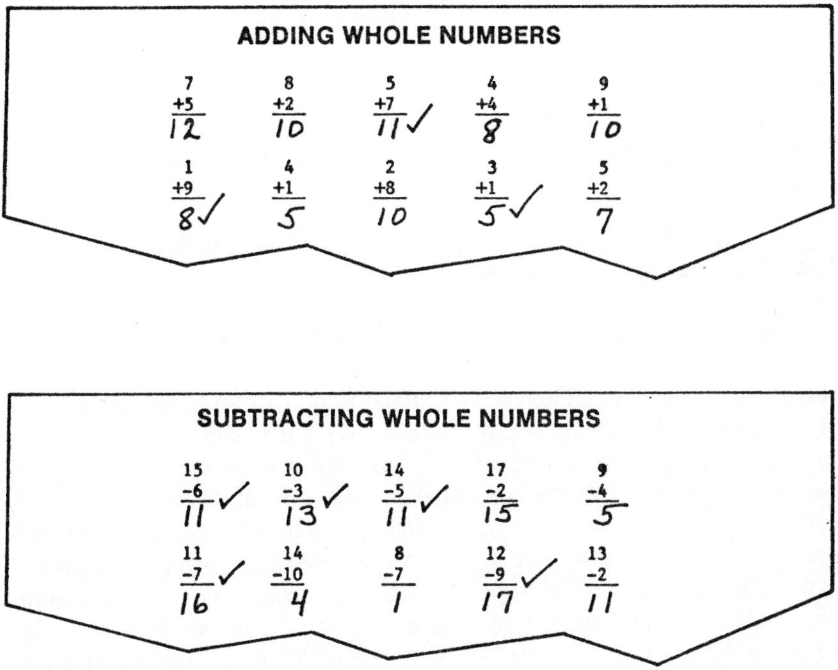

ADDING WHOLE NUMBERS

7 +5 12	8 +2 10	5 +7 11 ✓	4 +4 8	9 +1 10
1 +9 8 ✓	4 +1 5	2 +8 10	3 +1 5 ✓	5 +2 7

SUBTRACTING WHOLE NUMBERS

15 -6 11 ✓	10 -3 13 ✓	14 -5 11 ✓	17 -2 15	9 -4 5
11 -7 16 ✓	14 -10 4	8 -7 1	12 -9 17 ✓	13 -2 11

Figure 6-3. *Sample Error Patterns That Can Be Identified Through Error Analysis*

words for instruction according to a particular set of spelling rules, for example, "i before e except after c"; a common linguistic pattern, or words appearing at a high frequency in other content areas. In any event, evaluating children's errors in spelling can serve to determine a more useful means for selecting words to be taught. The following excerpt from a spelling test shows that this student's problem may be in the area of a mislearned concept (see definitions).

- olrite (for all right)
- atenchen (for attention)
- chair — correct

These findings suggest that attention should be focused on specific response deficits.

In contrast, we see that the error below is likely due to chance or "carelessness":

- whom (for who)
- stream — correct
- how — correct

Analyzing Handwriting Problems

In the area of handwriting, the use of error-analysis procedures has been particularly helpful. Samples of students' work can be obtained in several ways. Teachers can ask that children copy material from the board and put down on paper information presented orally. In this way, it is possible to obtain a permanent product of students' efforts with and without a model as a visual referent. Teachers have found that some students have difficulty in letter formation, as distinguished from problems in spelling. Children not possessing these difficulties, but who otherwise are unable to complete the "copying assignment" in the allotted time, may have poor motor coordination or simply lack sufficient motivation under existing conditions to complete the work successfully. To aid in the analysis of pupils' handwriting and to add a needed measure of objectivity, teachers are relying on transparent overlays or templates (Stowitschek & Stowitschek, 1979) for error-analysis purposes.

Error Analysis in Oral Reading

The concept of error analysis is widely applied to the area of oral reading instruction. Several individually administered diagnostic reading tests rely on a scoring procedure for classifying errors as "omissions, subsituations, repetitions," and so on. We have found that by supplementing this procedure, assessment can become even more useful. It is recommended that multiple samples (at least three) of students' reading be obtained so a more reliable indication of pupil performance is possible. Conventional reading scores are useful for selecting the level at which to initiate further evaluation, with the reading text corresponding with that level serving as the "diagnostic tool."

Measurement of student's oral reading can be accomplished by scoring passages as the student reads aloud or through the use of a tape recorder. Obtaining and maintaining a permanent response vis-à-vis audiotapes facilitates reading-analysis procedures. Recorded reading sessions serve as probe data for initial assessment and in attempting to evaluate the impact of specific teaching strategies. For assessment purposes, errors in oral reading might be subgrouped according to the following: (a) *substitutions*—any words read in place of those appearing in the selection; (b) *omissions*—any words deleted from the selection; and (c) *additions*—any instance in which the number of words read was increased from the number appearing in the passage. Split words, for example, two-thirds, might be defined as one word. Repetitions, hesitations, and disregard for punctuation marks may or may not be considered as errors, depending on the level of mastery demonstrated by the learner and the exact purpose of instruction.

The following sequence illustrates one way in which the principles of error analysis can be adapted to oral reading.

Analysis of Oral Reading

Step 1: Identify initial level of instruction.

Step 2: Identify type of error.

- A. Problem in discrimination.
  Probe with words erred out of context by using flash cards.
  1. If words read correctly to criterion, analyze contingencies.
  2. If errors persist during probe, identify errors and provide supplementary instruction designed to add to discriminative properties of words erred.
- B. Random errors.
  Probe with words erred out of context (flash cards).
  1. Probe for recognition.
  2. If errors persist during probe, provide supplementary instruction designed to teach new words.
- C. Waiting response.
  Probe with words erred out of context (flash cards).
  1. If student omits and/or waits for model of word, analyze data; then analyze contingencies.

Step 3: Devise and implement remedial instruction.

Step 4: Evaluate probe data—modify instruction as required.

As indicated, if errors continue to occur during probe sessions, the next step in the sequence is to ascertain if supplementary training appears to be an appropriate initial tactic. Teaching sessions would be designed, according to the type of error, to introduce new words or to enhance the discriminative properties of the words. That is, if the student repeatedly errs in correctly reading the terminal syllable, or phrase, or fails to include the word ending, for example, reads "careful" for "carefully," "tree" for "trees," the omitted segment of the word is given additional discriminative properties by underlining the erred-upon portion.

In sum, much is yet to be learned in regard to the analysis of pupil mistakes for the purpose of selecting intervention strategies and/or instructional materials best suited to their remediation. Increasingly, however, teachers are discovering that careful evaluation of students' errors can be of benefit when attempting to match materials and tactics to learner needs. The most significant feature of error analysis is that it provides a systematic approach to daily assessment of pupil performance.

QUANTIFYING DATA OBTAINED THROUGH DAILY MEASUREMENT

Some teachers tell us they can keep in their heads information on their students' performance as it accumulates on a daily basis. Some teachers also tell us they can leap tall buildings in a single bound. Other teachers tell us they would do a poor job of teaching if they did not have organized methods of keeping track of all the goings on of their students, at least in their daily work. Daily progress notes will not do it. Imagine reams of note paper, all hurriedly penned, and you have to run back through it to find important information. Quantification (scores) of daily work according to standard units is usually the only feasible alternative. Generally speaking, data is often quantified in one of three ways: (1) frequency of occurrence (tally), (2) percentage of occurrence, or (3) rate of occurrence.

Tally Summary

A tally of pupil responses represents one way to measure frequency of occurrence. A simple count of corrects and/or errors in, for example, completing single-digit addition problems probably is the most common means of classroom data collection. Although the use of a tally of daily academic responses (e.g., 13 words spelled correctly) is the stock in trade of many classroom teachers, several shortcomings mitigate against overdependence on this method. Unless the number of responses is held constant, that is, the same number of spelling words is tested each week, the utility of comparing performance across time is limited. As time is not usually considered to be an important variable in using a tally procedure, it is not possible to obtain a proficiency measure of pupil performance. Instead, only the question of accuracy can be addressed (White & Liberty, 1976). Shortcomings of a tally system notwithstanding, when properly managed, such recording can be useful. Some materials, such as audiotape units in drill and practice programs, contain a uniform number of practice items for each unit (e.g., 12 spelling words per taped unit), and a simple tally is sufficient to compare a student's progress across units. When units or lessons vary in length, tallies can be converted to percentage by simply dividing the number of corrects by the total number of responses and then multiplying by 100 (7 correct in 20 responses = 35 percent correct).

Percentage Summary

The advantage of percentage over tallying is that percent scores can be compared from one day to another even when different practice material is used and the number of possible responses differs. However, comparisons of correct responses across teaching sessions may be misleading when only a small number of academic responses are recorded. Also, if only the percentage correct is recorded daily and the number of problems vary from day-to-day (e.g., three reading work sheets, 8 items on the first, 3 items on the second, and 15 items on the third), results become extremely difficult to interpret accurately.

With the movement toward the use of diagnostic-prescriptive programs, teaching objectives are usually expressed in terms of a percentage, such as "95 percent correct on single-digit addition problems." When the number of responses per objective drops below 20, and particularly below 10, be extremely cautious in your judgments on the learner's performance, however well the materials appear to be constructed.

Converting a tally of the number of add-facts (if in sufficient number) calculated correctly permits one to fix the level at which a learner is performing. By transforming scores obtained through direct measurement to frequency correct and incorrect, teachers are able to make certain decisions regarding instruction and materials. One can substantiate that George has in two weeks' time improved in arithmetic by 30 percent. It would also be possible to say that this improvement has been demonstrated since the instructional materials were adapted by placing a permanent model on each daily work sheet. However, by using percent we impose a ceiling on performance, a ceiling of 100 percent. Admittedly, it is difficult to improve on 100 percent.

Rate Summary

Still, George can show further improvement if one takes into account the speed at which he performs or the total number of problems he is able to complete. A score of 80 percent correct does not yield knowledge of the number of errors, total number of problems attempted, or how long it took for the learner to complete the assignment. Another important consideration is that accuracy or percent data alone is not always sensitive to small amounts of academic change (White & Liberty, 1976). Again, this is particularly true when a student makes only a limited number of responses. For example, progress represented by an increase of 10 percent may be of greater educational signif-

Self-Check 6-3

Instructions

Analyze Gini's reading responses recorded on the tally sheet below as chance error, mislearned, or unlearned. Use the definitions as follows:

Unlearned: Two-thirds or more of the responses are in error and the errors are different.

Mislearned: Two-thirds or more of the responses are in error and the errors are the same.

Chance error: One-third or fewer of the responses are in error.

Mark your answers in the right-hand column headed "error type."

Response

DAILY / WEEKLY TALLY SHEET

Student Gini T.

Task calling out reading words

	Item	Date 3/4		3/5		3/8						item mastered	error type
	Time (min.)												
		cor.	inc.	cor.	inc.	cor.	inc.	cor.	inc.	cor.	inc.		
1	come		✓		✓	✓							
2		("cane")		("came")		("come")							
3	dome		✓		✓	✓							
4		("down")		("down")		("dome")							
5	here		✓	✓		✓							
6		("her")		("here")		("here")							
7	like		✓		✓		✓						
8		("look")		("lack")		("love")							
9	play		✓		✓		✓						
10		("plug")		("plug")		("plug")							
11	not		✓	✓			✓						
12		("Tom")		("not")		("Tom")							
13	had		✓	✓		✓							
14		("Dad")		("had")		("had")							
15	let		✓	✓			✓						
16		("tell")		("let")		("tall")							
17													
18													
19													
20													
21													
22													
23													
24													
25													
26													
27													
28													
29													
30													
	Total	cor.	inc.	cor.	inc.	cor.	inc.	cor.	inc.	cor.	inc.		
	Percent												
	Rate												

Percent Finder on reverse side of page.
Rate Finder on reverse side of page.

Compare your response to the sample responses in Appendix A.

icance when that 10 percent represents an increase of 10 arithmetic problems out of a possible 100 than when it represents only 1 out of 10 problems. Also, a 30 percent improvement from 10 percent (pretest) to 40 percent (posttest) can be considerably different in difficulty from a 30 percent improvement of 60 percent to 90 percent. By transforming the number of responses to the number correct and incorrect per unit of time, greater precision is possible. The major difficulty in using rate summaries is that almost all of the commercial materials available that include a measurement system do not have provisions for a rate summary. This means that the teacher will have to superimpose another or a different summary procedure.

When should teachers consider changing or supplementing the measurement system in a material? It depends upon the instructional purpose of the material. In the early stages of instruction, accuracy is critical. At more advanced stages, accuracy is not always the most important feature of pupil performance (Haring & Eaton, 1978). For instance, in oral reading, fluency is often the instructional goal. At first, of course, the objective is to teach the student to say the words accurately. Once the student is performing with a relatively high degree of accuracy (90-100 percent correct) in their readers, teachers often shift to attempts to increase the speed at which the student reads. Initially then, accuracy of percentage of words read correctly is sufficient; thereafter, the teacher's interest may move toward measuring accuracy and speed together. Only rate measures address the dimensions of speed and accuracy simultaneously.

The term *rate* is used to refer to an equation consisting of speed plus accuracy. Thus we measure not only the accuracy with which a learner performs but also the time required to perform the task in order to judge whether he or she has achieved proficiency. Knowledge of tasks accomplished to a specified level of accuracy (such as 90 percent correct) does not yield sufficiently precise information to evaluate performance. Using percent correct we know how well, but not how fast, the student performed. By specifying the number of responses divided by the time (usually in minutes) during which the response occurred,

$$\frac{\text{Number or Frequency of Responses}}{\text{Duration or Time to Complete These Responses}} = \text{Rate} \qquad \frac{\text{14 correct}}{\text{7 minutes}} = \begin{array}{c}\text{2 correct}\\ \text{per minute}\end{array}$$

we are able to obtain a performance figure referred to as rate (White & Liberty, 1976). Performance rates are especially useful for establishing proficiency criteria.

A major problem faced by teachers is establishing appropriate criterion levels. Although it is clear that a fixed and quantifiable criterion must be established before beginning instruction, few guidelines are available to assist teachers in accomplishing this important task. The goal of instruction can, of course, be arbitrarily established by selecting a certain number of corrects versus errors. Many published programs set a single percent-correct criterion for all objectives and all units of instruction. However, greater precision through the use of rate statements is advised. Rate criterion can be determined in several ways. For example, we can set rate goals by (a) identifying the performance of a competent peer (e.g., at what rate does the best reader in the fifth grade perform) or (b) by measuring adult performance and scaling that figure downward. Another, but more complex, way to establish rates is to set performance rates on certain academic responses and then evaluate the effect of those rates on the student's learning of subsequent higher level skills (Haring & Gentry, 1976). For example, a teacher could assess the effect of students' mastering simple addition facts at a rate of 30 per minute on their performance on multiplication facts. Teachers might sample student performance rates on various skills across classrooms and set the goal of instruction on the basis of others' performance levels.

Ways to Account for Differences in Work Complexity

Another aspect of quantifying data obtained through students' work in materials pertains to the complexity of pupil responses. Generally, teachers have evaluated academic behavior simply as "correct or incorrect." On the other hand, the steps required, for instance, to compute single-digit addition accurately are fewer than necessary to complete double-digit addition problems with carrying. Often a practice page in a published drill book will include items that vary in complexity. As shown below, more is demanded of the learner to complete examples in the left than the right column:

Variable Demands of Academic Responses

EXAMPLE 1: *"Complete the following problems."*

```
  2
 134        5
- 57       -2
  77        3
```

EXAMPLE 2: *"Spell these two words:"*

p-a-r-a-d-e c-a-t

EXAMPLE 3: *"Read the following passages."*

"The long day's march lead the small band of weary soldiers through an alligator-infested swamp."

"Jane give the candy to Sue."

In selecting a standard unit of measurement that is sensitive to the complexity of the responses, teachers have found it useful to slice the learning task into smaller and smaller steps. For example, in the area of arithmetic, it is possible first to list the number of subskill elements involved in completing a problem and then to record the number of correct operations completed. Rather than simply marking an answer as "correct or incorrect," one is now able to categorize learner behavior as precisely as is needed. In the area of spelling, it is sometimes useful to mark the number of letters consecutively placed in the right order or indicate the number of syllables spelled correctly (Haring & Gaton, 1978). More is demanded of the student in spelling "parade" than in spelling "cat."

As we suggested earlier, counting the number of syllables instead of whole words read correctly is one way to take into account the range in length and difficulty of words found in children's reading passages (Starlin, 1971). Of the two reading samples, not only would it take longer to read the selection on the left, but also it would require more knowledge of word recognition and word-attack skills.

Recalling the discussion on error-analysis tactics, you can see that a notable feature of slicing skills into smaller segments is that it has utility for uncovering deficits that might otherwise be overlooked. Rather than providing practice in double-digit subtraction, teachers can "zero in" on only that aspect, such as borrowing, that is troublesome for the learner. Teachers are daily placed in a position of choosing what is desirable and what is practical regarding measurement. It is no surprise that they are not always the same. However, slicing complex responses into smaller segments allows one directly to record behavior that is more descriptive of a student's performance. Choosing to record independently discrete segments of behavior rather than whole responses still permits one to quantify performance results as before — by frequency, percent, or rate.

Now, we know that one test, one system of probes, or one type of informal teacher checklist will not do it all. Teachers must use a variety of different measures for different purposes. A problem arises when a teacher must pull these different pieces of information together to make decisions about materials and instruction. Methods of summarizing results that span across differing measures sharing a common metric are going to be more useful to a teacher than are summary methods that can only be used with one test. The summary procedures described in this section are intended to be useful whether a teacher is simply scoring a workbook page at the end of the day or attempting to draw instructional information from an achievement test.

Although rather crude, and certainly not a procedure that allows for detailed analysis, a Daily Record Sheet (DRS), as shown in Figure 6-4, can be useful. The DRS provides a way to monitor the amount of work completed daily. We

	Daily Record Sheet									
	Monday		Tuesday		Wed		Thurs		Friday	
Name	pages	prob.	pages	prob.	pages	prob.	pages	prob.	pages	prob.
Sue	4	18	3	15	4	17	5	21	—	—
Bill	2	9	3	11	3	12	2	10	4	17
Fred	1	6	1	7	2	9	2	8	3	11
Mark	5	23	6	31	5	27	5	24	7	34
Bob	3	14	3	15	2	11	3	14	4	18

Figure 6-4. *Example of Summarized Work-Completion Information*

have written in the number of arithmetic workbook pages and total problems for a given day. This form of data collection can easily be accomplished by the student's themselves, and work in pages from different materials can be monitored. The subject areas being taught can be substituted where students' names appear below for purposes of individual rather than group record keeping.This type of summary information can help a teacher make decisions for grouping (e.g., faster students come to the reading circle for round 1, leaving slower students to complete their work and then participate in the round-two reading circle) and contingency management (e.g., Bill and Fred are going to need to complete two worksheets before being reinforced).

Although succeeding examples allow for more precise recording, some evidence suggests that a simple tally of assignments completed can offer a reasonable measure of pupil progress (Cooper, 1974). Of course, far greater specificity is required when collected data are analyzed for making instructional decisions that involve changing, deleting, or adding material.

Recall earlier that we discussed the use of error-analysis procedures in oral reading instruction. The Data Record Sheet pictured in Figure 6-4 represents an economical way of recording detailed information regarding such a program. Data recorded on a session-by-session basis can stand alone on this form or later be graphed for visual display. In either case one can easily see that such data go well beyond the observation that "Fred seems to be doing a little better in his reading these days."

Another way of recording pupil performance concisely is to use a Daily/Weekly Tally Sheet (Stowitschek, 1976). The following shows how a tally sheet (Figure 6-5), with items listed corresponding to spelling instruction, summarizes a pupil's progress. From left to right, after recording the student's name and indicating the task, one records the item (in this instance, new spell-

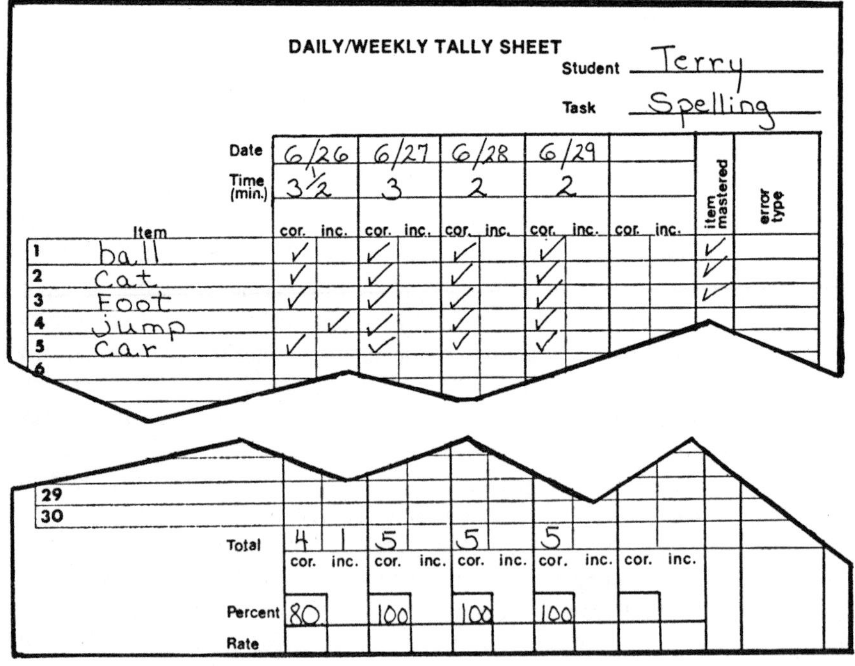

DAILY/WEEKLY TALLY SHEET

Student Terry

Task Spelling

	Item	cor.	inc.	cor.	inc.	cor.	inc.	cor.	inc.	cor.	inc.	item mastered	error type
Date		6/26		6/27		6/28		6/29					
Time (min.)		3½		3		2		2					
1	ball	✓		✓		✓		✓				✓	
2	Cat	✓		✓		✓		✓				✓	
3	Foot	✓		✓		✓		✓				✓	
4	Jump		✓	✓		✓		✓					
5	Car	✓		✓		✓		✓					
6													
29													
30													
Total		4	1	5		5		5					
Percent		80		100		100		100					
Rate													

Figure 6-5. *Summary of Spelling Performance Across Days, Computed into Percentages Correct*

Source: Reprinted from *Daily/Weekly Tally Sheets* by Joseph J. Stowitschek by permission of the author.

ing words), the date, the time required to complete the task, whether the task was performed correctly or incorrectly, whether the item was mastered—according to the predetermined criterion for mastery—and a notation regarding the nature of responses erred.

Looking at the lower portion of the Daily/Weekly Tally Sheet, space is provided for recording the total number of items correct and incorrect, which allows one to compute either percentage or rate of corrects and errors. The back side of this particular tally sheet contains matrices for summarizing quickly the rate and percentage correct.

In remembering the earlier discussion of trials to criterion measurement, it can be seen that the Daily/Weekly Tally Sheet affords an opportunity to check out consecutive correct responses until criterion is attained. We might feel confident that Johnny knows how to spell the word *window* correctly only after he has done so on three successive days. Then we would indicate that criterion has been achieved by marking "item mastered" to the right on the sheet.

Another type of summary form (Figure 6-6) accompanies a series of diagnostic arithmetic tests developed by Alan Hofmeister (1972). The number of problems correctly answered is individually recorded; scores can be summed across the bottom of the page. Data recorded indicate subskill areas of difficulty for a particular student as well as the entire class.

The "profile" for arithmetic that is pictured in Figure 6-6 can be modified so the vertical column on the right corresponds to scores obtained on daily probes—skill sheets. This adaptation is also illustrated in Figure 6-6.

Line Graphs

A *standard line graph* represents the simplest and most common form of plotting performance data (Hall, 1971). It affords the opportunity to inspect pupil performance data visually, allowing one easily to determine the extent to which a child's behavior corresponds with the goals of instruction. Many published materials include progress graphs. Steps to completing a line graph, like most graphs, follow a standard format (Figure 6-7). Along the vertical line, the amount of behavior is recorded, usually in terms of (a) frequency of occurrence, (b) percentage of occurrence, or (c) rate of occurrence. Information placed below the horizontal line corresponds to (a) sessions, (b) minutes, (c) days, or (d) weeks, according to the frequency with which assessment is conducted. The performance of several students can be charted together. Daily work can be summarized this way but it must be remembered that this is a group *average,* and information on an individual student cannot be drawn from it. A line graph is sometimes referred to as a *noncumulative graph* in that each score represents a single unit of measurement and stands independent of scores recorded before or after it (Cooper, 1974).

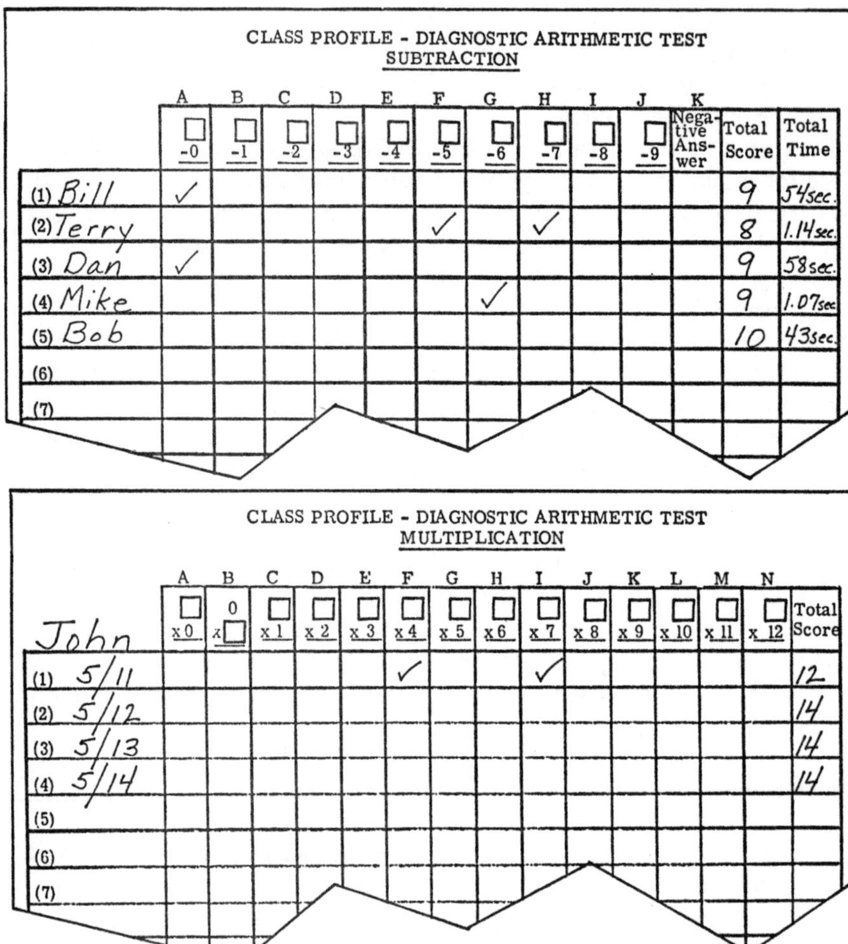

CLASS PROFILE - DIAGNOSTIC ARITHMETIC TEST
SUBTRACTION

	A □ -0	B □ -1	C □ -2	D □ -3	E □ -4	F □ -5	G □ -6	H □ -7	I □ -8	J □ -9	K Negative Answer	Total Score	Total Time
(1) Bill	✓											9	54sec.
(2) Terry						✓		✓				8	1.14sec.
(3) Dan	✓											9	58sec.
(4) Mike							✓					9	1.07sec.
(5) Bob												10	43sec.
(6)													
(7)													

CLASS PROFILE - DIAGNOSTIC ARITHMETIC TEST
MULTIPLICATION

John	A □ x 0	B 0 x□	C □ x 1	D □ x 2	E □ x 3	F □ x 4	G □ x 5	H □ x 6	I □ x 7	J □ x 8	K □ x 9	L □ x 10	M □ x 11	N □ x 12	Total Score
(1) 5/11						✓			✓						12
(2) 5/12															14
(3) 5/13															14
(4) 5/14															14
(5)															
(6)															
(7)															

Figure 6-6. *Class Profile for Summarizing Math-Computation Performance*

Source: Reprinted from *Diagnostic Arithmetic Test—Subtraction and Diagnostic Arithmetic Test—Multiplication* by Alan M. Hofmeister. Copyright 1973, by Alan M. Hofmeister.

Cumulative Graph

Cumulative graphs differ from noncumulative graphs in that the behavior recorded after each session is added to that which was recorded previously. In a cumulative graph of spelling performance, scores attained on daily spelling tests are summed across sessions. In Figure 6-7, the vertical line corresponds

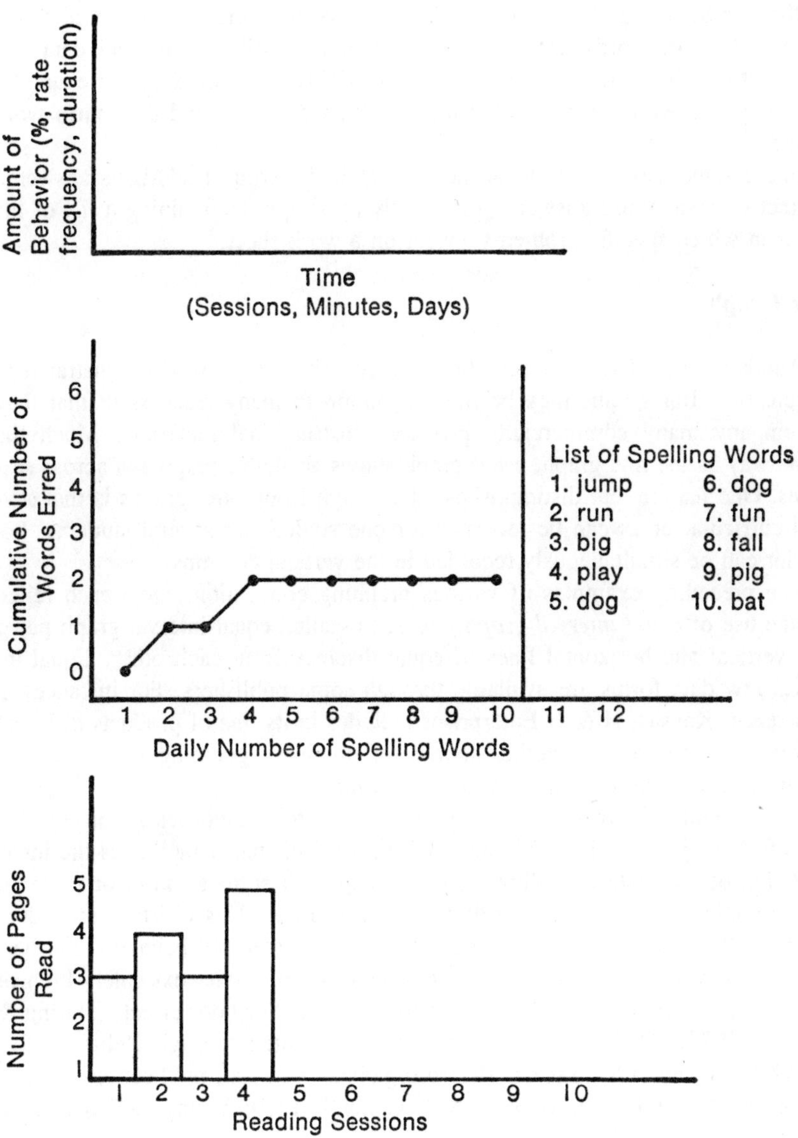

Figure 6-7. Examples of Graphical Summaries of Students' Performance in Daily Work

to the number of spelling words erred, whereas the horizontal line depicts the total number of words tested. In this way it is possible to present data that pertain to each discrete response (Cooper, 1974). We can see, for example, that only two words were spelled incorrectly, the second and the fourth word tested.

In the same way, teachers can keep a detailed record of add-facts answered correctly versus those answered incorrectly by simply maintaining a list of the order in which specific problems appear on a work sheet.

Bar Graph

Another form of data presentation, called a bar graph is also illustrated in Figure 6-7. Bar graphs may be more common to many teachers in that they accompany many commercially produced instructional materials. Much the same way as the line graph, a bar graph shows academic responses across sessions. One feature that distinguishes a bar graph from other graphs is that several curricular areas can be recorded for one student, or several students' behavior can be simultaneously recorded in the vertical columns.

The preceding examples of various graphing conventions have each relied on the use of *equal-interval graph paper*. So-called equal-interval graph paper has vertical and horizontal lines of equal distance from each other. Equal-interval raw data forms are available through some publishers. For instance, in Lawrence, Kansas, H & H Enterprises includes in its line of products different forms of graph paper. Another source for obtaining graphing forms is Academic Therapy Publication, Novato, California.

A less widely known means of plotting academic responses is through the use of a six-cycle semilogarithmic graph paper. This paper facilitates the interpretation of rate data and allows for graphing both correct and error rates in, for example, oral reading or arithmetic computation. This charting procedure is particularly useful in estimating future trends in rate(s) of behavior. Further, it is sensitive to performance data for behaviors with either extremely high or low rates; thus no data are "lost" due to ceiling and/or floor effects (Haring & Gentry, 1976). Daily behavior charts are distributed through Behavior Research Company, a Kansas City-based organization. Also, publications on precision teaching (Howell, Kaplan, & O'Connell, 1979; Young, 1972) explain the use of such graphing techniques.

Although not widespread, some commercially produced materials incorporate graphs to be filled out by either the teacher or the children themselves. The *Corrective Reading Program* calls for the daily graphing of errors exhibited during oral recitation (Figure 6-8). In addition, a point schedule is incorporated into the teaching sequence; points are summed on a weekly basis and then converted to a grade score of A, B, or C. In this way, motivational as-

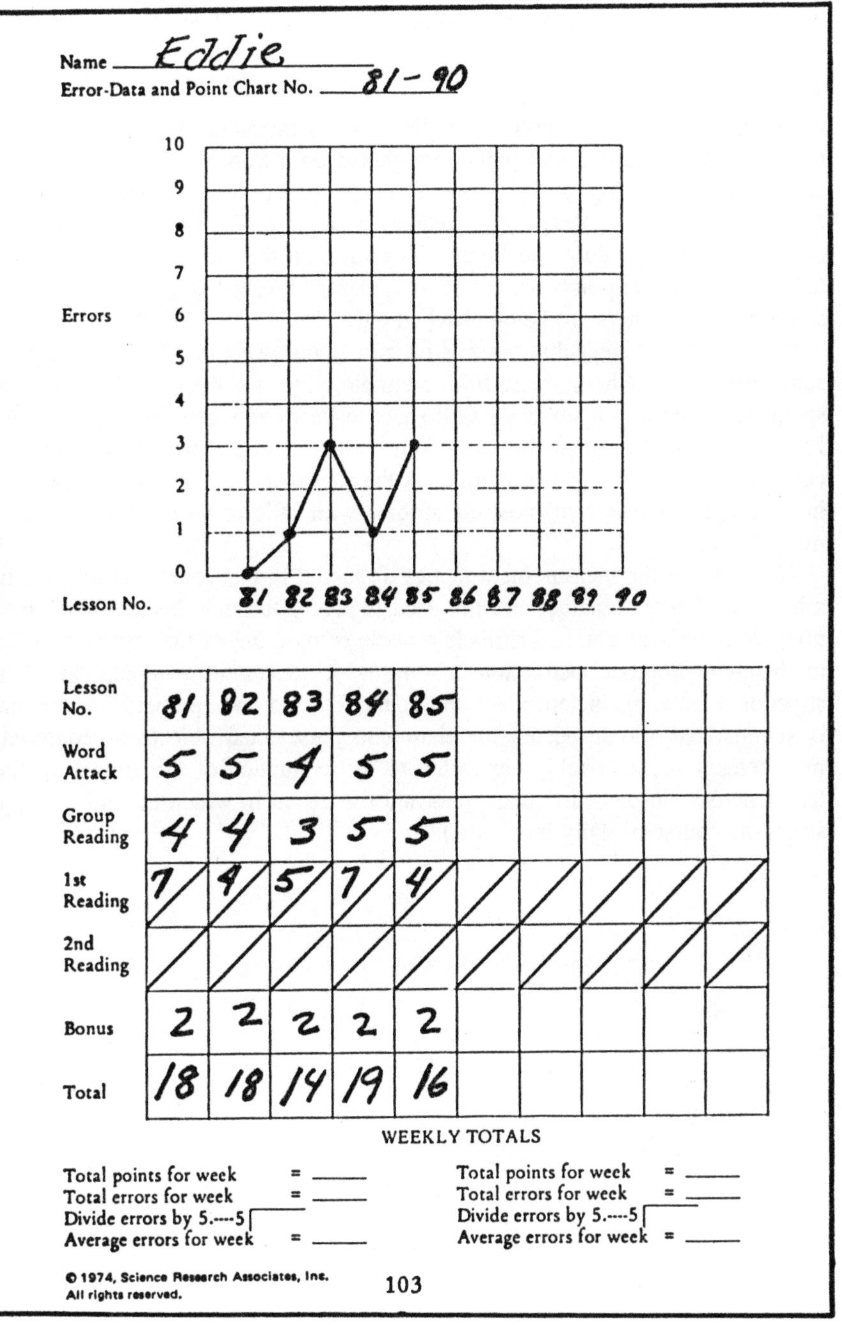

Name Eddie
Error-Data and Point Chart No. 81-90

Errors 10 9 8 7 6 5 4 3 2 1 0

Lesson No. 81 82 83 84 85 86 87 88 89 90

Lesson No.	81	82	83	84	85					
Word Attack	5	5	4	5	5					
Group Reading	4	4	3	5	5					
1st Reading	7	4	5	7	4					
2nd Reading										
Bonus	2	2	2	2	2					
Total	18	18	14	19	16					

WEEKLY TOTALS

Total points for week = ______
Total errors for week = ______
Divide errors by 5.----5
Average errors for week = ______

Total points for week = ______
Total errors for week = ______
Divide errors by 5.----5
Average errors for week = ______

103

Figure 6-8. *Combination Error Graph and Daily Work Summary in a Published Material*

Source: Reprinted from *Corrective Reading* by Siegfried Englemann and Wesley Becker with permission of the publisher. Copyright 1974 by Science Research Associates.

pects of teaching become an integral part of daily instruction. Figure 6-8 shows that errors are recorded and points distributed on a lesson-by-lesson basis. As can be seen, a maximum of five points can be earned in instruction for "Word Attack" and "Group Reading," whereas a variable number of points can be earned during individual checkouts, depending on the number of errors emitted. Finally, bonus points are given to students observed studying the reading selection while others are being checked out.

By now it is evident that there is no end to the ways in which data can be summarized. Procedures range from a simple tally of correct and incorrect responses recorded on a student's skill sheet to far more elaborate scoring of information gained through the use of an audio cassette recorder. One feature common to each of these techniques is the fact that they can be incorporated into the daily schedule of most classrooms with little or no disruption to normal routine.

The value of the measurement tactics discussed in this chapter is sharply diminished if scores obtained are not used regularly to guide instruction. Measuring children's educational skills is a waste of time unless the results are used to change or improve instruction in some way. Successful manipulation of instructional materials is dependent upon data obtained on pupil performance that is summarized and inspected in relation to preselected objectives. Materials management is inextricably connected to the evaluation of the impact of materials across various curricular areas and the extent to which this information steers the course of daily instruction.

CHAPTER 7

Daily Materials Management and Classroom Design

Objectives

1. Develop a systematic approach to managing daily instructional time and materials.
   - What materials-instructional factors do I need to consider in organizing daily teaching?
   - What options do I have to choose from in my classroom?
   - How can I organize the class so students engage in independent study?
   - How can I make use of pupils to make it work?

2. Prepare and maintain a skill file.
   - What is a skill file for?
   - How is a skill file initially organized?
   - How is a skill file maintained and further developed?

3. Use personal resources as an aid to instruction.
   - How can I use child-initiated instruction to promote better distribution of my instructional time?
   - How can I use cross-age peers and/or classmates as a resource for improving daily materials management?

4. Design (redesign) the physical arrangement of a classroom for efficient use of materials.
   - What materials-instructional variables should I take into account in arranging my classroom?
   - What social-interpersonal characteristics should I take into account in arranging my classroom?

At first it would appear that nothing less than sorcery is needed to be able to establish and maintain a well-organized, smoothly operating classroom. A closer look reveals that daily management of instruction consists of the skillful arrangement of time, materials, and resources. We hasten to add that this is by no means a simple undertaking; still, we are convinced that the benefits far outweight the demands.

When children do not improve their educational skills, a teacher's initial inclination is to say, "It's those lousy materials." Lack of academic gains can never really be attributed to materials. They may, of course, be ill-chosen or poorly applied, but materials themselves do not fail. Teachers need to manage, augment, or replace materials so instruction culminates in the attainment of the desired goals. To do this, a number of factors must be taken into account. The first section of this chapter pertains to scheduling for daily materials management and the use of materials that require less direct teacher management. Next, we present ways in which unbound and teacher-made materials can be organized into a skill file. In the third section there is a shift to discussion of instruction time and resources. A notable feature of the third section is a discussion of the use of a built-in classroom resource—children—to improve efficiency without diminishing the effectiveness of instruction. The final section of the chapter discusses and illustrates how the general arrangement of a classroom can facilitate appropriate use of materials and media, as well as various systematic instruction approaches.

SCHEDULING AND MATERIALS

Virtually every aspect of materials presentation not only calls for a well-defined plan of instruction but also its careful execution and thorough evaluation. In the end, scheduling of daily instruction depends on aligning learner needs with instruction capabilities. The amount of time (e.g., 20 minutes), how often (e.g., 3 days per week), the arrangement (small groups), and materials usage (teacher-constructed work sheets) are the ingredients that together constitute the daily and weekly teaching routine. We include daily and weekly arrangements because even though not all curricular areas are covered every day, it is still advisable regularly to schedule each instructional activity. For example, health might be taught Monday afternoons from 2:00 to 2:20 p.m.; whereas reading might be scheduled for 5 days a week, from 9:30 to 10:15 a.m. By maintaining a fixed schedule of instructional activities, the likelihood is increased that teachers will adhere to the plan developed for instruction and that greater student contact with instructional materials can occur. Conversely, those teachers who resist developing and following content- and child-specific plans in favor of so-called exploratory learning may find that a small variety of materials are amenable to that approach.

In short, daily materials management must take into account time, setting, and organization factors necessary to integrate the use of materials with the instruction process. Materials that pertain to a certain content area are generally placed in one locale in the classroom. For example, reading material can usually be found "stored on the three shelves against the back wall." In contrast, it may prove far more functional to group materials according to the manner in which they are presented (e.g., group versus one-to-one) or in relation to the stage of instruction for which they are designed (e.g., initial instruction versus proficiency practice). Then add-fact sheets may be filed beside audiotutorial spelling programs because each is devoted to drilling for mastery. An advantage to this arrangement is that measurement tactics matched to a particular presentation mode or learner response can be administered in one location. Thus record keeping becomes more manageable.

Arranging a Predictable Learning Situation

Numerous studies conducted in classroom settings have demonstrated the usefulness of posting and repeatedly referring to a set of simple classroom rules (Madsen, Becker, & Thomas, 1968). Experience has shown that a limited number of rules and procedures (four to five) stated in a positive tone (do's, not don'ts) will usually do the trick. Rules have been successfully combined with contingent use of teacher praise of desired behavior and ignoring of inappropriate behavior. These rules also pertain to locating and obtaining the correct materials as at the beginning of a work period, as well as returning them to their proper shelf at the end of a period. Teachers have found it necessary literally to "walk through" the list of rules, demonstrating the desired behavior for the class before problems arise. Modeling of classroom rules should be repeated for several days, making sure that students are reinforced for their compliance. Later, a short period on Monday mornings might be set aside for reviewing rules. The influence of classroom rules on the behavior of exceptional children and on materials management is increased when teachers routinely make reference to children's behavior that corresponds to established expectations: "Sally, I am so pleased that you found the right practice tape and, on your own, started your work right away?" or "I see that Maria and Doug put their finished work sheets on the correct pile without my asking for them."

Teachers have discovered that by maintaining a consistent daily routine, it becomes easier to follow the prescribed plan for instruction, and the chance of students mixing up materials is lessened. Here is the manner in which one teacher has chosen to structure the beginning of each school day:

1. Teacher initiates positive feedback to students concerning their previous day's efforts.
2. Teacher reviews classroom rules and daily routine of instruction.
3. Teacher makes announcements of the day.
4. Teacher instructs students to go to the designated distribution area(s) and pick up daily assignments.
5. Children are told and shown the kind of learner responses materials for *when, where,* and *how.*
6. Teacher reiterates the established consequences for completing assignments successfully.
7. Teacher individually reviews each child's behavioral goals, accompanied by modeling of the desired behavior, as needed. (Throughout the work sessions, the teacher singles out students, following the rules or otherwise engaging in appropriate behavior, and delivers precise praise: "I appreciate your waiting for instructions before beginning your assignments.")

Use of a Daily/Weekly Assignment Card

For each student to know what his or her assignments are, teachers have devised a variety of note cards, chalkboard lists, or wall charts for providing a record of assignments. With the example in Figure 7-1, each child is given a Daily/Weekly Assignment Card at the beginning of the week. As shown, the content area is listed in the left-hand column. Then for each day of the week work is assigned, the material, assignment, location, and criterion are indicated. Writing in the location of the materials (bottom shelf, folder R-12) will assist the student in finding his or her own materials. The inclusion of the criterion is not solely for the teacher's benefit but also informs the student of what the expectation is for that particular curricular area. It is widely recognized that providing a clear set of learner expectations is a powerful instructional tactic.

USING MATERIALS THAT REQUIRE LESS TEACHER TIME

As most seasoned educators will tell you, there simply is not enough time during the day to instruct every student directly in each curricular area. Not

Daily/Weekly Assignment Card

Name: ____________________ Week of: ____________________

Subject Area:	Monday				Tuesday				Wednesday				Thursday				Friday			
	Material	Location	Assignment	Criterion	Material	Location	Assignment	Criterion	Material	Location	Assignment	Criterion	Material	Location	Assignment	Criterion	Material	Location	Assignment	Criterion

DATA SUMMARY SHEET (DSS)

Date	Day	Con.	Name	Time/min.	#Wds.	Errs.	C. Rt.	E. Rt.	% C.
11/17	3	Model	David	1.5	97	2	63.3	1.3	97.9
			Bill	1.4	99	13	60.7	9.2	86.9
			Fred	.9	103	11	96.8	11.6	89.3

Figure 7-1. *Daily/Weekly Assignment Card Sample and Data Summary Sheet*

surprisingly then, teachers are finding that efficient teaching can result from the use of some form of self-instructional materials. Actually the term *self-instructional* is a misnomer. The term, when used in this book, refers to materials with which the learner can interact by himself or herself. The use of programmed learning is an example of the concept of self-instruction. We advocate the use of self-instruction when the opportunity to make academic gains is as great using age mates as when conventional teacher-controlled instruction is provided.

Admittedly, child-initiated programming sometimes requires a greater amount of planning time to begin with than when teachers plan for delivering most of the instruction themselves. Still, a number of benefits can be realized from investing the effort to develop child-initiated programs. First, once programming is underway, daily demands on the teacher are usually limited to intermittent checks on pupil progress. Second, little time is spent in correcting children's work since most child-initiated programs make provisions for self-evaluation of learner responses. Third, as fewer demands are made on teacher time, time saved can be reallocated for direct teaching when adult intervention is called for. Then programmed instruction eases the universal burden imposed by too little time and too much to be accomplished.

Not all content areas can economically be programmed for instructional purposes. Material that elicits "open-ended" as opposed to "binary" (wrong or right) answers is not suited to programmed presentation. Further, material that does not lend itself to step-by-step presentation may not prove worthwhile for programming; the uniformity of material must be such that a standardized presentation of a short segment of instruction is followed by a pupil response. The final consideration is the type of response, be it paper and pencil, oral, or motor. In any event, responses that require little or no inference concerning their correctness work best. Programmed materials are best suited to teaching discriminations that lead to a clear-cut choice between various possible responses. As an illustration of self-instructional materials designed to aid in the management of instruction, we have included a description of audiotutorial programming.

Audiotutorial Programming

Mediated instruction designed to complement existing materials for drill and practice purposes has much to offer the classroom teacher. The use of so-called audiotutorial (A-T) programmed learning illustrates another way of applying the concept of self-instruction. The adaptation of commercially produced materials to allow for mediated presentation serves several worthwhile purposes. First, it offers a means for individualizing instruction effectively. Second, it provides a remedial bridge between group-oriented teaching and the demands of one-to-one instruction. Third, it yields a flexible means for delivering child-specific instruction that requires extended drill and practice. Finally, A-T programming allows for independent learning experiences and thus offsets the sometimes negative teacher-pupil exchanges stemming from instruction based on repeated practice exercises.

Equipment necessary for using A-T programs include prerecorded tapes, cassette audiotape recorder, and earplugs and/or headphones. In incorporating the A-T concept of individualized instruction, programs are often established and maintained in one area of the classroom that may be designated as the "Center for Media Directed Programs." Once students are accustomed to the daily routine, little or no teacher time is spent distributing materials or providing direction. Children are often able to engage in the learning experience apart from the teacher's direct intervention.

An additional aspect of A-T programming that serves to underscore its value is the opportunity for including a self-correction component. Learner self-checks accompany several commercially produced programs. Furthermore, teachers can easily adapt materials so (a) a momentary pause for the learner to respond is followed by the correct answer, or (b) a portion of the audiotape provides corrective feedback at selected intervals. The first alternative may teach "patience" instead of the discrimination to be trained. For exceptional learners to function independent of teacher direction, it is advantageous to incorporate frequent self-checks during instruction if they are not included in the programs. Student records (e.g., response pages for each taped unit) also serve as a ready reference for teachers in monitoring and evaluating pupil progress. Evaluation procedures discussed in Chapter 6 can, with little effort, be applied to A-T programming.

Training Children in the Use of A-T Programs

Understandably, an important aspect of A-T programming is the adaptation of materials. A second and related factor pertains to preparing students to manage instructional materials and equipment successfully.

To increase the likelihood that children will gain educationally from such a program, a series of supervised practice exercises may be needed in which students are led step-by-step through a sample unit. During training students should be taught how to operate equipment plus how and when to respond. In this way, teachers are able to demonstrate to children each step of the program. Students are afforded ample opportunity to try out each component of the program and obtain feedback before being permitted to begin working independently. This period of preparation will reduce problems later when careful supervision may not be possible.

Audiotutorial programming represents a useful strategy for delivering self-instruction whereby students can engage in repeated learning experiences, progress at their own pace, and receive frequent confirmation regarding their progress toward mastery of selected materials. At the same time, A-T programming enables classroom teachers to divert time and resources to those curricular areas that call for a greater amount of direct instruction. The following guidelines are offered to teachers interested in further exploring the concept of A-T programming.

Self-Check 7-1

MATHEMATICS—Numeration

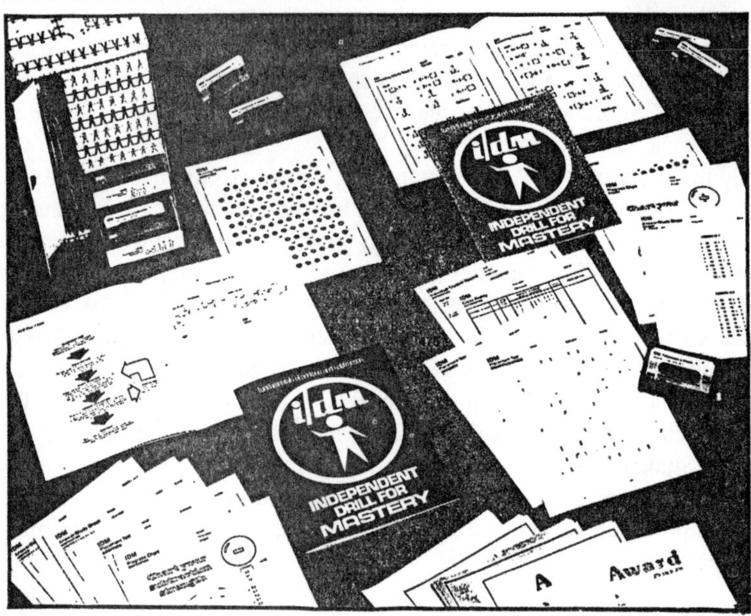

IDM

INDEPENDENT DRILL FOR MASTERY:

Fundamentals of Addition and Subtraction

Fundamentals of Multiplication and Division

Research has identified poor recall of math facts as a major source of students' skill deficits. Designed to increase students' speed and accuracy in math computation, Independent Drill for Mastery was developed and field tested under the direction of Alan M. Hofmeister, Ph.D., Exceptional Child Center, Utah State University.

This individualized program features placement tests to determine students' entry levels and to assess progress in the program. Scoring overlays and a class profile assist the teacher in scoring and recording test results and prescriptions.

Self-study lessons on tape are assigned and students independently listen, write, and correct their practice papers with the answer/study sheets. Students exercise their own judgment as to when they are prepared to be evaluated on a lesson and chart their progress on a student progress record. The teacher monitors and corrects a study-test and when the criteria are met, the student proceeds to the next sequential lesson. Award certificates provide recognition of a student's efforts and achievement.

Fundamentals of Addition and Subtraction covers 42 lessons on 11 tapes—6 addition and 5 subtraction—and 16 spirit masters. Fundamentals of Multiplication and Division has 46 lessons—a total of 12 tapes, 6 for each skill area, and 18 spirit masters.

A tape presents two lessons per side, and each lesson runs approximately four minutes.

Each program provides a teacher's manual, 50 award certificates, scoring overlays, and spirit masters for the placement tests, class profile, student progress record, culminating worksheets, and answer/study sheets. Replacement award certificates are available in packages of 50.

#474 Addition and Subtraction	**$46.50**
#475 Multiplication and Division	**$50.75**
#501 Award Certificates (Package of 50)	**$ 1.75**

Instructions

The description of the individualized mathematics practice program shown above is admittedly limited. However, you may be able to make some judgments on how the management of this program may affect the daily class schedule. Assuming that all necessary materials are duplicated and equipment is available but stored away, list what your best estimates may be for (a) daily management steps, (b) whether the teacher *must* or the pupils *can* complete the step, and (c) the number of minutes involved for each step.

Responses

	Management Steps	Teacher Conducted or	Pupil Conducted	Minutes
A. Setup (to the point where the student is working in the unit)				
B. Operation (to the end of the practice period)				

Compare your response to the sample responses in Appendix A.

Source: Reprinted from *Developmental Learning Materials Catalogue* with permission of the publisher. Copyright 1979, by Developmental Learning Materials.

A Guide to Developing A-T Instruction

1. Preassess students' present knowledge in a specific skill area.
2. Establish short-term educational objectives in relation to learner needs.
3. Identify necessary entry-level skills, that is, the prerequisites to using the program successfully.
4. Prepare materials packets to include material adaptations based on learner needs and content areas.
5. Develop administration procedures either written or audiotaped; develop monitoring-evaluation systems that include instructions for students, record sheets, and so on.
6. Place students in programs according to information obtained during preassessment period.
7. Select method(s) for providing further remedial instruction, as needed.
8. Implement A-T program; observe and evaluate student performance for purposes of additional program modification based on learner needs.

Materials that are particularly adaptive to teacher-free instruction include those calling for repeated drill for mastery such as in arithmetic, spelling, handwriting, and language development.

PREPARING AND MAINTAINING A SKILL FILE

Not all materials are bound in a book or packaged in a self-contained kit. In fact, many of the practice materials teachers use, particularly in remedial situations, are loose paper. These materials include teacher-made work sheets, single workbooks, duplicator pages drawn from available materials, skill tests, demonstration sheets, and so on. New teachers find that they can rapidly build a collection of individual practice and test pages that help to fill in the gaps in commercial materials.

It is not unheard of for a teacher to have from 75 to 150 separate practice pages (and the same number of skill test pages) covering a variety of subject areas and subskills within these areas. Multiply this number by the number of copies that must be duplicated (often two or more per student) and you can see how disorganization rears its ugly head. Materials piling up, duplication masters lost, skill test papers that do not match with practice pages, work sheets for different skills getting mixed together, running out of some pages while running off too many others, all can add up to inefficient classroom operation and teachers overdosing on Rolaids.

Many teachers have successfully coped with these problems through the use of a skill file system. Such a system involves some initial work to set up but, if organized properly, a system can be cumulative, employ the assistance of pupils in maintaining it, and save teachers from a lot of headaches, not to mention purple fingers (e.g., from spirit masters).

What Is a Skill File?

Skill files vary from teacher to teacher. Different formats are designed depending upon their purpose. Whatever the format, a skill file should incorporate the following: (a) practice material sequenced according to skills, (b) matching skill tests sequenced according to skills, (c) a means of organization so students can locate and retrieve practice materials, (d) a system for routine replenishment of the material.

The components of a sample skill file system are shown in Figure 7-2 (top). These are the steps we took in preparing this sample:

1. *Prepare and tape on the front of a file box or drawer a sequence of skills for a given subject area.* This sequence may be drawn from the materials-management system described in Chapter 5, a scope and sequence chart, or the skill sequences found in many published tests. This sequence should be coded so the contents of the drawer can be matched to it. If all students who use it can recognize numerals, simply number the skills 1, 2, 3, and so on. You may also letter the sequence but then you are limited to 26 skills. If students do not recognize numerals or letters of the alphabet, you may decide to use a color-shape combination (e.g., red triangle, blue triangle, yellow triangle, green triangle, red square, and so on). With this code, teachers can then request students to locate a work sheet and simply tell them to find the symbol used in the code.

2. *Collect all available work sheet, practice-page, and skill-test sheet masters* for a given subject area and determine which skill(s) on the skill sequence they provide practice for. Code the masters to correspond with the skill sequence and at the top of the page note the type of duplication required (e.g., spirit master, thermofax, ditto, xerox, and so on). Place the masters in a folder apart from the copies, say, in the back of the file. When no master is available for a designated skill, you will have to decide whether you can locate one in available material or whether you will have to prepare a master. For every skill in the practice material, there should be a corresponding skill-test master, whether it be from published material or an informal teacher-made probe (see Chapter 5 for procedures on adapting practice materials for testing purposes).

3. *Collect or duplicate copies of available practice and skill-test sheets.* Two major choices are open to the teacher on this step; (1) to duplicate materials from all available masters in advance or (2) to duplicate materials for given skills as the need arises. We suggest that, at the least, duplication is completed several skills in advance of the progress of the class. Otherwise pre-

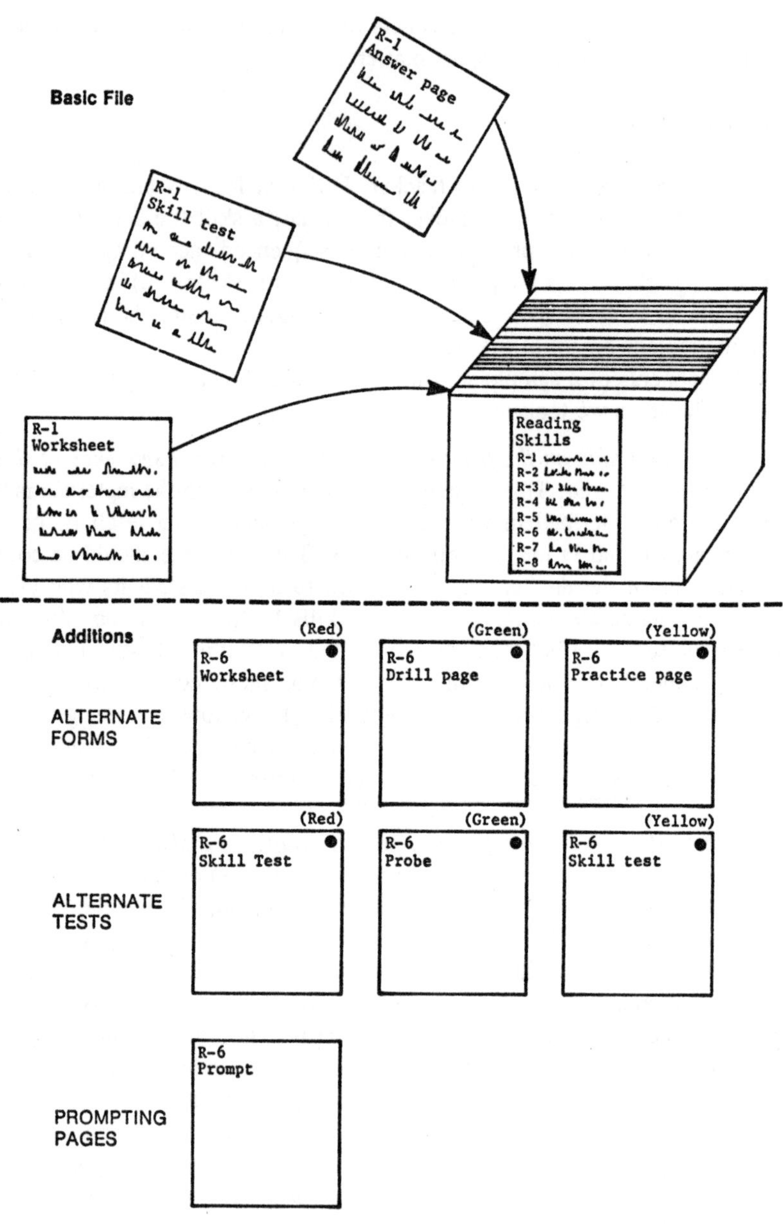

Figure 7-2. Components of a Sample Skill File System

cious class time can be wasted if materials are not ready and the teacher will be placed in a position of making decisions for "what to do today" based on what is expedient and not on what is most needed by the students. Teachers who are working with handicapped learners are best advised to duplicate materials for the entire skill sequence in advance because of the wide range of skill levels students may demonstrate. How many copies? The rate at which practice materials are used depends upon several factors: how many students there are in the class, how many students require practice on the same skill, how much practice is required to master a given skill, and so on. Duplication of too many copies (100-200) will load the file and force the teacher to consume more space. Duplication of too few copies (5-10) may increase the number of duplication times. We suggest you start with a sample number, say 20 to 25 copies of each master and then adjust this amount according to the rate of use.

4. *File practice and skill-test material copies in folders coded by skills.* The file box or drawer for a given skill should contain folders of (a) practice pages in the front, sequenced to match the skill sequence taped on the outside, (b) test pages next to the same coded sequence, and (c) answer pages (1-5 copies each). For security purposes, the teacher may consider placing answer pages in a more controlled location if all students have access to the file.

This is the basic skill file—practice, test, and answer pages. The following are additional considerations for maintaining and using a skill file with handicapped children:

1. *Replenishing materials.* Copies of materials will run out before you know it if there is not a systematic method for replenishing the file on an ongoing basis. We suggest that a colored page be placed somewhere forward of the last copy, say, leaving five copies in the folder. This colored page can signal the teacher or the student that the file must be replenished. Each colored page should contain the skill code, a notation for whether it is a practice or a test page, the type of duplication, and number of copies required. The teacher will have to instruct the student to place the colored sheet on her desk so the teacher may duplicate the necessary materials during planning time. Knowing how little planning time some teachers actually have, we suggest that capable students in the class may be able to help replenish the file. For instance, the student who pulls the practice or test page that reveals the colored sheet gets to leave class, say during home room or free time, and run copies for the file that has run low. If all students cannot do this, the teacher may select and train a small number of peer assistants who can perform this function contingent upon successful completion of their own work. Some words of caution are offered on this option. The approval of the use of students in this manner should be first obtained from both the immediate supervisor and the parents. Second, safety

precautions regarding the operation of equipment by students should be undertaken. Third, the amount of student training required to operate duplication equipment safely and proficiently should be weighed against the time it would take the teacher to complete the task.

2. *Alternate forms*. Since many children require a repeated practice-test-practice cycle to attain mastery, a skill file for handicapped learners may include different forms of practice and test pages on the same skill (see Figure 7-2). This can increase the complexity of the file. In this instance we suggest that colored dots be placed on folders having the same code. The colors can represent different forms of practice or tests (e.g., R-10-red, R-10-blue, R-10-yellow).

3. *Prompting pages*. Many children fail at completing their work, not because they cannot perform the skill, but because they do not know which skill must be performed (Englemann, 1970). Also, teachers can often spend a lot of time trying to pinpoint what problem a learner is having in completing a work sheet after the fact when this could have been prevented. A prompting page can be devised using a work sheet that has already been prepared. The teacher simply fills out answers on the sheet beginning with a complete model or demonstration at the top of the sheet and then progressively removes or fades portions of the answers or responses. The student then has a work sheet that (a) demonstrates an answer and (b) gradually provides less help on items while requiring more of the student. In Figure 7-3 the first problem of row one contains a complete model. The rest of row one requires only one response of the student. In the second row the student must complete the multiplication, including carrying and the final addition. For the third row the student has only the first multiplication operation completed for her and must complete the rest. By the time the student completes the prompting sheet the teacher will know two things: (a) whether the student is ready to work on unprompted materials or (b) which of the responses for a problem item a student can or cannot successfully perform. Prompting pages may be used only for trouble spots. It will require the preparation of a master containing the prompts.

For many teachers, a skill file may well be the most commonly used material resource. For teachers of handicapped children, the flexibility a skill file permits in handling many practice and prompting versions of the same skill sheet may prove to be a useful remedial resource. Self-Check 7-2 allows the reader to practice preparing a prompting work page.

PEERS AS AN INSTRUCTIONAL RESOURCE

Sometimes teacher educators make recommendations for the classroom as if they think that teachers are not limited to two arms, two legs, two eyes, two

Self-Check 7-2

Instructions

Ms. Henson has found that her class of young, mild to moderately retarded learners requires some assistance in completing practice work on an audiotape-work sheet spelling program. The sentence shown on the work sheet is heard on the tape followed by a request to spell the word. Help her to devise a prompting page for Unit 1 shown below. Use the step procedures described earlier for preparing a prompting page.

Response

GET HIGH ON SPELLING

UNIT 1 NAME

I
A. THE DOG CHASED THE .
B. GIVE ME ANOTHER PIECE OF BIRTHDAY .
C. THE CAT CLIMBED THE .

II
A. SALLY IS NOT A BOY, SHE IS A .
B. THE COLOR OF THIS APPLE IS .
C. LET'S AND JUMP AND PLAY.

III
A. EVERYTHING THAT GOES UP MUST COME .
B. THIS HAT IS NOT NEW, IT IS .
C. I'LL BE AND YOU BE SECOND.

IV
A. LET'S PLAY A AND SEE WHO WINS.
B. THE SUN IS OUT. IT IS A FINE .
C. DADDY, PLEASE TAKE ME FOR A RIDE IN YOUR !

Compare your response to the sample responses in Appendix A.

[3] [6] [1] [2] 2 3 7 X 9 4 9 4 8 2 1 3 3 22,2 7 8	[3] [3] 3 8 8 X 4 1 3 8 8 1 5 5 2	[4] [4] 9 0 7 X 6 6 5 4 4 2 5 4 4 2	[5] [4] 4 7 5 X 1 9 4 1 8 5 4 7 5
□ [3] 1 1 8 X 4 4 4 7 2	□ [1] 7 2 1 X 2 7 5 0 4 7	□ □ [7] [5] 4 8 6 X 3 9 4 3 7 4	□ 5 0 0 X 9 1 5 0 0
□ 3 7 2 X 6 8 6	4 4 6 X 1 0 0	3 9 3 X 3 1 3	□ 8 7 6 X 5 4 4
2 3 5 X 7 5	4 1 9 X 2 7	3 7 1 X 2 0	4 0 4 X 9 0

Figure 7-3. *Example of a Work Sheet Modified as a Prompting Page*

ears, and so on. They act as if the teachers need only have the inclination to implement the gems of wisdom they are spewing forth. Special educators often prepare materials that are appealing and highly useful for remedial and other instruction with the handicapped. They also should have supplied a 36-day monthly calendar and a 28-hour watch with some of those materials because that is what it would require for a teacher to use them fully in consort with other responsibilities. The truth is teachers need help. They must capitalize on all available resources for providing assistance in instruction. Peers (the students in the class) are some of the most reliable and useful resources. It has been shown that children are capable of carrying out, at times, complex procedures and, in turn, systematically influencing the academic behavior of their classmates. Specifically, students can function as scoring monitors, tutors, or as managers of motivational systems.

Peers as Scoring Monitors

The use of peers as scoring monitors means students are responsible for checking other children's assignments. This task usually includes maintaining a daily performance record on peer behavior to which the child and teacher can make frequent reference. For peers to function successfully in this capacity, it is suggested that one section of the classroom be designated as a paper turn-in area for assignments. Use of file folders or plastic office organizers aid in managing student's assignments. Use of this area should be restricted to scoring and filing children's work. Answer keys or access to the teacher's manual should be distributed on a lesson-by-lesson basis or stored in the appropriate skill file. Students who have mastered the exercises and preferably achieved proficiency should be selected as monitors. In employing peers as scoring monitors, teachers should routinely make reliability checks of their work to help ensure continued accuracy in their assignment correcting.

Peers as Class Tutors

Students as peer tutors are ideally suited to efforts of special educators to achieve fully individualized instructional programming. Peer-tutoring programs can be developed that rely either on the use of across-age peers, older students working with younger students, or children working with their age mates. Peer tutoring is particularly applicable to tasks and materials requiring oral drill and practice (e.g., with flash cards, spelling lists, and so on). Before selecting students to be trained as peer tutors, teachers should first single out those children who repeatedly engage in some form of positive social interaction with other children. Second, only those students who are able to exercise some measure of self-control by remaining "on-task" during daily instruction should be considered. Third, candidates should be those children who can locate answers to teaching tasks or who have demonstrated mastery over the content area they are to train. Finally, it is worthwhile to take into account a student's academic and social-interpersonal deficiencies when making the decision of who will tutor, since children often benefit not only academically but also in improved confidence and self-esteem. Finally, opportunity to manage one's own behavior in independent learning experiences is in itself a valuable lesson.

Training Peers as Tutors

As one might imagine, peer tutoring by no means implies simply assigning classmates an academic task on which to work cooperatively. Instead, peer tutoring means a student is chosen to teach another a particular task and has been properly trained in skills necessary for accomplishing that goal. It follows then that peer tutors must possess knowledge of (a) how to give instruction, (b) what pupil responses to expect, and (c) how to react when an expected response is obtained. We recommend that peer tutoring begin with a series of training exercises that cover at least three major areas: (1) instructional procedures corresponding to the specific subskills to be taught and the use of materials that aid in that instruction; (2) use of appropriate motivational techniques; and (3) use of selected progress monitoring procedures. Training should be geared to provide appropriate practice in those aspects of instruction-materials usage judged to be relevant to the content to be taught. Instructional objectives must be defined so each subskill statement can be matched with a simulated training activity. These "tryout" sessions are intended to give opportunity to apply a particular teaching tactic and receive teacher feedback and then to reapply that strategy before its use in a tutoring situation. It is suggested that a preselected criterion level (e.g., correctly engaging in a three-step instructional sequence five consecutive times) serve as a means for ascertaining when the student has mastered a given teaching technique. Since peers may experience frustration when instructing classmates, training sessions should be structured so they are prepared to deal with the occasional "unresponsiveness" of the learner. In this way, tutors are better able to deliver instruction under various conditions.

Peer tutors must become skilled in discriminating *when* and *what* child responses to reinforce. They also must know *when not* to consequate child responses. Reinforcement procedures can be as complex as the student is capable of applying. Our experience has been that most children can quickly be taught to do this and then consistently deliver praise statements for corrects, ignore errors, and/or engage in further instruction.

Finally, the tutor must be trained in the use of progress monitoring and recording procedures. The selection of the daily monitoring and data-collection system should correspond with the instructional task. A simple daily probe administered at the end of each lesson is usually sufficient to provide comparative data across tutorial sessions (see Chapter 6 for discussion of measurement tactics).

Matching Material and Instruction

Selecting instructional materials represents a third major issue to consider when instigating any peer-tutoring program. The materials to be used should be chosen on the basis of several factors. As with any instruction, attention must be given to the learner's entry-level capabilities, not only in selecting instructional materials but also in matching appropriate teaching strategies. Materials should be selected that allow for active learner responding and that call for responses requiring little or no inference as to their accuracy. More precisely, we have adapted and applied a list of variables reported by Morrissey (no date) to the development of our peer-tutoring projects: (1) the skill area should lend itself to instruction that includes repeated drill and practice; (2) the skill should be clearly defined and arranged in sequence with discrete subskill statements for each objective; (3) tasks should allow for active participation by the tutor and learner in almost equal proportions; and (4) learner responses should be able to be recorded reliably as correct or erred.

When children just begin to learn a new task, such as calling out sight words, naming pictures, or spelling words, we have found that training tutors to engage in modeling tactics is of particular benefit. One such modeling tactic, modeling before requiring a response, is shown below:

Model	"This word is cat." "This word is spelled *c a t*." (cover word)
Question	"How is it spelled?"
Response	"*c a t*"
Praise (and go on to next item)	"Good spelling"
Model	"This word is dog." "This word is spelled *d o g*." (cover word)
Question	"How is it spelled?"

Response "*d a w g*"
Model This word is dog.
This word is spelled
d o g.
(cover word)
Question "How is it spelled?"
Response "d o g"
Praise "Nice spelling."

During more advanced stages, when the learner has begun to master the fundamentals, modeling paired with corrective feedback can be an effective technique. Later, as children approach a level of proficiency, manipulating the contingencies of reinforcement appears preferable.

Peers as Deliverers of Reinforcement

One of the most commonly deficient aspects of materials is any provision or instructions for providing systematic reinforcement. Often a teacher must devise supplementary motivation procedures. Exceptional children are capable of participating in the administration of relatively sophisticated motivational programs. For example, classmates have been trained to dispense points contingent upon a peer engaging in specified behavior; they have consistently provided verbal praise and/or feedback to others; and they have been successfully taught to initiate contracting arrangements for managing their own academic behavior.

General programming principles apply to the use of peers as an instructional resource. In many situations, it is exceedingly difficult to initiate a complete peer-initiated program. Instead, it is often necessary to train skills successively that together lead to independent material-instructional management. Use of a task-analysis approach to planning of training permits teachers to "zero in" on discrete behaviors to be trained. By accepting successive approximations of the desired goal, the likelihood that teachers will be able to incorporate the use of peers into daily materials management is significantly increased. Self-Check 7-3 focuses the reader's attention on prerequisites for tutoring.

CLASSROOM ARRANGEMENT AND DESIGN

At last most exceptional children have been rescued from dreary basement classrooms. Special education programs now enjoy a standing that is comparable to other programs. It is surprising then when special education teachers fail to attend to the aesthetic aspects of classroom preparation since no one en-

Self-Check 7-3

Instructions

A special education teacher who is planning to use his pupils as teaching assistants in mathematics is trying to determine what prerequisite skill a tutor may need to be able to tell the learner whether she is correct or incorrect. The students will be using flash cards. Your task is to (a) identify whether the learner must have mastered the skill to provide feedback on it and, if not, which skill is prerequisite to providing feedback (*hint:* this list assumes that the tutor will be supplied with answers or answer keys in writing).

Response

Skill	*Mastery yes*	*Required? no*	*Prerequisite Skill Required?*
1. Say the number pictured on flash card (0–10).	____	____	____________
2. Say numbers pictured from left to right in sequence (0–10).	____	____	____________
3. Count by ones to 10.	____	____	____________
4. Count by twos to 10.	____	____	____________
5. Write numbers in sequence from 1 to 10.	____	____	____________
6. Say answers to math facts pictured on flash card.	____	____	____________
7. Write answers to math facts displayed on skill sheets.	____	____	____________
8. Write answers to two-, three-, and four-place computational problems for all four operations.	____	____	____________

Compare your response with the sample response in Appendix A.

joys spending most of the day in a drab, nonstimulating environment. It is even more remarkable that some teachers do not take full advantage of improved classroom facilities to maximize the impact of materials instruction. Unfortunately, uncovering solutions to the problem of appearance is easier than resolving those problems associated with instruction. The cost of several plants, a throw rug, posters, or a table lamp and chair is not prohibitive, even with a teacher's limited budget. The following discussion focuses on ways in which teachers can integrate physical aspects of the classroom with daily instruction and materials usage.

Careful arrangement of the classroom can contribute significantly to more efficient materials management and instruction. A range of variables together influence the way in which a classroom is organized. The size of the room; the number of children (and adults); furnishings; materials and equipment; and the amounts of shelf, cabinet, and closet space play an important role in determining possible classroom arrangements. Issues regarding curriculum, measurement, and instruction dictate certain needs that must be taken into account. Not only do materials and instructional variables relate to room arrangement but so also do behavior-management factors. Even the best materials will be useless if children persist in engaging in inappropriate behavior while a teacher is attempting to provide instruction.

Before proceeding, it should be recognized that research on the influence of classroom design on children's learning is scant. No one perfect classroom arrangement yet exists. However, certain arrangements do appear to be more effective for some children than others. It has been our experience, and that of others, that even limited modification in classroom organization and use of space can remarkably improve the educational program. Whenever possible, special educators should take an active role in the planning and design of new classrooms and in the renovation of existing facilities to accommodate exceptional children. As more and more handicapped learners enter the public education system, teachers have the opportunity to voice their opinion regarding the kind of physical facilities best suited to a particular population of students.

VARIABLES TO CONSIDER IN ARRANGING THE LEARNING ENVIRONMENT

Earlier in this chapter, we talked about the scheduling of daily materials and instruction. The physical arrangement of the classroom should be designed to accommodate a wide range of instructional activities and materials used for that instruction. One way of approaching this is to devise a list of factors corresponding to each period of instruction. For example, a teacher might routinely schedule several teaching situations: one-to-one, small group, and independent desk work. A distinction should be made between those situations that are teacher directed and those that include self-instruction assignments. Added to the list are the materials corresponding to the aforegoing inventory and the measurement tactics to be applied. It is useful to indicate not only textbooks, workbooks, or skill sheets but also audiovisual equipment and multimedia materials, such as Systems 80 units and Language Master lessons. Next, consideration must be given to storage of materials and their daily distribution. These factors are important in that the distribution and collection of daily assignments should not result in "traffic jams" that are likely to cause confusion and even lead to major behavior problems that could be avoided by improved classroom organization.

Certain classroom-arrangement factors will inevitably be given more weight than others on the basis of the particular needs of the students being taught. In some instances classrooms must be arranged to make provision for children with multiple handicaps. Then, use of special equipment may be an integral part of daily instruction. Some children need opportunity for increased peer contacts when they are exceedingly withdrawn. Although close proximity will not necessarily lead to positive initiations among classmates, decreasing the social distance of withdrawn children can set the occasion for further intervention on the part of the teacher. Situations will exist in which it is advantageous to be able to use physical barriers to separate children exhibiting limited self-control over aggressive behavior. Arrangements to allow for spaces for children to work apart from others, of course, do not represent the final solution for dealing with acting-out behavior. Nevertheless, the classroom setting can be organized to mediate a wide range of social-interpersonal as well as academic problems. In all, teachers are faced with considerable diversity among children within a class. Because of this, we recommend that thought be given to conceptualizing a classroom that has utility for integrating children with divergent behavioral as well as academic needs.

Use of Cubicles, Carrels, and the Like: Some Cautions

For years debate has centered on the wisdom of isolating children who have extreme difficulty with conventional group-oriented instruction and who exhibit a wide range of inappropriate, off-task behavior. Use of cubicles, carrels, partitions, or strategically located cabinets do afford an opportunity to separate these children physically. However, it has been shown that this tactic alone is not always sufficient to ensure that learning will occur. Although attending behavior may increase, gains in children's ability to attend to material are not necessarily linked to improved academic achievement (Haubrick & Shores, 1976; Shores & Haubrick, 1969). Often children need material especially adapted so smaller segments of instruction are presented that enable them to discriminate and attend to the relevant features (see Chapter 9). Reinforcement tactics, also discussed in Chapter 9, may need to be introduced to motivate children to complete assigned work. In that event, consequences should be imposed according to work accomplished instead of time engaged in the assignment.

We do not want to discourage the use of cubicles. Indeed, many children make significant gains when given the opportunity to function independent of the group and when provided with a program adapted to their needs. Yet even if individual instruction were feasible throughout the day, the learning experience does not correspond to demands on children in the mainstream of public education. Since many exceptional children are being integrated at least on a part-time basis with their normal counterparts, they should have the opportunity to learn to interact positively in group instructional situations. Although use of cubicles may prove to be a useful beginning strategy, in the end it is usually advantageous to include an opportunity for children to acquire classroom skills that will be judged acceptable to the larger educational community.

Independent Instructional Activities: The Learning Center

Previously we discussed the use of isolated situations within the class for instruction. An example of independent instruction that is useful for one or several children is the use of learning centers. Located in various areas of the classroom, learning centers are usually organized around specific curricular areas: the Spelling Center, Math Center, or Science Center. Use of the learning center concept allows one to individualize instruction according to content and performance level. In contrast to teacher-directed instruction, material is programmed so students can independently engage in learning experiences. Earlier discussion on the skill file and the use of peers as instructional resources is worth recalling as we consider ways of managing a learning center. Flexibility is a key element to instructional-materials interaction so teachers can be delivering direct instruction to a small group while others are working independently in various learning centers. As a result of pretesting, materials placed in the learning center are adapted to meet the instructional needs of each learner. The learning-center approach works well with material that requires repeated drill for mastery and in curricular areas where skills are presented sequentially. As before, the use of learning centers calls for the introduction of a measurement tactic that can be applied without the presence of an attentive adult. So regularly employing peer or self-monitoring strategies is an economical way of obtaining detailed records of pupil performance. Because mutual use of learning centers by students sometimes leads to social interactions that are not compatible with academics, it is suggested that individual contracts be tailored to a specific child's assignments to be completed at a learning center. Since audiovisual equipment accompanies many materials placed in learning centers, instruction and practice in its proper use should come before children are permitted to work independently at a center. Finally, it is often worthwhile to begin giving small assignments for short periods at a learning center. The "red-line" procedure, presented in Chapter 9, is one means for introducing succeedingly longer assignments. Teachers should arrange to provide ample feedback regarding established rules for working at a learning center combined with instruction on particular programs. In this way, children are gradually given more responsibility for engaging in independent materials-instructional activities.

MODEL-CLASSROOM ARRANGEMENTS

Figure 7-4 represents an "engineered classroom" as advocated by Hewett (1968). This plan rejects the contention that exceptional children need a drab, nonstimulating classroom situation. Instead, the teacher engineers an environment in which appropriate task assignments are defined, meaningful rewards are provided for learning, and well-defined limits are maintained to reduce or eliminate the occurrence of inappropriate behavior. The physical environment is composed of three major areas: order, exploratory, and mastery centers.

The *order center* usually includes puzzles, exercises, and material aimed at helping children learn to adapt to routine, follow directions, and complete assignments, while exercising self-control.

In the *exploratory-social center,* opportunity is provided for multisensory learning experiences. In one section materials for science experiments and demonstrations might be available. Simple games for two or three children, and an audiotape recorder might be arranged in another area for communication and social skills. Another section might comprise the art area in which material is provided for arts and crafts activities. The goal at the exploratory level is to involve children in active learning with their senses, to maintain interest, and to provide "intriguing information and experiences through exploration of the environment." In such situations the teacher usually demonstrates different science experiments weekly. The experiments are illustrated on large poster cards and filed at the center so they can then be independently replicated by students assigned to the center.

According to Hewett, the *mastery center* is established for the purpose of engaging children in a certain amount of academic work each day, including reading, written language, and arithmetic skills. At the mastery level, attention is given to attaining a level of self-control that enables children to function independently and to promoting cognitive development in areas such as speech, concept formation, and problem solving. Within such a classroom arrange-

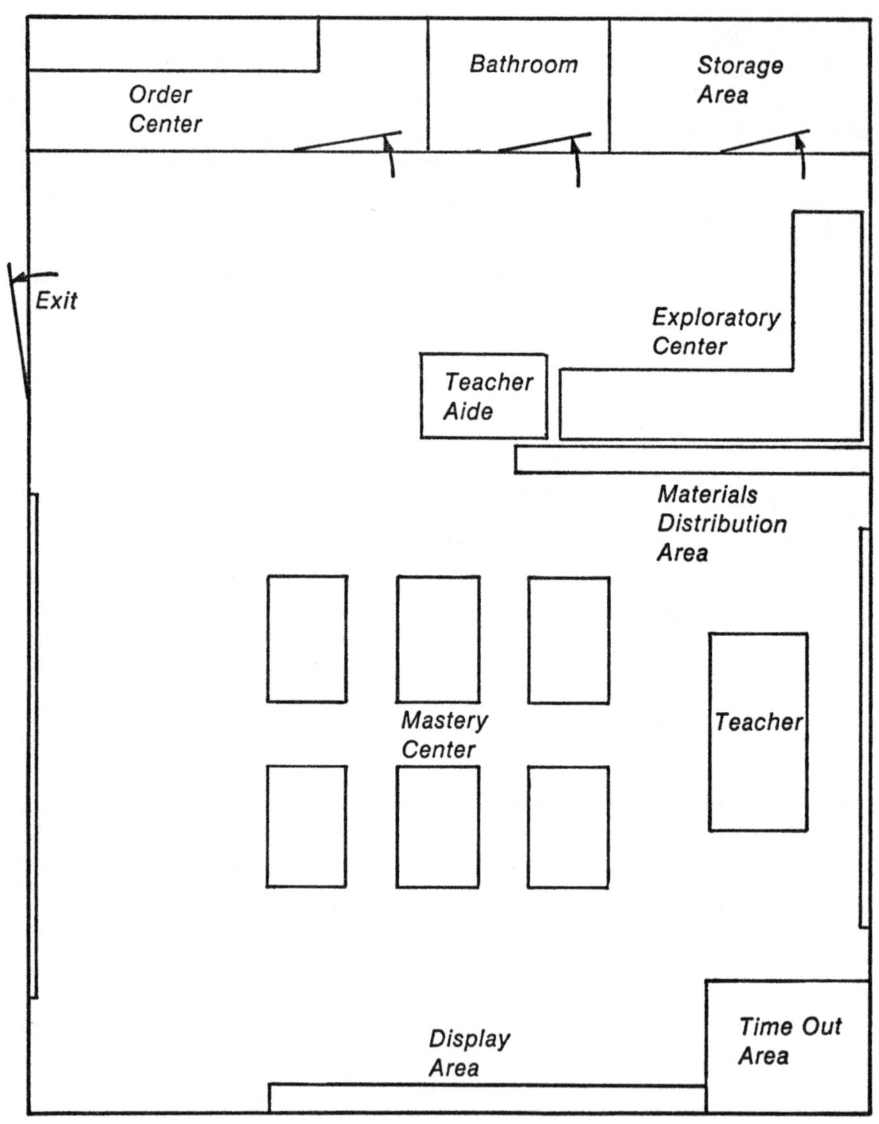

Figure 7-4. *Example of an "Engineered Classroom"*

ment, students can be shifted to various areas, as when a student is given an assignment to be completed in the order center, for purposes of managing problem behavior and minimizing stress.

Figure 7-5 illustrates another possible classroom design. As can be seen, provision is made for several different materials presentation formats. Specifically, one-to-one, small group and whole group instruction is possible. Further, in Figure 7-5, the classroom is organized so as to accommodate a range of equipment and material that rely on child-initiated application. Storage cabinets and movable partitions are used to subdivide the classroom. As shown, Systems 80, Language Master Units, audiotutorial and slide/sound projectors are strategically situated so that youngsters can: (a) locate materials in adjacent cabinets, (b) engage in independent and self-instructional activities, (c) self-correct assignments, and (d) return materials/equipment to its proper place. The bulk of mediated instruction is devoted to drill of newly acquired skills or to strengthen already existing skills in content areas that do not require direct adult intervention. Selected use of audiovisual equipment and material allows one to individualize materials usage that, in turn, facilitates self-pacing and repeated practice until mastery is attained. Available shelf and cabinet space is made use of not only for organizing material according to curricular area and instructional level but also for daily distribution and collection of assignments.

Also shown is a section of the classroom designated as a "Reinforcing Event" Area. Furnished with a sofa, armchair, circular rug and with magazines, games, puzzles and so on, as will be discussed, entry is predicated on completion of a specified amount of work.

Classroom Layout for Motivational Purposes

Class "engineering" can have utility for daily management of noninstructional problems. For example, classrooms may be organized so certain sections are designated for academics and other areas for activities children usually find more pleasurable. The classroom is arranged so students having satisfactorily completed a specified amount of work may enter the "high-probability" area of the room. The *high-probability area* contains either instructional activities judged to be more desirable or an assortment of material considered to be reinforcing to children (Homme & Tosti, 1971). Also called a Reinforcing-Event Area (RE Area), games, books, record players and headsets, puzzles, and the like are made available to children contingent upon completion of certain assignments. In some classrooms, entry to the RE Area is based on expending a certain number of points earned for appropriate behavior and/or academic achievement. Thus activities that generally are "low probability" or "low strength," namely, most academics, are paired with the opportunity to engage in high-strength events. The arrangement of high-strength events, for example,

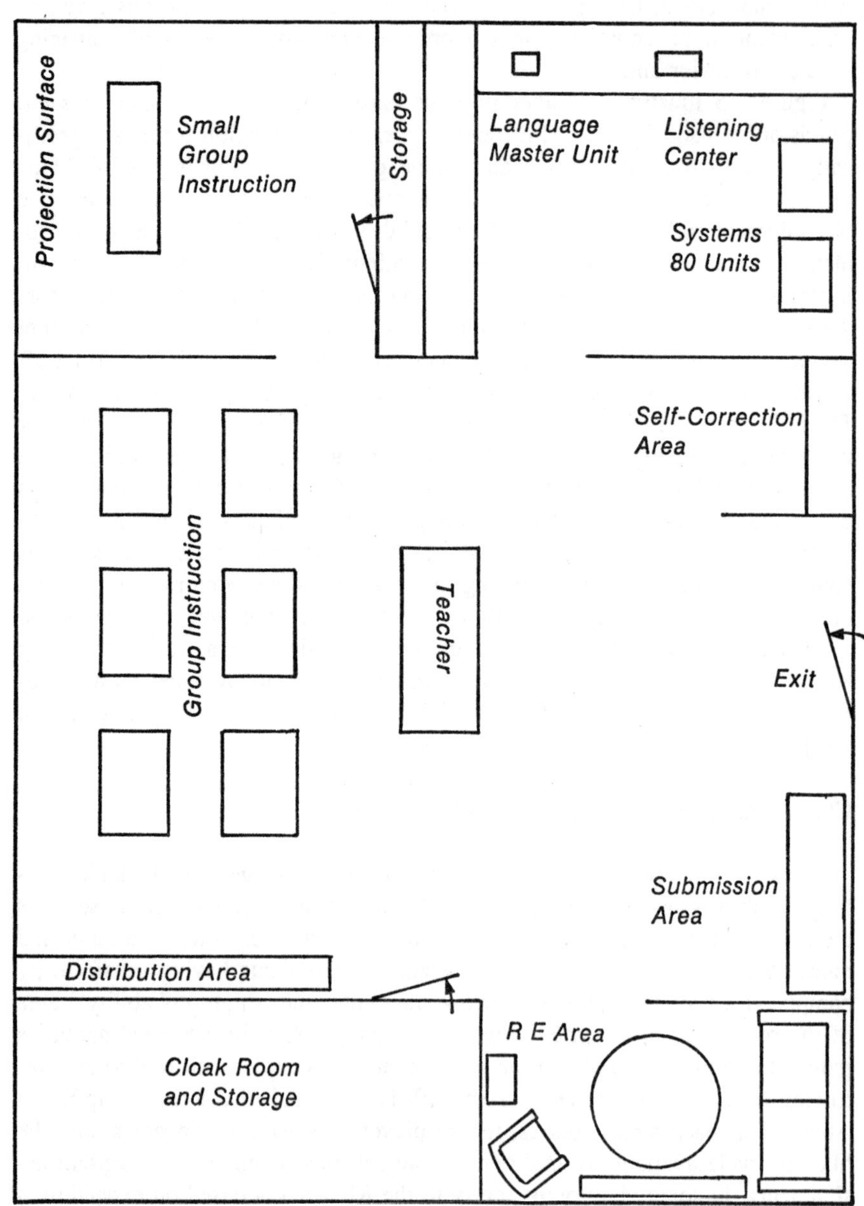

Figure 7-5. *Modification of an Engineered Classroom Layout*

ten minutes for reading comic books and assembling puzzles, contingent upon completing a specified low-strength event, for example, five add-fact sheets, has proven to be an effective means for increasing the likelihood that children will engage in future academic tasks (see Figure 7-6).

Designating a Behavior-Control Area

For many exceptional children, interpersonal and/or behavioral problems sometimes interfere with the learning experience. To clarify the connection between behavior and its consequences, teachers have designated one portion of the classrooms as a "time-out area." Simply stated, *time out* exists when the opportunity to obtain reinforcement is removed for a specified period, which, in turn, can serve to decrease inappropriate or disruptive behavior. Procedurally, time out can be varied according to the teaching situation. For example, during one-to-one instruction, the teacher can simply (for several seconds) turn away from a child who emits an inappropriate response; then the same stimuli can be represented. A similar tactic can be used during group instruction, namely, ignoring undesirable behavior and, instead, attending to those students engaged in appropriate behavior. Time out also exists when access to material is interrupted; that is, when a teacher simply takes away the audio cassette recorder for five minutes contingent upon a child's engaging in off-task behavior. Teachers have further applied the concept of time out by assigning children to the "time-out chair" situated away from the group. Finally, in some classrooms a booth or room is available to place children whose behavior is otherwise too disruptive or unmanageable during instruction (See Figures 7-4 and 7-5).

As time out has sometimes been misapplied, its classroom use raises a number of issues teachers must resolve before it is advised that one physically isolate a child from the group (Gast & Nelson, 1977). It should be stated that use of time out presupposes that a child indeed finds class participation and obtaining available reinforcement desirable. As we know, this is not always the case. A second factor to consider is that during the time-out period, no instruction is provided, and opportunity for learning is completely interrupted.

A Materials-Based Resource Program

A resource program can make a significant contribution to the total education program of a school if it is well organized and closely related to the aims of the regular education classes it serves. When there is little interaction between the resource teacher and his or her colleagues, or when the resource program is viewed as having a purely clinical function, its impact may be diminished. When this is the case the resource teacher is often found to be a

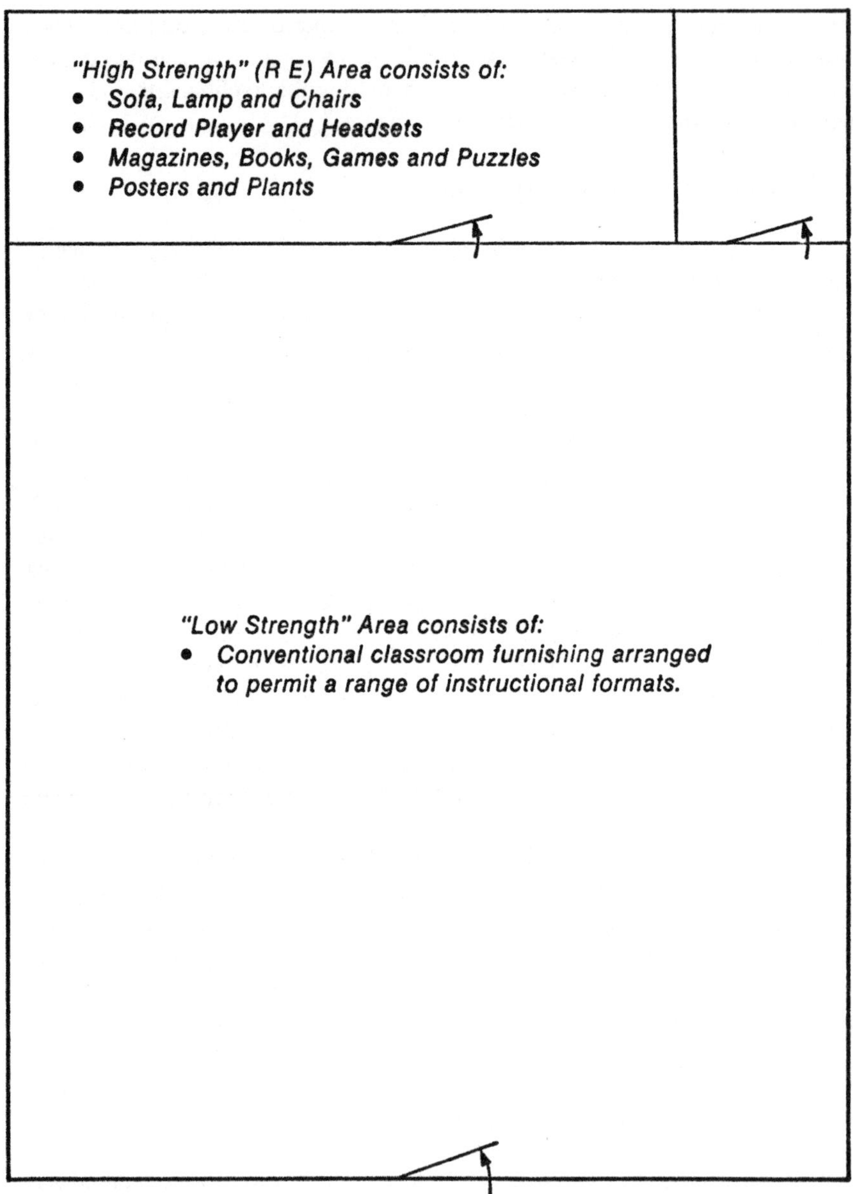

Figure 7-6. *Classroom Designating Behavioral Control Areas*

"high-priced tutor." The organization of the program to enable the teacher to approximate from a range of remedial to more normal classroom conditions, both in instructional format and in materials usage, is important.

A materials-based resource program and room, organized to accommodate a variety of teaching formats, is illustrated in Figure 7-7*. Materials are grouped in central locations relative to the type of use and for ease of access by students. Copies of materials are organized in a skill file, similar to that described earlier in the chapter, which has ready access by students en route to individual work carrels. Also, students daily work folders, arranged on a stand next to the file, are easily supplied and replenished. Master copies of practice materials are kept in a teacher-access file. Media materials, such as audiotapes, filmstrips, and slide carousels and corresponding response pages are located in a cabinet close to their area of use. Visual displays of progress and points earned are grouped on a large bulletin board.

The furniture and equipment in the room are organized so a variety of instructional activities in differing formats can occur singly or simultaneously. A "small-group instruction" area is located close to a blackboard. Individual work carrels are arranged so students pick up their days' materials en route to them. The audiotutorial carrels permit students to work through media-paced practice materials while the teacher supervises other students. Since student teachers often assist in the classroom, and they need to build competencies in one-to-one or small-group teaching, an additional area is designated for this purpose. The free-time area is one in which students earn time to themselves contingent upon successfully completing the day's assignments.

In all, a range of factors should be taken into account in attempting to arrange the classroom to maximize its usefulness as an instructional variable. In the final analysis only time and careful evaluation will lead to discovering the best organizational plan for you. The following summary questions are presented to stimulate further thinking about factors surrounding classroom arrangement to accommodate daily materials management. Adopted from a list reported by Hewett (1971), items are organized around the theme of integrating classroom arrangement and instructional-materials management.

1. Are cubicles conducive to increased attending behavior and control over competing stimuli or do they promote isolation and set the stage for off-task behavior such as "daydreaming"?
2. Would the use of enclosed areas in which visual and auditory stimuli are controlled positively influence attending behavior or are difficulties concerning supervision apt to arise?
3. Will movable walls or partitions make an opportunity to change the size

*Our appreciation is extended to Vickie Henson-Edwards for enlightening us.

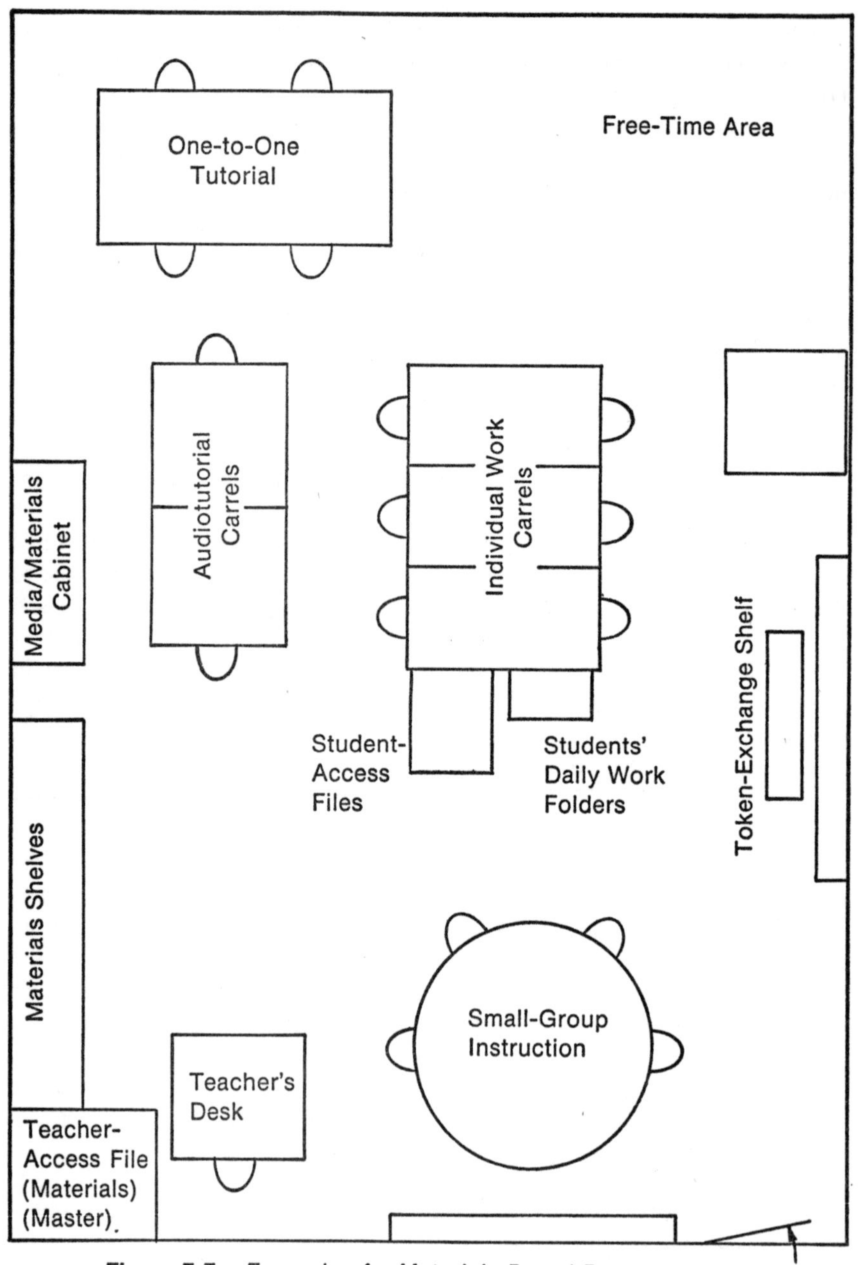

Figure 7-7. *Example of a Materials-Based Resource Room*

of the room so small-group instruction and use of materials that aid that instruction would be more feasible?

4. Will separation of children through use of individual work stations increase the usefulness of instructional materials and decrease the amount of distractibility and disruption?
5. Should learning centers and accompanying materials be located out of view to reduce distraction?
6. How can the classroom be arranged so movement either from one instructional activity to the next or to pick up or submit assignments and so on creates minimum disruption?
7. If high-strength areas are used for motivational purposes, should they be located in another room? What about supervision?
8. How should academic work be displayed in the room? Should there be display cases, tables, and bulletin boards for children's work?
9. What, if any, connection is there between wall color, presence of display areas, bulletin boards, and instructional materials and distractability among exceptional children?
10. Should the teacher forgo use of a stationary desk and maintain a "roving pattern" of student contact, or should a well-defined teacher area be established with children called up for one-to-one attention?
11. How can learning centers be organized so more than one child can simultaneously use a headset and a set of instructional materials and have sufficient space to make written responses?
12. How can the use of peer monitors or the opportunity for self-checks be arranged so one area of the room is used for only this purpose?
13. Will teaching machines and/or audiotape recorders promote responding for learners who dislike written assignments or oral class recitation? Should this equipment be built into the room or housed in a separate area?
14. Do large, open areas encourage more acting-out behavior than do small, screened-off areas? Can a room be arranged so one can create a full range of instructional settings: teacher-whole group, teacher-small group, child independent, and one-to-one tutorial?
15. If high-probability activities (e.g., use of record player, slot-car racing, model building) are used as reinforcers when children complete an academic task, should these items be in the room or in a separate area?

Overlooked in planning the physical arrangement of the classroom is the location of the teacher's desk. Often it is suggested that the teacher be situated so he or she can oversee all areas of the classroom. We concur with those who advocate the need to be able to supervise children directly throughout the day. We are not, on the other hand, convinced that this should be carried out from a stationary position. For example, attempting to place the teacher's desk strategically in the "middle of the action" can lead to unforeseen problems. Classroom observation has shown that some teachers remain seated for the majority of the day and consequently engage in only limited pupil contacts. Then the area immediately surrounding the desk becomes congested with children seeking the teacher's attention. Other children find ways of surreptitiously entering into a wide range of off-task behavior, unobserved. Since habits of long standing are usually resistant to change, some teachers faced with these and related problems have actually removed their desk from the classroom in an effort to increase direct pupil contacts significantly.

III

Adapting Instructional Materials

CHAPTER 8

Field-Tested Materials? Who Cares?

Objectives

1. Describe the negative consequences of using materials that have not been field tested.
- How is teacher time affected by the use of validated versus non-validated instructional materials?
- What kinds of information should a teacher seek that will help determine if a material is likely to be appropriate to the children in his or her classroom?
- How will using field-tested materials affect the teacher's ability to prepare meaningful individual educational plans?

2. List the kinds of validation information a teacher should seek regarding an instructional material.
- Why is objective field-test information important?
- How does knowledge on the precise manner in which the material should be presented to students facilitate the teaching process?
- Why is it easier to adapt materials that have been field tested than materials that have not been thoroughly validated?
- What is the difference between formative and summative evaluation?

3. Identify whose responsibility it is to ensure that instructional materials have been adequately tested and are updated frequently.
- What steps can a teacher take to be an advocate for well-designed and well-tested instructional materials?
- How can teachers, teacher-training institutions, and publishers work together to ensure that handicapped children are receiving the best materials that modern technology and the current state of knowledge can offer?

No competent diagnostician would consider giving a child a test without being thoroughly familiar with the test as well its administration. An accountable diagnostician knows the precise purpose of each test and how well it assesses what is claimed. Should a competent teacher be less than thoroughly familiar with the instructional material and procedures he or she will be using than a diagnostician is with test materials? Can teachers be optimally effective without a broad yet specific understanding of any given instructional material and how it can be expected to affect student performance?

SUBJECTIVE OR OBJECTIVE EVALUATION OF MATERIALS?

One publisher of special education materials has a toll-free telephone number for anyone desiring information on the instructional materials he publishes. He notes that teachers rarely request information on how a material was field tested. Apparently they are unaware of the utility of such information. In the end teachers generally select materials based on subjective reasons rather than objective data (Bliel, 1975). When this happens they are actually turning their classrooms into catch-as-catch-can laboratories. The teacher who selects an instructional material based on subjective measures is imposing a possibly untried material onto his or her students. Would a hospital do the same with a new drug? The fact is that teachers who do not use objective information to evaluate instructional material will be much more limited in their ability to predict how the material will affect their students than teachers who do use such information.

So why don't teachers base their decisions on objective field-test information? If materials have been field tested, does it make sense to expend student time in further "testing" of the material? It would seem much more profitable to evaluate the objective information provided by the publisher and then make adaptations, rather than immediately to begin using and changing an instructional material.

Unfortunately, teachers have not had an opportunity to gain skills in evaluating instructional materials. In contrast, educational diagnosticians have been trained to expect and inspect a wide variety of objective field-validation information. They know the importance and relevance of examining information on the normative population, test administration, scoring, and interpretation of test results. Anecdotal accounts of how well a test is "liked" takes a back seat to objective information on test construction, validity, and reliability. The time has now come for teachers to learn how objective information on the effectiveness of instructional materials can facilitate the teaching process. In a time when the marketplace is flooded with "junk," dare teachers be less informed and skilled in their approach to daily instruction than the diagnostician is to comprehensive assessment? Dare teachers act as though daily instruction were less important to the goal of delivering appropriate educational services than is diagnostic testing? The answer is clearly no. Educators cannot underestimate the importance of daily learning. The magnitude of the task confronting the classroom teacher is becoming increasingly apparent. Today it is commonly accepted that the classroom teacher will have an effect on the learning of special children that is greater than that of any other professional. It is the child's daily classroom experiences that will be the backbone of his or her achievement.

Teachers must act now in accordance with the current understanding of the significance of their role. They must demand any information that will enhance delivery of appropriate, effective instruction to children. Clearly, a most important factor in delivering effective training is the instructional material used. To be most effective, teachers must have objective evaluations of instructional materials. The information available to teachers must be as precise as the information a diagnostician expects on an assessment instrument.

WHY IS OBJECTIVE FIELD-VALIDATION INFORMATION NEEDED?

The teacher's task of providing daily instruction is no less sophisticated or important than the diagnostician's. Only with complete information on the appropriate way to use materials and their effectiveness when used as tested can teachers hope to maximize instructional outcomes. By using validated instructional materials in the prescribed manner, the teacher can expect that planning and adaptation time will be greatly reduced. The reasons planning time is decreased and adaptation is easier are twofold. First, the teacher does not have to spend a great deal of time planning and perfecting a suitable way to implement instruction with the materials since the teaching procedure is already clearly articulated. Second, the teacher can *systematically* begin materials adaptation if it is necessary, varying one element at a time and witnessing its effect on student performance, because the teacher began instruction by using the materials in the precise fashion they were intended. Further, since the implementation of P.L. 94-142, it has become the teacher's responsibility to prepare meaningful individual educational plans (IEPs). IEPs must allow for the attainment of objectives by combining effective instructional materials with efficient teaching tactics. Yet how can teachers be expected to select appropriate instructional materials if information pertaining to child characteristics and the correct way to use the materials is not available? Even worse, how can teachers wisely choose from materials that have not been field tested? Without information on how materials may be expected to change child behavior and under what conditions that change occurs, how can educationally sound decisions be made? How can meaningful IEPs be designed and the most effective materials and procedures be identified without data directly related to child performance, the materials, and teaching procedure accessible to teachers? In response to this question, many educators are taking matters into their own hands. Two states, Florida and California, now require learner verification data (i.e., data on materials that show use of the materials in a prescribed way leads to verified changes in learner performance) as a requisite for state adoption of instructional materials (Fuchs, 1979). Legislation on documentation of learner verification as a requirement for materials is a trend that can only increase in the future.

A teacher will need to ask many questions regarding instructional materials and procedures before determining which are likely to be most effective. As a first and basic step, the teacher will simply pose two questions:

1. Has the material been tested and are the results reported?
2. Is the teaching procedure precisely described so the material can be reliably used?

Screening materials according to these criteria is essential. If an instructional material has not been tested, how can the teacher have any confidence in how it will affect his or her students' performance? The teacher also needs to know with whom it was tested, when and where testing occurred, and what the specific results were. If a material was field tested and shown to be magnificently successful with gifted 9, 10, and 12 year olds in Seattle, Washington, in 1955, it is very likely to be quite inappropriate for severely retarded teenagers living in group homes. Finally, if the precise manner in which the materials are to be used to obtain specified objectives is not clearly described, how can the teacher hope to gain results similar to those witnessed during field tests? The teacher must be provided with an exact description of the teaching procedure to reliably implement the program and achieve similar changes with his or her students.

As an illustration of how a teacher might use these two criteria, consider a hypothetical situation where the teacher wants a program to teach children to write their names. The teacher might take the following steps:

1. Identify potential programs (Figure 8-1).
2. Retrieve the Materials Review Form (see Chapter 2) on each program from the Materials Information File (do an initial review, if necessary).
3. Compare the programs based on the information on the Materials Review Form.
4. Answer these two questions about each program:
   a. Are results of field testing reported?
   b. Are the instructional procedures clearly and precisely defined (Instructional Characteristics Section)? Note which program is preferred.
5. File the Materials Review Forms and teacher note in folder files by major subject areas such as reading, hand washing, and self-help, in the Materials Information File (see Chapter 2). The teacher may use file cabinets, a portable file box, or shelves to serve as his or her Materials Information File.

In the present example (Figure 8-1) the teacher wants the name-writing instructional material that seems most likely to require the least amount of planning time and adaptation. Of course, the teacher also wants a program that results in predictable child skill acquisition. Hubbard's Name Writing Program is selected. From the teacher's inspection, she found that this program has been field tested and leads to positive gains, and the procedure for using the material is presented in detail. If the teacher did not need to have the program immediately, the Materials Review Forms and her notes on each program would be filed for future reference or for use by other teachers. Information on other programs would be added to the Materials Information File as the teacher reviewed other potentially useful materials. This handy reference system can be used by the teacher across the years or shared by all teachers in the school and serve as an inventory of current materials.

ACCOUNTABILITY . . . WE'RE IN IT TOGETHER

Much of what might be considered the burden of accountability falls most squarely on the shoulders of teachers. In fact, the delivery of an appropriate education to handicapped children depends on a number of persons, organizations, and agencies: teacher-training institutions, the government, state and local education agencies, material developers, publishers, and many others. Nonetheless, it is the teacher who is expected to demonstrate that children are learning. Therefore, the question again arises: how can teachers be expected to

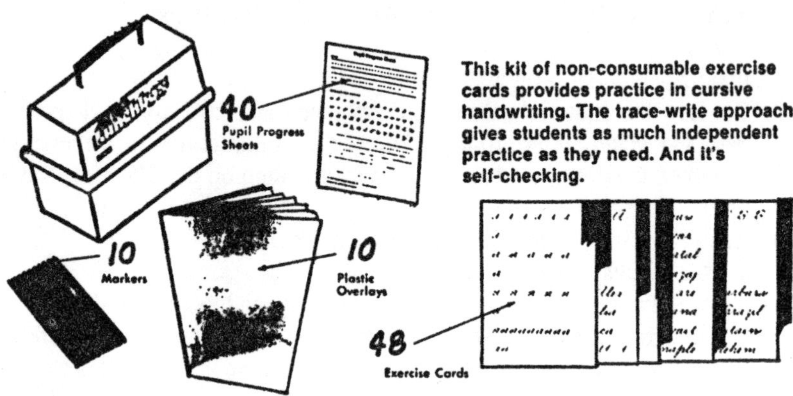

LETTER ORDER

Begin with L-1 and S-1 daily lesson plans

wha

★ **Name Lotto: All cues**	**L-1**
O t i s	O t i s

Figure 8-1. *Teacher Comparison of Two Name-Writing Programs*

Source: From *SRA Lunchbox™: Cursive Handwriting.* Copyright 1977, Science Research Associates, Inc. Reprinted by permission of the publisher.

Source: Reprinted from the *1979 Special Education Catalogue* of Hubbard Scientific with their permission.

implement IEPs that combine effective materials and efficient teaching procedures if (a) publishers do not provide appropriate information on their instructional materials or (b) teachers by lack of appropriate training are not skilled in evaluating the information that is provided? How can teachers or even educational administrators be expected to select effective materials from the proliferation of attractive "junk" (Bliel, 1975)?

One answer might be to buy only materials that have demonstrated effectiveness. Unfortunately, few publishers have thoroughly field tested materials and still fewer publishers provide objective data on field-test results. Often reports are so obtuse, they are close to unintelligible and virtually useless to the teacher. While director of NCEMMH, Dr. Sam Ashcroft (1979) estimated that less than 1 percent of the material on the market had been adequately field tested. Berman (1977) contended that most products for learning disabled children, for example, show little if any effectiveness. Rather, Berman (1977) asserted that sales promotion tactics, elaborate packaging, and the principle of supply and demand direct the sale of instructional materials. Consequently, inflationary prices are paid for materials of questionable worth. Numerous material specialists and consumers agree that materials are generally produced and sold based on Madison Avenue advertising tactics. Criteria related to how a material affects a student or teacher is seldom used to market materials. Few publishers give any guarantee on their products. Performance guarantees that would be demanded by the same individuals when they buy a car, appliance, or other item are seldom even discussed in relation to instructional materials. However, there are some examples of noteworthy exception to publishers' lack of concern for student outcomes.

Figure 8-2 presents one example of an advertisement that appeared in a 1979 issue of the *Journal of Special Education Technology*.

It is outstanding in several ways. Primarily significant, however, is the warranty that accompanies the advertisement. The publisher has emphasized student performance outcomes. Consequently, the consumer begins to view performance outcomes as the major criterion for selecting and assessing this program. The advertisement goes one step further and takes the position that "Dollars Spent for Educational Products Should Produce Predictable and Measurable Student Benefits." Other publishers are implicitly challenged to demonstrate the worth of their materials as well. This advertisement, hopefully, will be a prototype for all instructional-materials advertisements in the not-too-distant future.

Lack of field-test information handicaps teachers. To make matters more difficult, most colleges and universities still do not train teachers to make decisions based on field-test results. Courses are provided on testing and measurement. Special courses for assessing blind, multihandicapped, and severely and profoundly mentally retarded persons are available. Practica and supervision

performance warranty
Edmark Associates, Bellevue, Washington

Dollars Spent for Educational Products Should Produce Predictable and Measurable Student Benefits.

SOUNDER—*a reading skills tutoring program — is warranted to produce specific measurable student reading gains, or your money will be refunded in full.*

If you are faced with students who are deficient in word attack skills, **Edmark Associates** is prepared to offer what we believe is an unprecedented warranty. Try **Sounder** with 20 students, using **Sounder** exactly as specified. (Our price includes complete on-site inservice training.) If, at the end of the program, your students have not on an average *gained a minimum* of two months gain in reading word attack skills for each month of use as measured by the *Word Attack Test* of the *Woodcock Reading Mastery Tests*, you may return the materials for a 100% refund.

The initial package for 20 students, including our consultant's on-site inservice, is $487.50. Since the **Sounder** package is non-consumable, additional students may use **Sounder** for a recordkeeping supplies cost of only $3.75 per student. And I.E.P.'s, for compliance with Public Law 94-142, are part of the package.

For complete information, call or write Edmark ASSOCIATES, 13241 Northup Way, Bellevue, Washington 98005 - Toll-Free 800-426-0856; Washington State 206-746-3900.

Figure 8-2. *Example of a Program Accompanied by a Performance Warranty*

Source: Reprinted from *Performance Warranty* advertisement as it appeared in the *Journal of Special Education Technology* with permission from the publisher. Copyright, 1979 by Edmark Associates.

stressing the use of various teaching tactics are commonplace. Yet courses on curriculum and instructional materials often do little more than survey available materials. Although all of these courses are relevant to providing good instruction, they are not sufficient. Teachers continue to graduate without the ability to prepare meaningful IEPs confidently and skillfully, a main reason being that they lack an understanding of the practical significance of publisher information on instructional-material development and field testing. They do not know how to relate instructional materials to teaching procedures (Berman, 1977).

In spite of extensive preservice and inservice training, few teachers have learned how to improve child performance through direct use of validated field-tested materials. One special education teacher-training program based at Utah State University has made a significant beginning. Trainees in this program begin their practicum experience by using a series of field-tested instructional packages with handicapped learners exactly as the packages were designed, to a criterion level of performance. At the least, these trainees gain a healthy respect for field-validated materials and a basic understanding of the validation process. At best, they have a solid baseline against which future training and materials usage can be compared (Hofmeister, Personal Communication, 1978). Shores (1979) described a course offered at The University of Wisconsin (Madison) that tied evaluation of instructional materials to practicum experience teaching exceptional learners. By combining these activities systematically, students were able to acquire competencies relating to instructional materials and the delivery of educational services infrequently achieved in teacher-training institutions. Graduates of most training institutions, however, do not realize they must demand validated instructional materials from publishers. They must insist on having materials of demonstrated worth. Making such demands is not only important to implementing effective educational plans but should be a part of teacher professional accountability. By demanding high-quality, well-designed, field-tested materials such materials may become available. Teachers may need to boycott publishers who do not demonstrate efforts toward improving their current products and changing the criteria they use to market materials. By demanding publisher accountability in terms of child performance and precise descriptions of teacher usage there will be increased hope of improving our choices of instructional materials.

A TIME TO BE AND A TIME NOT TO BE CREATIVE

Teachers select materials to accomplish any of a number of instructional goals. Instructional materials are selected because they pertain to a subject area such as self-help, mathematics, or spelling or because they are purported to be designed for a certain type of handicapped person. They are selected because they are believed to lead to remediation and worthwhile criteria. But are they selected because they have been demonstrated to be truly effective? Many publishers say no. Further, if there are valid materials, that is, materials that have been shown to improve student performance if used as prescribed, do teachers understand that getting desired results directly relates to using the materials as they were used during field testing? Just as the diagnostician must conform to the constraints and conditions specified in the text manual, so must the teacher conform to the guidelines for using validated instructional materials if they expect to achieve reported gains. This is not to say that adaptations may not be required. It is to stress that there are times to be creative and times to capitalize on the efforts of others.

The design, development, and testing of instructional materials is a long process that requires the consultation and direct input of highly trained specialists. Although the individual teacher knows the needs of his or her students better than anyone else, teachers in general simply have not been trained to "know better" than the experts with regard to designing instructional materials. In fact, it is highly probable that a majority of the spontaneous modifications that a teacher might choose to make had already been considered and perhaps even tested. It is likely that many alterations teachers might make were eliminated at some point during the development process. Empirical evidence may have shown that a given modification was detrimental or simply that it was not of any additional worth. In short, it is to the teacher's advantage to capitalize on the work of the specialists and minimize his or her own work load by adapting and modifying materials only when it is truly required.

As an example, this is how a resource teacher employed in the Fairview Tennessee School System* went about using instructional materials. She had access to and used a number of field-tested instruction materials. One set of materials, a mathematics facts teaching program using audiotapes, published by Developmental Learning Materials (Hofmeister, 1979), was heavily relied upon. This program contained a detailed teachers' manual, tests, tapes, and practice sheets. The program had been thoroughly field tested with both handicapped and nonhandicapped populations. An audiotape play-back practice center capable of accommodating four students at one time was set up in the classroom. The program was employed with several students in need of this type of instruction. Measurements of student performance during baseline and instruction were carefully recorded. The program was successful with most of her students when the teacher's manual was followed. A few students, however, did not make progress at an adequate rate, even with use of the program's remedial procedures. At this point, the teacher decided to supplement

---

*Our appreciation is extended to Vickie Henson-Edwards for her assistance.

the audiotape-controlled practice with self-rehearsal (using flash cards) preceding each tape lesson. The students began making adequate progress and the basic precepts of the program were not violated.

The important point here is that the teacher's decisions on how to use a program, how to determine its effect, and how to adapt the program were not based on her ego involvement but on student outcomes. This approach did not make the teacher any less competent or the program any less successful. Do not mistake our intent. This objective approach is not easy. It requires a sort of courage, by the teacher, because in many cases he or she must diverge from what was advocated in teacher-training programs. Also, it requires as much inventiveness and creativity as do more subjective approaches to using materials. The difference is that it is not measured on a creativity scale but in terms of progress made by students.

At this time you should stop and complete Self-Check 8-1. It is simply a review of material presented to this point.

HOW ARE INSTRUCTIONAL MATERIALS EVALUATED?

The development and validation of instructional materials involves a lengthy sequence of activities (Armstrong, 1971). Throughout the total process of designing and developing any material, evaluation activities may be continuously occurring. The early process of developing and evaluating an instructional material is often referred to as formative evaluation. Once a material has been developed, revised, and refined, further evaluative measures may be undertaken. Evaluations that follow the initial development efforts are usually referred to as *summative evaluations*. Summative evaluations occur in field situations and are *not* under the control of the author or publisher. Summative evaluation or field testing of an instructional material is an assessment that should indicate how successful materials are in achieving specified objectives in the "real world."

In the not-too-distant past many instructional materials were designed, produced, and published with little or no evaluation obtained beyond the opinion of experts. The author(s) of a given material and a team of selected consultants may have joined together, planned, and evaluated its merits. *Evaluation* generally consisted of careful inspection of the material followed by recommendations based on the experts' personal experiences and biases. The "experts" might be teachers, other educators, or the publisher. Next, the author(s) or publisher would choose to incorporate these recommendations into the material or decide to ignore the recommendations. Many times publishing companies rather than the "experts" were the catalysts for the production of materials. Based on marketing research (an activity to which companies devote incredible

Self-Check 8-1

Instructions

Answer each of the following true-false questions.

Response

1. Most special educators are aware of the significance that field testing of instructional materials has to educational decision making.
   True *False*
2. Often subjective information on instructional materials is used as the main kind of information that teachers consider when selecting a material.
   True *False*
3. In spite of many advances in the content of university teacher-preparation programs, many graduating students are not trained to evaluate and constructively use field-test information.
   True *False*
4. Two basic questions every teacher selecting any instructional material should ask are: (1) Has this material been field tested and are the results reported? (2) Is the teaching procedure described precisely enough to allow the teacher to replicate it?
   True *False*
5. Teachers do not demand objective field-test information on child performance because they realize that it is better to "test" a material in their own class than to use materials in prescribed ways.
   True *False*
6. Educational accountability pertains to the roles and functions of many people, organizations, and institutions; however, it is the teacher who most often is held accountable for demonstrating gains in student performance.
   True *False*

Answer the following questions briefly.

1. Is there any hope of ever having the majority of instructional materials field tested? What can teachers do to contribute to the process of gaining such materials?

   ____

2. Name one unique aspect of the advertisement shown in Figure 8-2.

   ____

3. How might teacher creativity interfere with the predictability of student gains when materials that have been thoroughly field tested are used?

   ____

Now, compare your response with the sample response in Appendix A.

time and money), they would determine which materials were likely to be in high demand, would sell at premium prices, or had a potentially large market. Next, "experts" or willing others who might be considered authorities were solicited to endorse the material or assist in the development of promising products.

To substantiate the worth of these materials, testimonials to their value and effectiveness and consumer delight were gathered. In some cases comparative studies may have been backed and undertaken, comparing material A to material B. Usually these studies occurred late in the development process or after the material had already been marketed. Generally student-performance measures and teacher-satisfaction data also were collected and statistically analyzed. Group-performance data taken on a pretreatment and posttreatment basis were typically the primary empirical evidence collected. In some instances only one group of students was used. In more adequate studies, comparison and control groups were added to enhance the credibility of the results.

Although all these approaches to evaluation are still being used, a trend is growing to evaluate materials at each stage in the developmental process in terms of specific student outcomes. Evaluation is increasingly being viewed as a continuous process, and many kinds of data are collected to improve products and ensure that prespecified outcomes are attained when materials are used according to specification. One evaluation process particularly worth mentioning is known as the learner-verification-revision (LVR) process (Komoski, 1973). LVR is attractive because it is not as extensive as standard program-evaluation techniques; yet it yields information directly pertinent to assessing the effectiveness of instructional materials. Basically LVR is a series of activities centered around an instructional material. It employs a limited number of learners trying out the material and involves in-depth analysis of the performance and attitudes of the learners. Typically, individual or group learner tryouts provide information, objective and subjective, that leads to material revision and refinement, additional learner tryouts, and further revision and refinement. The entire process is repeated until satisfactory learner verification is achieved at a given level. Broader field testing is then ready to be undertaken. American Guidance Service, Hubbard Scientific and Edmark Associates are examples of publishers who make it a practice of publishing instructional materials that have been evaluated using the learner-verification-revision process and extensive field testing. Their resulting materials are of outstandingly high quality when set against the majority of comparable, less adequately evaluated instructional materials. Table 8-1 presents advantages and disadvantages of the materials-evaluation procedures that have just been discussed. The different types of evaluation procedures and their relative merits should be considered by the teacher when he or she attempts to assess any instructional material and the appropriateness of the evaluation procedure used in that assessment.

Awareness of these different evaluation procedures and when they are most

Table 8-1 Evaluation Procedures and Their Advantages and Disadvantages

Procedures	*Advantages*	*Disadvantages*
1. Expert appraisal (Teacher, publisher)	• Important to analysis of content scope and sequence of an instructional material, particularly during the initial phases of development. • Important to the development of a sound rationale, goals, and specific objectives. • Important to anticipation of potential problems with content or teaching procedure.	• The expert is limited by experience and personal biases. • A subjective information base. • Opinions are to be regarded but not necessarily relied upon. • Teacher or school-system testimonials are often "selected" and may not be representative of wide opinion. • Opinions may reflect other characteristics of materials, for example, entertainment value verses instructional worth.
2. Marketing research (Publishers)	• May lead to the identification of materials that are needed but currently unavailable.	• The purpose is to find a product that will sell and the outcome may be material of decreased quality accompanied by misleading advertising and publicity that creates a market for a product of minimal utility or relevance.
3. Learner verification	• Results of evaluation directly tied to scope, content, and pace of the material in most instances in terms of child performance.	• Does not assess the generalizability of the material. • Generally requires construction of all instrumentation used in assessment

	• Performance of individual learner assessed in depth. • Specific teaching procedure is likely to evolve. • Generally yields teacher- and child-performance data. • Limited persons, expense.	process.
4. Comparative-materials research	• Compares effects of one material to others. • Provides objective, empirical data on child or adult behavior or attitudes. • May assess the generalizability of the material.	• The results may still not indicate whether the materials successfully teach the skill(s). • All materials tested may be of poor quality and this research may only serve to identify which material is significantly less poor than another. • Requires a large number of participants, may be expensive. • Instrumentation used may not be appropriate to evaluation of the material since previously standardized instruments are often required. • Evaluation data does not often lead to specific modifications or revisions that would improve the material.
5. Validation research	• Includes both learner verification-revision research and summative evaluation.	• Involves extensive time and financial expenditure.

Table 8-1 Evaluation Procedures and Their Advantages and Disadvantages (continued)

	• Focuses on two questions: Do the materials work? Do users in the schools get satisfactory performance results similar to those obtained in most controlled field tests? • Employs criterion-referenced materials. • Refers directly to skills being taught.	

effectively employed should allow teachers to improve their assessment of information reported by publishers. For example, if detailed information on the learner-verification-revision process is presented, the teacher can be relatively confident that the materials and the teaching procedure are directly related and well specified. On the other hand, if postmarketing evaluation in the form of anecdotal information is all that is presented, it is likely that the reader should be cautious if he or she is about to make a purchase.

The Materials Review Form presented in Chapter 2 will assist the teacher in analyzing and selecting materials using field-test information as a criterion measure. The second page of the form has a section entitled Field-Test Results.

The reader can see that several kinds of evaluation approaches are represented in Figure 8-3, generally ranging from most subjective to increasingly objective. The teacher evaluating an instructional material would simply place a check mark (√) next to the type(s) of procedure used to evaluate any given instructional material. Several categories might be checked. For example, "expert appraisal" and "no field test" may both be checked for many materials.

```
Field Test Results:

     Subjective 1  expert appraisal...............___
                2  publisher testimonials.........___
                3  teacher testimonials...........___
                4  marketing research.............___
                5  no field tests reported........___
                6  individual learner verification___
                7  one group field tests
                   (pre--post-tests)..............___
                8  controlled study comparing
                   one material to another........___
                9  controlled study comparing
                   material to objectives
                   (validation research)..........___
     Objective 10  performance warranty...........___
```

Figure 8-3. *Portion of Materials Review Form That Pertains to the Assessment of Field Testing Done on Materials*

The teacher should be particularly alert to the last two categories, "controlled study of material in relation to achieving specific objectives" and "performance warranties." Any material with data demonstrating that objectives have been reached and/or that student performance gains are guaranteed is likely to be a good investment. On the other hand, material that has been evaluated solely on subjective measures, for example, expert appraisal, or for noninstructional goals, for example, marketing research, will require careful scrutiny. "No field testing" alerts the reviewer to the fact that the materials are still in a de facto developmental phase. They may or may not be effective with your students. Teachers are usually taking a relatively high risk if they purchase materials with no-field-test information whatsoever. Individual learner verification is an important evaluation process and should provide the teacher with confidence in the specific effects of the instructional material in question. One group pretest-posttest research and controlled comparative studies of other instructional materials may be very relevant or totally irrelevant to any teacher's particular needs. These data must be reviewed cautiously. If material A is five times more effective than material B, for example, one might conclude that material A is the material to buy. However, if material A and B are both poorly organized, difficult to implement, and do not lead to the specific gains a given class of students must achieve, neither may be the right selection. (At this point the reader is invited to complete Self-Check 8-2.)

WHAT ASPECTS OF AN INSTRUCTIONAL MATERIAL SHOULD BE EVALUATED?

The previous examples show how instructional materials have been evaluated in the past and the kinds of procedures that are currently being used to assess the worth of different material. Some evaluation procedures are more appropriate for answering certain questions than others. For example, to answer the question of *which* material is better for raising children's reading performance, a comparison study of two or more groups of children would be used. To answer the question of whether a particular material will sell, a survey of administrator and teacher opinion might be conducted. However, teachers need to ask only one major question when selecting an instructional material: Do the evaluation procedure and results relate *directly* to the measurement of the skills and concepts being taught? When this question can be answered affirmatively, the teacher can be sure that he or she is starting with an instructional material that is basically desirable and worthy of further investigation.

Teachers need to ask a number of other questions. These questions may or may not have been evaluated by the producer of the instructional material. If the publisher does not provide the information pertaining to these questions, the teacher is advised to request it. The following list is not exhaustive but illustrates the issues that will be extremely pertinent to whether or not instructional material will be of utility in any given classroom:

1. Was the rationale for developing the program clearly stated, followed by goals and specific statements of objectives? Do they match your needs?
2. Was the quality of the content, the scope of the program, and the sequencing of the skills or items evaluated? Was a learner-verification strategy used?
3. Does the publisher present information on the format of the material and the effectiveness of that format? Is the format feasible for you to use with your students.
4. Is the population upon which the material was validated clearly described? Does it fit your students?
5. Is information on how the material is paced presented, on how this pacing was evaluated? Are the steps too large or too small for your students?
6. Are both child-performance outcomes and teacher-instruction variables evaluated? Were they evaluated independently of each other? Will the results of their evaluation generalize to you and your students?
7. What types of evaluation information have been employed? Subjective evaluation only? Objective evaluation? What kinds of evaluation were used and how thorough were the evaluations?
8. Is there evidence that revisions have been made based on evaluation data? It is important to note if the publisher-author(s) have been improving this program.
9. Is there evidence that the assessment instruments or procedures validly and reliably measure the skills and concepts purported to be taught? This is critical.

Some of these questions the teacher can answer by looking back at the Materials Review Form that was completed on the material. The section on Instructional Characteristics should contain some of this information particularly the teacher comment sections (see Chapter 2).

FIELD TESTED? WHO CARES? WHO SHOULD CARE?

Review of instructional materials, the manner and extent to which they have been field tested, would imply that few if any teachers care whether materials have been field tested. One might deduce that field evaluation of instructional materials is of such minimal value or great expense that it is not worth being undertaken. To the traditionally trained teacher, the first deduction might suf-

Self-Check 8-2

Range:
Average three-year-olds, advanced two-year-olds, less mature four-year-olds, and children who need practice with standard English.

Time:
About 25 minutes per lesson.

Group Size:
Up to 12 children.

Description
The *Peabody Early Experiences Kit* (PEEK) is a program that helps young children to think more effectively and to express their thoughts and feelings more clearly. The 250 daily lessons, which include 1,000 activities, provide a rich variety of detailed plans for the teacher, and spontaneous, play-like learning experiences for the children. PEEK is appropriate for both full-time or half-day prekindergarten programs. Its easy-to-follow lessons can be presented by prekindergarten educators, day-care workers, community volunteers, and parents. There are enough lessons to provide one lesson per school day for a full calendar year.

PEEK is designed to assist in the development of abilities that are unfolding naturally. It is based on the premise that social, cognitive, and linguistic skills develop in an interrelated fashion and should be fostered that way.

The lessons have been sequenced in a spiral fashion, by level of difficulty, so they can easily accommodate children with different levels of ability as well as children who enter after the program has started.

Because the lesson contents have been balanced to teach to both strengths and weaknesses and are constructed to avoid omissions, lessons should be taught in sequential order. However, an index classifies the activities under 17 varied content areas, such as body parts, sounds, and weather. A second classification system codes the 1,000 PEEK activities by subtypes under the affective, cognitive, and linguistic domains. By using these classification systems, the teacher can selectively teach to one or more facets of the program.

About 50 percent of the PEEK activities focus directly on cognitive development. The affective area is emphasized in 25 percent of the activities, and oral language development in the remaining 25 percent. Usually at least one activity in each lesson is an action game for developing body coordination and awareness.

Development and Field Testing

The lessons and instructional materials in PEEK are products of five years of development. Two years were spent generating the initial pool of activities and assembling prototypes of the materials. Lesson refinement took another year. During the fourth year, the experimental edition of PEEK was widely field-tested. The fifth year was spent modifying and replacing activities and changing the materials in keeping with field-test feedback.

Field testing was carried out in the United States and Canada and, to a lesser degree, in Australia and New Zealand. In the United States, the PEEK draft lessons were taught and evaluated by 50 prekindergarten teachers in seven states: California, Colorado, Hawaii, Minnesota, Pennsylvania, South Carolina, and Virginia. In Canada, the program was field-tested in Ontario and Saskatchewan. Field testers were asked to point out ethnic and gender stereotyping and other possible prejudices. Thus, social bias has been minimized in the final edition.

Instructions

Read the preceding excerpt from a brochure and determine the type of field-test results described. Use the Field-Test Results section of the Materials Review Form reproduced below. Place one or more checks beside the list.

Response

Field-Test Results:

```
Subjective 1  expert appraisal..............___
           2  publisher testimonials........___
           3  teacher testimonials..........___
           4  marketing research............___
           5  no field tests reported.......___
           6  individual learner verification___
           7  one-group field tests
              (pre--post-tests).............___
           8  controlled study comparing
              one material to another.......___
           9  controlled study comparing
              material to objectives
              (validation research).........___
Objective 10  performance warranty..........___
```

Compare your response with the sample response in Appendix A.

Source: Reprinted from *American Guidance Service, 1979 Catalogue* with permission from the publisher. Copyright 1979 by American Guidance Service.

fice. To the publisher, the second deduction might be embraced. To the accountable educator and increasingly aware public, neither are satisfactory. In fact, research continues to show that adequately tested instructional material leads to predictable gains in student performance regardless of the general instructional conditions as long as the specified teacher procedures are employed. This data strongly supports the contention that accountable educational planning and instruction may most efficiently be reached by employing tried and proven materials and procedures. Rather than attempting to be innovative within all classroom-learning situations, teachers should use materials and methods that lead to demonstrated outcomes in student performance. This will make instruction more efficient and learning more predictable.

Unfortunately, a dearth of instructional materials have been carefully developed and fully evaluated. In the final analysis, it is likely that market research will continue to shape the direction of future materials development and teachers will continue to take what is dished out. Unless teachers, students, and other interested persons become outspoken, make their requirements for instructional materials known, publishers and teacher-training colleges will be slow to change their established routines. Influence must be applied with all who are involved directly and indirectly in the education of handicapped children or improvements in our materials will not be forthcoming. Influence must be applied to demonstrate that teachers are serious, that if they are going to be held accountable by parents, colleagues, and the educational system, they will demand validated instructional materials. The time to begin is now. Present the demand for sound, proven materials to the colleges, publishers, state and local education agencies, and all others influencing the delivery of appropriate education to handicapped learners. (It is now time to complete Self-Check 8-3. Good luck.)

Self-Check 8-3

Instructions

Based on the exerpts of the sample advertisement of instructional materials shown in Self-Check 8-2, answer the following questions.

Response

	Yes	*No*
1. Was the rationale for developing the program clearly stated, followed by goals and specific objectives?	________	________
2. Is the population upon which the material was tested clearly described?	________	________
3. Is there evidence that revisions have been made based on evaluation data?	________	________
4. Is there evidence that the assessment instruments used in the material reliably and validly measure the skills and concepts purported to be taught?	________	________

Compare your response to the sample response shown in Appendix A.

CHAPTER 9

Adapting Instructional Materials

Objectives

1. Describe the process of material adaptation—using material in a way that makes it work.
- What child characteristics do I need to consider in adapting materials?
- What materials characteristics do I need to consider?

2. Identify critical features of curriculum, measurement, and instruction for analyzing instructional materials.
- How can I systematically analyze material variables?

3. Adapt materials to meet individual learner needs by supplementing them.
- What alternatives for supplementing existing materials are possible?

4. Adapt materials to meet individual learner's needs by modifying them.
- What alternatives for adapting selected materials are possible?

What do teachers find is their greatest need once they leave a teacher-training institution and begin teaching handicapped learners? A recent national survey of personnel involved with handicapped children shows that concern for obtaining increased knowledge in the area of curriculum programming and materials resources ranks second only to instructional procedures and classroom management (Rude, 1978). Another survey, conducted with graduates of a special education teacher-training program (Shores & Stowitschek, 1975) revealed that knowledge about procedures for adapting materials was one of the highest rated needs.

Unfortunately, from our experience and that of others, it is abundantly clear that the skill whereby teachers are able to "make the match" between learner needs and instructional materials has been largely ignored by most teacher-preparation programs. Few classroom teachers are in a position to select judiciously from the wide array of commercially produced materials and then systematically adapt materials to meet learner needs. To compound the problem further, publishers annually lay claim to the development of materials best suited to the demands of a changing field. Rarely are these claims justified! Few materials on today's market have been adequately researched and sufficiently field tested to warrant such claims. Only after considerable time and effort is expended by classroom teachers are many materials able to measure up to the publisher's original claims.

Before discussing the adaptation of materials for exceptional learners, two closely related issues deserve mention. First, as no one set of materials is effective with all learners all of the time, the selection and adaptation of materials must correspond directly to the goals defined for instruction. Second, certain child-specific characteristics may influence the appropriateness of materials X over materials Y.

Even though exceptional children are diagnostically classified as "mentally retarded, hearing impaired, learning disabled, partially sighted" and so on, they share a number of similar learning characteristics. Differences among exceptional children are sometimes as great within as across traditional categories of exceptionality. No doubt this realization has contributed to the recent movement toward cross-categorical teacher preparation and, to a lesser degree, declassification of educational services.

It would be unwise to make too broad statements regarding the learning characteristics of exceptional children. Indeed, differences do exist. However, several general observations seem appropriate. A growing body of information suggests that many exceptional learners are "slow to catch on," requiring greater instructional time to master a particular set of materials than other students. A number of factors could serve to explain this. One possible solution rests in the selection and adaptation of materials matched to fit such a need. Not only is it necessary to adjust the content of instruction, but also the sequence of its presentation. Exceptional learners sometimes experience difficulty in attending to those aspects of instruction that would normally lead to mastering a particular learning task. Materials may need to be altered so smaller segments are presented while other aspects of instruction not judged to be relevant are dropped. Still other learners evidence a diminished ability to acquire abstract concepts, particularly through conventional instructional means. Again, the question of materials adaptations come to the fore. It is not uncommon for deficits to be present in a learner's short-term memory or information retention. Then material analysis may show that supplementary practice exercises need to be developed to improve retention following instruction. Finally, some children exhibit a variety of social-interpersonal problems such that traditional group-oriented presentation of material proves unsuccessful.

In all, discrepancies clearly exist between exceptional learners and their so-called normal counterparts. It is less certain to what these shortcomings can be accurately attributed. Yet practitioners are faced daily with the need to accommodate a wide range of learner needs. No other avenue of instruction is more directly related to meeting these needs than the manipulation of instructional materials. Simply stated, our purpose is to provide a practical yet systematic way of integrating information pertaining to learner needs and materials characteristics so what follows is a worthwhile learning experience. In that effort we have identified three separate but related aspects of instruction that must be looked at in selecting materials: (1) curriculum, (2) measurement, and (3) instruction. Viewed together, these three factors play a pivotal role in determining the appropriateness of materials and the extent to which they must be adapted to meet learner needs. The term *adapt* is somewhat misleading in that certain materials may be useful supplemented by additional practice exercises, whereas teachers will find that other materials require actual modification, sometimes in a number of areas. Only after recognizing the individuality of each student and determining child-specific instructional objectives can we move toward examining materials with the hope of arriving at a wise decision.

Individualized instruction necessitates that we first determine the curriculum needs of our students; second, that we plan a sequence of instruction corresponding to individual entry level skills; third, and relatedly, that we apply some form of direct measurement to our instruction; and finally, that we pursue a course of instruction matched to each learner's requirements.

WHAT DOES OR DOES NOT NEED MODIFICATION?

The Material Analysis and Adaptation Form (see Appendix B) is a unified approach to the adaptation of instructional materials. "Curriculum," "measurement," and "instruction" are divided into subelements that allow one to "zero in" on only those areas of an instructional program in need of adaptation. In succeeding discussion we explore the use of this form in detail and show ways in which materials can be improved in the areas of curriculum, measurement, and instruction. The form is arranged so that for any instructional program, subelements corresponding to each "Area" can, on the basis of a materials analysis, be singled out for adaptation purposes. The "Problem" that a particular subelement poses is pinpointed and recorded in narrative form so possible "Solutions" can be formulated.

This form is designed to correspond with the second page of the Materials Review Form (Chapter 2) so the "Problem" section can be drawn from it if the materials have already been reviewed. Probable problems include:

Curriculum

(A-Obj) Objectives	No objectives, objectives too general to permit precise direction, a mixture of specific and general objectives.
(A-Prereq) Prerequisites	Program starts too high, directions for how to work in the materials are too complex, prohibitive reading prerequisite.
(A-Seq) Sequence	Lock-step to sequence (linear), no alternative instruction sequence if the first does not work, steps out of sequence.
(A-Cont) Content	Gaps in the sequence, steps too large and must be broken down into subunits, irrelevant steps in the sequence.

Measurement

(B-Pre) Preassessment	Not enough test items to permit a judgment about mastery of subskills, test doesn't pertain to practice in materials,

	no assessment provided, assessment provided but doesn't permit placement in the instruction sequence of the materials.
(B-Prog) Progress assessment	Assessment is not sensitive enough to measure subskills in the material sequence, no progress assessment, progress assessment too infrequent.
(B-Vis) Visual Display	No visual display of assessment results (chart or graph), visual display is inadequate.
(B-Crit) Mastery criteria	No mastery criteria, mastery criteria fall short for determining proficiency or retention.
Instruction	
(C-Prac) Practice	Materials provide practice on several subskills (steps) at once, materials provide insufficient practice on certain subskills, irrelevant practice mixed in with relevant practice.
(C-Dir) Learner directions	Directions for learner are not explicit enough, the learner could perform the task but would be unsure about which task is to be performed.
(C-Prog) Programming	No assistance or prompts provided in the materials, prompts are provided but are removed too rapidly.
(C-Teach) Teacher activity	The teacher activities for helping the learner are not specific, no consistent helping tactic provided.
(C-Reinf) Reinforcement	General or no instructions for providing reinforcement, no supportive materials provided, suggestions in training guide do not specify contingent relationship between student performance and teacher attention.
(C-Redir) Redirection	No instructions for what to do if the program doesn't work (if the student doesn't make progress), instructions limited to recycling the student through the same material.

ADAPTATION OF CURRICULUM

Most commercially produced materials follow what might be described as a lock-step or set sequence of presentation. That is, most materials follow a fixed course requiring students to progress at the same rate as their classmates. The content of instruction is intended to be group oriented. Little provision is made for those children who do not "get it the first time." This so-called linear form of instruction not only minimizes one's ability to assess small amounts of change from day to day, but also hampers efforts by practitioners to rediagnose pupil needs during instruction. As we pointed out in our discussion of child-based evaluation, exceptional learners may require instructional materials that afford greater flexibility in regard to the manner in which they move from one subskill objective to the next. The following illustrates two courses of instruc- n, one requiring students to interact with the same material at the same pace l the other shows one way to overcome the obstacle of step-by-step materials presentation. As can be seen, aspects of curriculum, measurement, and instruction are singled out for adaptation to child-specific instruction.

Fixed Order of Instruction

Entry —— *Step 1* —— *Step 2* —— *Step 3*

Child-specific Instruction

Preassessment ——	*Step 1— Probe*	*Step 2 —*	*Probe*
	Pass		Pass
	Fail		Fail
	Step 1a		Step 2a
	Step 1b		Step 2b

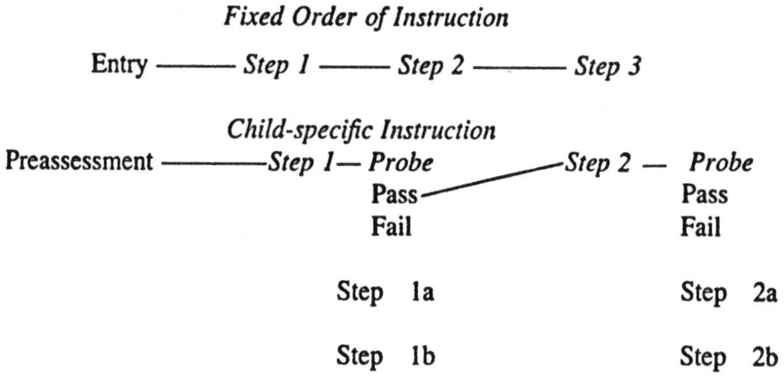

Objectives

It may be that our analysis shows the purpose of the materials is stated only in global terms. Lacking a fixed and quantifiable objective, we would indeed find it difficult to judge the impact of their usage. Then objectives must be written that clearly specify the instructional intent of the materials, and that describe in observable terms anticipated learner behavior. Only by stipulating the objective in this manner is one able to measure accurately the relative success of students in relation to instruction and materials that aid in that instruction.

Sequence and Content

Teacher adaptation often follows when the course of instruction specified in commercial materials requires too large or rapid a jump from one subskill to another. Then teachers faced with this problem often "slice" existing units of instruction into smaller, more manageable steps. In other instances, the sequence of instruction does not correspond to the objectives for which the materials are selected. Before actually modifying materials, it is advisable that we examine our goals of instruction. This analysis should yield information regarding two important points:

1. Do the materials include all subskill objectives I want to teach?
2. Do the materials contain any steps not directly related to my objectives?

By asking these two questions we are able to alter the sequence and/or supplement the content of existing materials. If it is found that the materials do not include certain aspects judged important to our instruction or that movement from one subskill to the next is too rapid, provisions must be made to accommodate learner needs. Smaller segments of instruction can be introduced. Should we discover material not directly related to instruction that can be dropped without adversely affecting the content, we can alter the scope of our instruction by simply deleting irrelevant material.

For exceptional learners to interact successfully with certain instructional materials, teachers will need at times to supplement commercial materials; in other instances, more extensive adaptation may be necessary. In supplementing existing materials, it may be fruitful to develop work sheets corresponding to exercises found in students' workbooks. As shown in Figure 9-1, we have constructed a work sheet on double-digit addition. In this example, students are given an opportunity to "tryout" skills during the beginning stages of instruction and obtain immediate teacher feedback concerning the accuracy of skills being applied. Also, as one can see, since a model of the steps leading to completing the problem is included, students can refer to the work sheet, which serves as a ready operation. As teachers increase the use of these simple yet effective tryout sheets, they will be able to assess the amount of warmup practice and immediate feedback students require to proceed independent of direct instruction. In some instances, the tryout sheets may need to be broken down into even smaller steps. Teaching "frames," if needed, may be developed for each discrete suboperation (Figure 9-1).

Self-Check 9-1

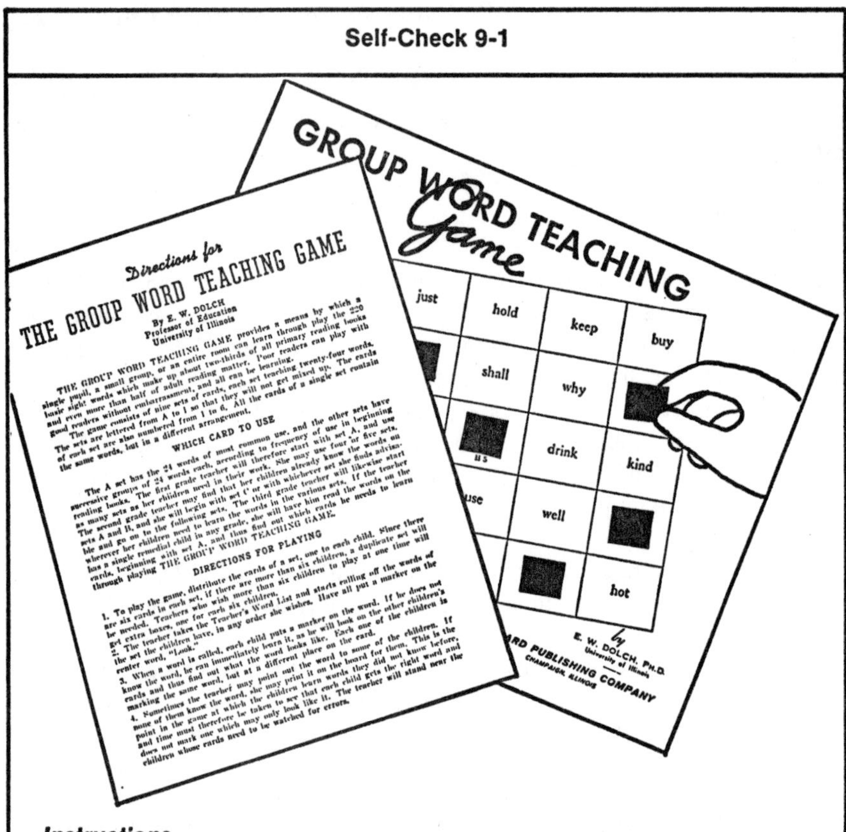

Instructions

Please read the following teacher description and excerpts from directions accompanying the Group Word Teaching Game, an instructional material to which the Materials Analysis and Adaptation Form (Appendix B) is to be applied. Then fill in the responses called for at the end of the paragraph:

To teach sight vocabulary words to seven nine- and ten-year-old mentally retarded children, you have chosen to incorporate a word game into the practice aspect of instruction. In analyzing the material, you find that the stated purpose of the program is that "Children will learn sight words." The objective is to have each child locate a word on a "bingo-type grid" and then place a marker on it.

We find that materials consist of 9 sets of word cards, each set containing 24 words. It is not clear, however, whether these words are presented in sequence even though the directions tell us they were selected on the basis of "frequency of use in beginning reading books." With the aforegoing in mind, please complete appropriate subelements of the "Area" and "Problem" sections of the Materials Analysis and Adaptation Form pictured below. (*Hint:* It has been repeatedly shown that children can't always learn 24 new words simultaneously.)

Area	*Problem*
A. Curriculum	
_____ (A-Obj) Objectives	________________________
	________________________
_____ (A-Seq) Sequence	________________________
	________________________
_____ (A-Cont) Content	________________________
	________________________

See sample answer in Appendix A.

Source: Reprinted from *Group Word Teaching Game* by E.W. Dolch with permission of the publisher. Copyright 1964, by Garrard Publishing Company.

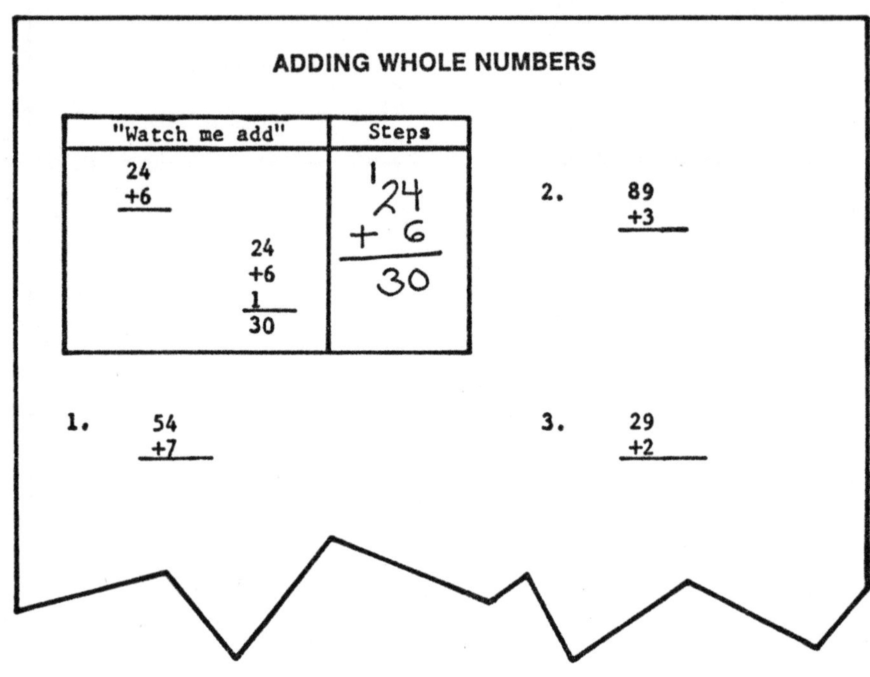

Figure 9-1. Sample Item from a "Tryout" Sheet

ADAPTATION AND MEASUREMENT

Discussed at length in Chapter 6, the second major aspect of materials analysis pertains to measurement. A growing number of commercially produced materials make provisions for assessing pupil performance. Few materials, however, enable teachers to pinpoint entry-level skills, directly and repeatedly monitor pupil progress, and finally evaluate retention following instruction. Still, child-specific materials management necessitates that one devise a method for assessing continuously students' knowledge or skill in relation to the specified objectives.

Some instructional programs make provisions for administering a placement test to assist teachers in matching a child's skill level with corresponding program segments. Often, however, test items do not directly relate to the goals singled out for instruction. In other instances, procedures call for only one testing session. If in our analysis it is found that a satisfactory means of assessing entry-level behavior does not exist, tactics must be developed to accomplish this task. Without specific knowledge of learner abilities, selection and adaptation of materials are not feasible. Moreover, it is likely that plans devised in the absence of a uniform measure of pupil behavior will resemble a "shotgun" approach, in that a little bit of everything is thrown into classroom presentation lest some aspect of instruction be overlooked. Understandably, such an approach has proven less successful than one in which teachers are able to zero in on discrete subskill deficiencies. Not only is preassessment essential for accurate curricular placement but, thereafter, continued evaluation is called for to enable teachers to precisely assess the influence of materials instruction.

Visual Display

The visual display of learner responses may be another needed adaptation to materials. A range of procedures are available from simple tallying to more elaborate graphing conventions. Depending on the kind of performance data, teachers may prefer to use a skill chart such as that discussed previously (Chapter 5). Whatever means for visually presenting data is selected, it is also suggested that one consider instructing students to chart their own academic responses. Ample evidence supports the fact that engaging learners in daily charting can serve as a powerful reinforcer of improved performance.

Mastery Criteria

The final measurement item pertains to establishing acceptable performance criteria for making decisions regarding students' progress in materials. Materials analysis may show that no measurable criteria are provided. If materials do not make provision for repeatedly and reliably measuring learner behavior, satisfactory criteria must be set. Some materials will identify criteria as percentage correct. A few will specify the number of consecutive correct trials. Rarely do materials specify criteria for proficiency or retention.

ADAPTATION AND INSTRUCTION

In turning to aterials analysis and instruction, we have singled out major problem areas for possible adaptation. As shown on the Material Analysis and Adaptation Form, provision is made for examining materials in relation to six common problem areas of instruction and for choosing what appears to be the most feasible solution. Now let us more closely inspect each aspect of instruction and materials that aid in that instruction.

Self-Check 9-2

Instructions

In Self-Check 9-1 you identified deficiencies in the area of "curriculum." Now we need to analyze possible problems pertaining to The Group Word Teaching Game on "measurement." The following is taken from instructions accompanying the game. "The ________ grade teacher will start wherever her children need to learn the words in the various sets." "The child wins who first finds on his card five words in a row in any direction. . . . The teacher may check to be sure the child has marked the right words." When the teacher knows that she is calling familiar words, she may call them rapidly to develop quick recognition."

On the basis of the aforegoing information, complete the appropriate areas of the "Measurement" section below:

B. Measurement

_____ (B-Pre) Preassessment ______________________________

____

____

_____ (B-Prog) Progress-mastery assessment ______________________________

....

....

_____ (B-Vis) Visual display ______________________________

____

____

_____ (B-Crit) Mastery criteria ______________________________

____

____

See sample answer in Appendix A.

Practice

An important area of materials analysis pertains to the amount of practice and application provided by materials. It is widely recognized and supported by research in the field that exceptional learners need repeated opportunity to interact with materials if they are to be mastered. We have often heard teachers remark that they cannot understand why Fred appeared to grasp, for example, double-digit addition operations on Tuesday, but failed Friday's test. One possible explanation is that Fred was not afforded enough opportunity to practice his add-facts following Tuesday's instruction. Ample evidence exists that exceptional learners generally require repeated chances to engage in a particular skill before mastery is attained. Unfortunately, many commercially produced materials are "too lean" in the amount of practice provided in a particular subskill area. Indeed, we have seen some materials that introduce a given concept, provide limited opportunity to practice it, and then require students to apply that concept to new learning experiences in the space of one or two workbook pages.

The use of practice exercises is usually limited to areas of learning not yet mastered. Effort should be made to pinpoint child-specific instructional needs and to tailor assignments accordingly. Children, of course, should be spared the tedium of completing exercises containing skills they already know how to perform correctly. The number of items per exercise and the time allocated for them should remain constant; as few as ten minutes a day often is enough if practice is concentrated. A fixed criterion and evaluation procedure should be used to measure pupil gains from day to day. Once a child has attained the preselected performance level, instruction can be shifted to new learning experiences.

The need to provide sufficient drill so each discrete subskill is mastered extends beyond initial acquisition stages. It is equally important that children not only receive repeated practice but also the opportunity to apply newly acquired skills systematically. A persistent problem is that skills are not always extended to new learning situations. One cannot, for example, assume that students who have mastered double-digit addition will be able correctly to calculate reading problems requiring the same operation. Therefore, further instruction is often necessary to ensure that children are capable of transferring skills successfully to other curricular areas. This is accomplished much the same way as with earlier learning experiences, by using materials that provide a bridge between existing skills and new areas of application. It is often necessary to pair familiar with new materials and gradually introduce novel applications of existing skills. As before, this calls for additional steps to be built into materials and that students be given supplementary instruction focusing on the transfer of discrete subskill operations.

Learner Directions

It is not unusual for a teacher to introduce the day's lesson and assignment only to observe a bewildering array of "blank stares" or "what was that again" looks. The fact is that many exceptional children have difficulty following verbal instructions or complying with directions that accompany written materials (Englemann, 1970). Experienced teachers have found it necessary to supplement commercial materials with more detailed directions. Even so, many children continue to experience difficulty until teachers actually demonstrate the desired operation, procedure, or response. Indeed, as we previously commented, the step-by-step performance of a task by the teacher and the provision of a permanent model for future reference has proven to be a useful technique. In other instances, directions can be recorded on audiotape for repeated play. Overall, certain instructional materials necessitate that the directions themselves be analyzed in an effort to add clarity and to remove any confusing or unnecessary information. Much as when instructional tasks are sliced into smaller segments and taught individually, a sequence of directions can be devised that calls for students to demonstrate understanding at each step.

Checkpoints can be built in—"point with your finger and show me where you are to write the answer"; one does not move ahead until each learner has demonstrated that he or she can perform the desired behavior. Finally, at the risk of stating the obvious, if materials are divided into smaller units of instruction, one need only provide children with those directions directly corresponding to the first unit. Then as they complete that segment, directions can be repeated, or new instructions provided, as needed.

Programming or Prompting

For even the most accomplished teacher, gaps may exist between the principle of individualization and its current classroom practice. Although federal legislation stipulates that an individualized educational program be developed for each exceptional learner, such mandates have not resolved the many practical problems faced by classroom teachers. Accordingly, limited instructional time and resources dictate that decisions regarding which content areas require the greatest amount of planning and instruction must sometimes be made. Then, to the extent that materials can be adapted to allow flexibility in pupil responses, for example, written versus oral, and to the degree that teaching time can be held constant in each content area, groups of students can be taught in several curricular areas simultaneously.

To accomplish this, a uniform presentation mode represents one area for adaptation by the teacher. In developing a so-called individualized group format, clear instruction is needed so students understand not only *how* but *when* to respond. A warmup period during which time prompting in following the instructional routine is given is often helpful. Similarly, teachers should plan and provide ample feedback (verbal or nonverbal) at selected intervals according to each student's observed need. Even though child-specific instruction within a group format necessitates incorporating a high degree of uniformity in relation to instructional management, a variety of content-specific material at various instructional levels can be presented.

Most commercially produced materials rely on visual presentation. Often materials are designed to elicit a written academic response. For many exceptional learners this poses immediate problems: first, many students evidence reading deficits that adversely affect their ability to acquire new information; and second, many students have spelling and/or handwriting problems that further decrease their ability to communicate in writing the acquisition of that information. On the other hand, a child may show little or no difficulty when materials are adapted to his or her needs. For children with reading difficulties that cause independent reading before recitation to be troublesome, one might prerecord audiotape passages presenting pertinent material. In this way, students are able to progress at their own rate. Students can review materials as often as necessary and even be able to self-correct, given that an answer key has likewise been prerecorded and/or is available in written form. Not only are children able to participate in a group-oriented lesson, but they are also able to engage in independent remedial instruction until the material is mastered.

Many teachers have found that the content areas of spelling, arithmetic, and phonics are most easily adapted to such instruction. Following the aforementioned procedure, teachers are able (a) to use different instructional materials matched to individual learner needs or (b) to apply the same materials but with different instructional objectives, for example, percent versus rate criteria. The following serves to highlight the manner in which "multilevel instruction" can be a solution to programming problems.

Mrs. L has identified seven students for whom further drill exercises are indicated, three in add-facts, two in subtraction, and two in spelling. Students are first pretested and then placed according to skill level and matched in relation to response mode. Three children are designated as oral responders and four will be asked to respond in writing. Material selected consists of teacher-made work sheets in arithmetic and a prerecorded audiospelling tape. Mrs. L further adapts her instruction so a uniform number of responses, each demanding a similar number of suboperations, is introduced: ten double-digit addition, ten double-digit subtraction problems. Spelling words are choosen that are four or fewer letters. Finally, Mrs. L stipulates that each child is to "self-check" his or her work with answer keys furnished following the daily probe. To increase the prospect that the small-group format will be successful, Mrs. L schedules a series of three warmup exercises. During these sessions children are prompted when and how to respond individually to instruction. During actual instruction a signal or cue can be routinely provided and serve as a prompt for responding.

Faced with the problem of providing enough feedback to students to maintain on-task performance, one can select from several alternatives. Teachers may wish simply to "red-line" the number of subtraction problems a student should independently calculate.

As shown in Figure 9-2, seven subtraction problems have been singled out for the student to complete. In this way a child is not confronted with a full page of problems; rather, only a few are to be calculated at one time. Then, following teacher feedback, regarding the accuracy with which problems were worked, the child is either instructed to complete seven more problems or, depending on the correctness of the answers recorded for the first seven problems, told that is "all for today." By breaking down conventional materials into smaller units of instruction, the amount of work demanded of a child can be gradually increased over time. In succeeding sessions the number of problems can be systematically increased, thus affording an opportunity to provide continued feedback and instruction while approximating the goal of completing the entire page.

Programmed learning is another possible solution to certain instructional problems. Although a growing number of programmed materials are on the market, certain adaptations are usually necessary to maximize their worth. Ad-

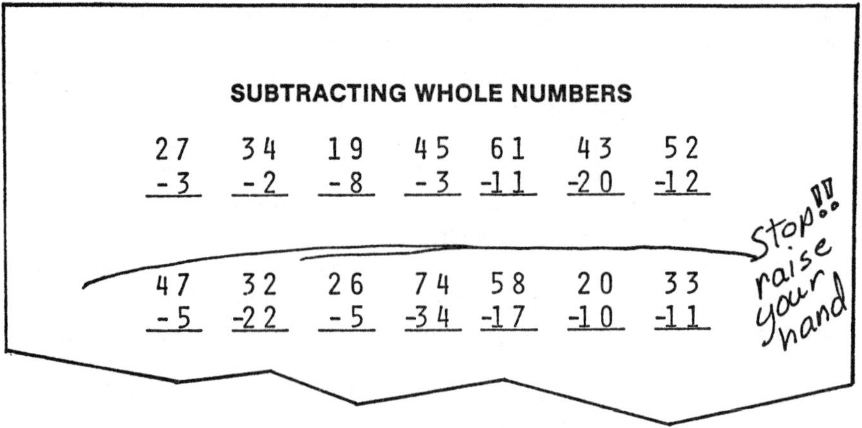

Figure 9-2. Example of a "Red-Line" Procedure for Breaking Up Work on Skill Tests

aptation procedures discussed in this and other chapters are applicable. One of the problems with programmed materials (linear) is that students must work through all frames of a unit between tests. This means that much of the practice can be inappropriate. One adaptation may be to "lean out" the program by providing a guide so the student can skip some sections until he or she reaches portions where practice is needed.

The following illustrates how programmed materials can be subdivided into three areas of instruction:

1. *Test frames* — for assessment purposes
2. *Rule frames* — for review purposes
3. *Prompt frames* — for practice purposes

Accompanying the example on teaching the concept of a decimal point is a Program Prescription Sheet. The Program Prescription Sheet affords an opportunity to categorize each "frame" (Figure 9-3) according to its purpose. Then, depending on learner performance, it is possible to modify further the instructional sequence. For example, should we wish to obtain more test data, additional test frames might be constructed. If our analysis reveals that additional instruction seems warranted, more rule frames could be added, whereas if materials do not appear to afford enough practice, the number of prompt frames could be increased. In contrast, analysis may show that certain portions of instruction can be deleted without negatively affecting the program. Overall, the use of the Program Prescription Form has utility for subdividing programmed material and for singling out only those aspects of instruction needing attention.

In sum, programmed instructional materials are materials that give learners an opportunity to progress at a rate independent of other students. Self-pacing, however, often necessitates that teachers pay particular attention to providing feedback, checking pupil progress, and reassessing and adapting materials.

Teacher Activity

As we previously discussed, teachers are discovering that more efficient materials management can result from the wise use of some form of self-instruction. *Self-instruction* can include child management of certain aspects of instruction that permits children systematically "to teach one another." Although it is the stock-in-trade of many special educators, such instructional management has rarely been approached in a systematic and consistent manner. As classmates represent an economical and readily accessible resource to teachers, we advocate their use in instances where self-instruction or peer instruction affords as much opportunity to progress academically as more con-

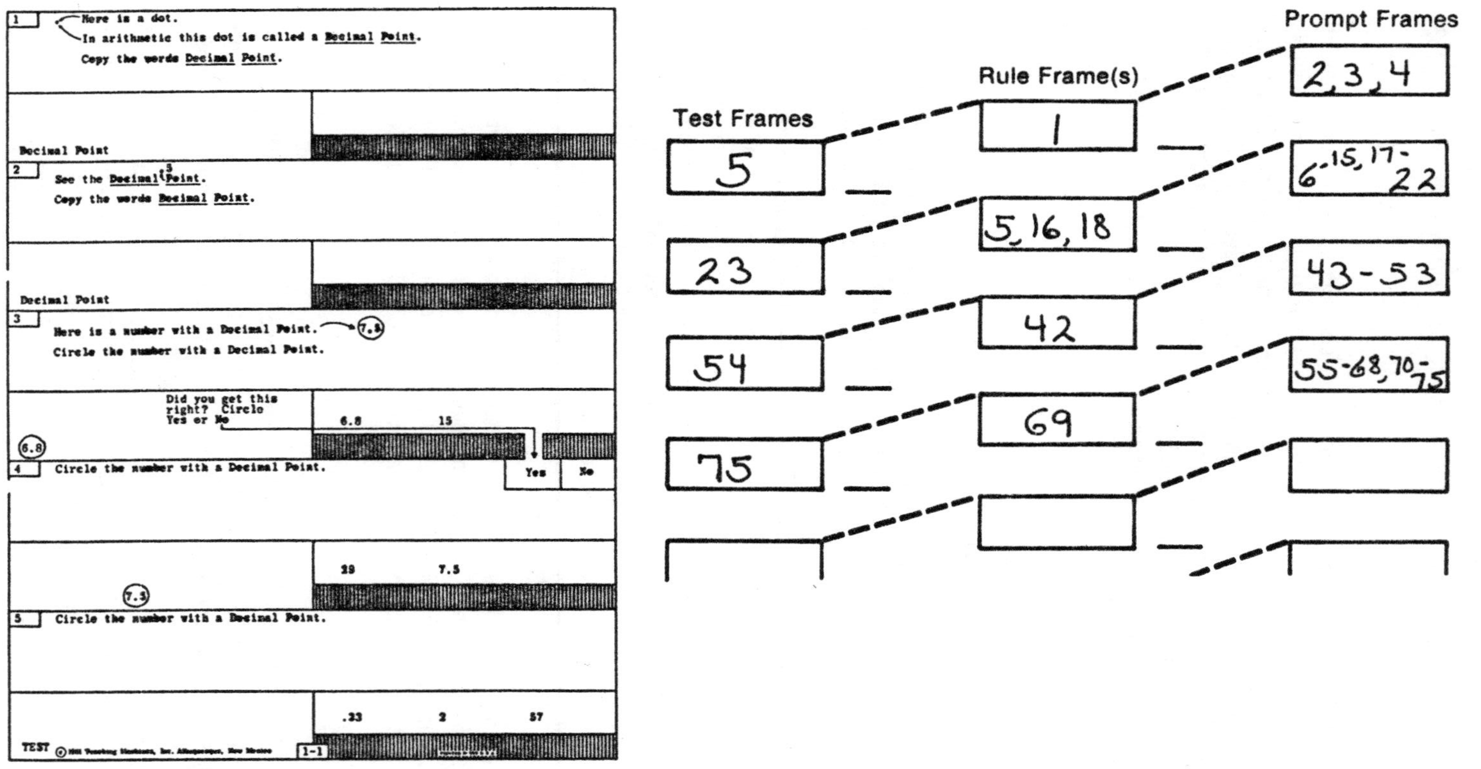

Figure 9-3. *Sample Page of Programmed Material and a Program Prescription Sheet*

Source: Reprinted from *Elementary Arithmetic Series: Decimal Numbers, Self-Tutoring Course* by TMI Grolier. Copyright 1961 by Teaching Machines, Inc.

ventional teacher-directed instruction. Materials that are particularly adaptive to peer instruction include those calling for repeated drill for mastery such as in arithmetic, spelling, handwriting, and language development. As discussed in Chapter 7, the use of peers, preferably for tutorial instruction, can be arranged in a variety of ways, depending on learner needs and capabilities. Teachers interested in a limited form of peer or self-instruction can develop a scoring key for use with conventional materials so students can immediately and independently evaluate their own efforts. Still another option would be for the teacher to engage one student as the correcter-of-the-day. In the case of both self-corrective and peer-assisted alternatives, caution of course is suggested lest the students prove unreliable in their evaluations or negative in their interactions with classmates. One way to minimize the likelihood that students will deliberately or otherwise err in this is for teachers to (1) establish one area of the classroom solely for checking work, (2) intermittently evaluate the efforts of the student(s), and (3) praise students frequently for their accuracy and honesty in performing the task of correcting their own or a classmate's work.

Reinforcement: Its Relationship to Materials

The issue of pupil motivation may seem less directly linked to materials analysis and adaptation than previous discussion. Yet we recognize the central role reinforcement plays in the overall success of instruction.

A wide range of strategies for delivering reinforcement has been proven effective in classroom settings. Contingent teacher attention has been repeatedly shown to influence behavior positively. An "inventory" of other classroom-related events deemed to be rewarding can be obtained in several ways. First, teachers can observe and record the activities in which children freely engage during noninstructional periods. Second, teachers can prepare a list of potential reinforcers and have children indicate preferred ones. With younger children it is suggested that either a picture or an example of the reinforcers be presented from which they may sample several possibilities. Third, teachers can simply poll students regarding activities they may want to earn. A note of caution is in order concerning the selection of reinforcers. No single item or event will necessarily have the same impact on each child. Reinforcers need to be matched with children's preferences to increase the probability of their being effective. Finally, only by measuring the impact of selected reinforcers can we actually be certain of their utility as a motivational tactic.

Redirection or Correction

Finally, instructional problems sometimes stem from the fact that many children find needed repetition in skill development less than enjoyable. To offset this potential stumbling block to repeated practice for mastery, researchers (e.g., Lovitt & Hanson, 1976) and practitioners have applied a strategy referred to as contingent skipping and drilling. Simply stated, *contingent skipping and drilling* exists when a student, having acquired the fundamentals of a task, that is, single-digit addition, is permitted to skip selected exercises or, conversely, is required to engage in further drill. The choice between skipping and drilling rests with the child's performance in relation to a preselected criterion. Say, for example, that we have established mastery as 120 words per minute, 2 or fewer errors, and 80 percent correct on comprehension questions in a series of reading exercises. Next, we determine the minimum number of days each student is required to meet that standard; three consecutive days should satisfy our requirements. Then all students attaining or exceeding this criterion level are permitted to pass over succeeding passages; children failing to do so are required to engage in further drill. By applying a skipping and drilling tactic, teachers can arrange practice exercises that serve a useful purpose. No longer are students forced to engage in endless repetition; instead, motivation exists for children to put forth their best efforts.

Another possible solution to problems in this area is the use of alternative materials. Often children find it difficult to interact daily with the same material, especially if they are experiencing problems mastering skills being presented. It is not unusual, however, for children to evidence renewed enthusiasm over a change in materials. Indeed, it has been shown that they are sometimes better able to select appropriately from several material alternatives best suited to their needs. Teachers tend to overlook the fact that regardless of the effort invested in "making the match" between learner and materials, only the outcome is important. It is useful to observe children as they interact with material X and material Y for the purpose of discovering problem areas otherwise overlooked. With this goal in mind, teachers have scheduled a limited number of one-to-one sessions for attempting to analyze specific aspects of instruction systematically. In some cases this period of teacher-directed instruction is extended until the child demonstrates skills prerequisite to more independent learning experiences. Earlier comments regarding contingent teacher attention and use of feedback is worth recalling here, too. With a history of repeated failure in the classroom, many exceptional learners will respond positively only when they discover success is attainable.

EXAMPLES OF ADAPTING BY SUPPLEMENTING

When materials do not work, the decision to dig right into materials and attempt to change them can lead to a time-consuming and unnecessary process. Materials cannot be made to work by supplementing or adding something to them. One example of adapting by supplementing is related to an instruction kit that is commonly found in many special education classrooms.

The Peabody Language Development Kit—Level 1 (American Guidance Service) contains a collection of stimulus cards, an activity manual, and other supportive materials (e.g., puppets, plastic chips, and so on). The manual describes types of teacher activities and requires some fairly sophisticated judgments about the conduct of lessons and when to move on to another activity. Two teachers of moderately retarded children who had teacher aides and volunteers working for them found that more specific teaching instructions were required. The teachers got together and prepared a supplementary guide so aides and volunteers could conduct supportive practice activities on selected language skills. The guide contained instructions for how to employ a simple teaching tactic (in script form), how to check and record students' responses, and how to correct errors. With this supplement, teachers could effectively use aides' and volunteers' time without taking large amounts of time away from their own teaching or letting volunteers stand around waiting for some direction.

One of the more involved supplements to published instructional materials is that described by Rosen (1973). This supplement pertained to the Programmed Reading Series published by McGraw-Hill Book Company. Programmed reading is one of the more commonly available materials in special education classrooms, because it includes placement and mastery tests and it is amenable to remedial instruction (divided into 21 books and highly sequenced). Some of the more common complaints of teachers include the following:

1. Practice is focused on written responses and must be supplemented with oral reading instruction.
2. Reading comprehension is less emphasized than are decoding skills.

The supplements completed for this program include teacher instructions and materials for oral reading activities (teach sounds and words books) and timed practice (read sounds and words) before the learner works in the programmed reader. Once approximately eight to ten pages have been completed, additional supplements pertaining to oral reading rate and reading comprehension are used. The cycle of supplements plus programmed reading are repeated for the next set of pages. An individual progress chart for each of the 21 books displays the results of the learners performance in each of the supplements as well as in the pages of the reader. In this case the carefully sequenced and well-programmed individual practice of the reader was capitalized on without violating the design of a field-tested program. Yet the supplements served to render it a comprehensive and complete reading program that permits teachers to use what they have and avoid the expense of purchasing a completely new program.

A simpler example of adapting materials by supplementing them pertains to problems that preadolescent and adolescent handicapped learners have with materials, say in biology, social studies, or business education subjects. The complaints that teachers in these subjects have about handicapped learners is often not related to deficiencies inherent in the subject areas but concerns the fact that they cannot read the materials. If the content of the subject is important to learn, regardless of whether learners can read it, a simple supplementary process can be to audiotape pertinent material. For instance, instructions for biology lab exercises can be prepared by willing students in advance of each lab. The tapes are inexpensive and reusable so it only needs to be done once for a given exercise.

EXAMPLES OF ADAPTING BY MODIFYING

Another adaptation of Programmed Reading (Hofmeister, 1969) was less involved but modified the criterion performance tested, the frequency of progress testing, and the page-by-page practice procedure used with trainable mentally retarded adolescents. Instead of testing reading responses given the sounds or words and a pictorial stimulus, Hofmeister modified the testing condition so sounds or words were read without external prompting stimuli. Instead of taking a test at the end of each programmed book, students took a progress test after every five pages. Instead of making written responses on a program and moving on to the next page, students' oral reading of each page was also checked by the teacher.

Some supplemental adaptations were also made to aid the teacher in managing the modified program. For instance, to avoid having students leave their desks, interrupt the teacher, and possibly cause disruptions, a moveable flag was attached to each desk. When a student completed a page he or she flipped the flag up to signal the teacher to come and check the student's oral reading of the page. Another supplement related to converting the materials from consumable into reusable pages: Each student wrote on a transparent overlay that was wiped clean by the teacher after checking the student on the page. A token economy was also added to aid in managing the students.

Evaluation and Adaptation

In all, most curricular areas lend themselves to some form of materials "tryout." Such a tactic provides first-hand knowledge regarding the appropriateness of instructional materials and yields valuable clues about the extent of

Self-Check 9-3

Instruction

Recalling Self-Checks 9-1. and 9-2, you have analyzed and adapted the Group Word Teaching Game in the areas of curriculum and Measurement. The final area of evaluation pertains to "instructions." The following is taken from the directions of the material:

> To play the game, distribute the cards of a set, one to each child. The teacher takes the Teacher's Word List and starts calling off the words of the set the children have, in any order she wishes. When a word is called, each child puts a marker on the word. If he does not know the word, he can immediately learn it, as he will look on the other children's cards and thus find out what the word looks like. Sometimes the teacher may point out the word to some of the children. If none of them knows the word, she may print it on the board for them. This is the point in the game at which the children learn words they did not know before, and time must therefore be taken to see that each child gets the right word and does not mark one which may only look like it. The teacher will stand near the children whose cards need to be watched for errors.
>
> When the child finds new words, he is learning new sight vocabulary. When he finds already known words, he is practicing his word recognition and speeding it up. If the teacher knows that she is calling familiar words, she may call them rapidly to develop quick recognition.

On the form below, complete those aspects of instruction that, because of the aforegoing, seem to be potential problem areas. (*Remember:* In special education settings, it is likely that not all children will always choose to participate in instruction).

Instructions

_____ (C-Prac) Practice _____________________

_____ (C-Dir) Learner directions _____________________

_____ (C-Prog) Programming or prompting _____________________
____

_____ (C-Teach) Teacher activity _____________________

_____ (C-Reinf) Reinforcement _____________________

_____ (C-Redir) Redirection or correction _____________________
____

adaptation required to fit learner needs. Once teachers have uncovered each learner's needs, the selection and adaptation of materials can easily follow. We would also add that this diagnostic process by no means represents a singular act; instead, as instruction moves forward, progress monitoring helps ensure the continued appropriateness of selected materials. This ongoing evaluation has the advantage of yielding additional information on the pace of instruction and the amount of feedback necessary to maintain progress, as well as aspects pertaining to actual materials adaptation, such as the need for selected practice exercises or the need for further manipulation or reinforcement tactics.

Materials analysis and adaptation are purposeful only to the extent that their use leads to the desired outcome. Expanding the adaptation period to include a short series of trial lessons allows one to determine functionally the appropriateness of materials.

To summarize, the preceeding discussion has focused on the systematic analysis of materials and included a range of strategies for adapting materials for exceptional learners. Understandably, we have not exhausted the possibilities; instead, we have offered tactics selected on the basis of their applicability to solving problems common to many teaching situations. You should now complete Self Check 9–3.

CHAPTER 10

Child-Based Materials Evaluation

Objectives

1. Define and describe a child-based materials evaluation.
   - What is the purpose of a child-based materials evaluation?
   - Why is a child-based materials evaluation particularly important to special educators?
   - What are the major steps in a child-based materials evaluation?
   - How feasible and justifiable is such an evaluation?

2. Name two direct measurement systems that should be used in a child-based materials evaluation.
   - What are the different purposes of each?
   - Which system provides more specific information on the learning process?
   - What should a teacher do if the instructional material does not have a measurement system built in?

3. Name the three components of the material-adaptation strategy that are evaluated to improve an instructional material.
   - What is the CSR adaptation strategy?
   - Why are modifications made one at a time?
   - Why is changing the child's response the last step in the adaptation strategy?
   - What kinds of modifications might be considered stimulus adaptations?

4. Conduct a child-based materials evaluation with one to three children.
   - Did you initially select a couple of programs upon which to complete a Materials Review Form?
   - What was the source of the child-behavior measurement system you used? Selected or self-made?
   - Did you think each of the steps in a child-based materials evaluation were important?
   - How many steps in the adaptation strategy did you require?

Would you buy a car after reading a brochure describing its merits? Would you buy the car after simply inspecting it on the showroom floor? This is how teachers generally purchase instructional materials. However, when buying a car most people try out a model of each car they are considering. They test drive it in the manner they will be using it. When purchasing materials, why do not teachers try them out in the manner they will be using them?

Before committing a substantial portion of the budget to the purchase of an instructional program it is highly advisable to assess directly the potential utility of that material. Child-based materials evaluation is one of the most productive, money-saving approaches to the assessment of instructional materials. The materials-analysis and review procedure described in Chapter 2 is a first step in materials evaluation. The child-based materials evaluation is a follow-up to that first level of analysis. A child-based evaluation will support or disconfirm the conclusions made from the teacher's first material analysis. It allows the teacher to evaluate the effect of an instructional material on students in the classroom conditions under which it will be used. This process enables the teacher to predict with relative certainty the likelihood that the material will be worth the investment of time, money, and energy that will be required to make it work effectively. A child-based materials evaluation will provide information on whether and to what degree a material must be modified to maximize its impact on learning. Equally important, a child-based materials evaluation can be accomplished with surprisingly little alteration in the instructional day and will require few additional demands upon teacher preparation time.

WHAT IS A CHILD-BASED MATERIALS EVALUATION?

A *child-based materials evaluation (CBME)* is precisely what its name suggests. It is an assessment of the worth of an instructional material based on the performance of the actual learners with whom it is intended to be used. It is a short-term assessment tactic that employs a limited number of pupils and affords information on the nature and rate of their learning. Child-based evaluation is particularly important to special educators because few instructional materials have been field tested and validated on special student populations. Furthermore, the statistical analyses used in most evaluations of instructional materials are based on group performance and often are not generalizable to individual students.

In a child-based materials evaluation, only a few students and a small amount of time are needed. Usually two to three students, perhaps in high-, medium-, and low-performance ranges, are selected to work with the material on a tryout basis. The materials are used in accordance with publisher guidelines. The total number of days involved will vary depending on the skill or concept being taught, the manner in which the materials are organized, the progress monitoring procedures or tests to be used, and the students' learning characteristics. The teacher may expect to spend from 1 to 3 weeks, perhaps 15 minutes a day, using the materials in a child-based evaluation.

Child-Based Measurement

It is recommended that assessment of students be done by using one of two measurement systems. Depending on the purpose of a specific CBME, the teacher should select either a pre-posttest mastery measure or a continuous daily monitoring system. Some materials the teacher may want to evaluate will already have adequate pre-posttests or daily progress monitoring tests, and these can be used without modification. Other materials will require preparation of simple probes or tests by the teacher. Several progress monitoring procedures require minimal effort to select or prepare and validly assess student performance. Suggestions for designing your own monitoring procedures are presented later in this chapter and are discussed in Chapter 5.

For the most part, the decision to use a pre-posttest measure or a daily testing procedure to assess child learning will depend on the teacher's purpose. If the major purpose of the CBME is to determine if the material works with a specific group of students, a pre-posttest tryout will suffice. If the purpose is to pinpoint specifically when learning occurs and determine the kinds of changes that will be necessary to make the material work better, a continuous monitoring system should be used. For both purposes it is best to use a simple, direct-measurement system, that is, a procedure that directly assesses the behavior of interest. A direct measure tests the exact concepts or skills to be learned. For instance, if the material was designed to teach students to spell one-syllable words ending in a "silent" *e*, the test would require the students to spell one-syllable words. The words would be presented during the test in the same mode (e.g., orally by the teacher) as they had been during the learning process. The student would respond in the same mode during the testing as he or she had done during instruction (e.g., a written or spoken response).

Materials Evaluation: A Three-Step Process

Pre-posttest and continuous monitoring of child behavior in a child-based materials evaluation are conducted in a sequence of three steps. The steps in a pre-posttest evaluation include:

1. Administering the pretest and assessing the child's entry level performance
2. Applying the instructional materials and teaching tactic
3. Administering the posttest and assessing the child's final performance level

When using a continuous monitoring system, there are also three basic steps to follow:

1. Pretesting or collecting baseline data on child performance, generally for three or more sessions
2. Applying the instructional material and teaching tactic while continuing to collect data on child performance
3. Posttesting or collecting data on child mastery performance and level of maintenance

If the materials prove to be successful using either procedure, the teacher can begin implementation in the classroom on a larger scale. If little or no improvement is evident in student performance, a continuous monitoring system will provide information on how to improve the materials. The following strategy for adapting instructional materials is recommended. It is designed to permit teachers to expend the least possible effort and achieve the greatest gains.

Materials Adaptation: A Three-Step Process

It is recommended that changes in instructional materials be made by using a systematic, three-step adaptation strategy designed to facilitate easy implementation and achieve rapid results. The three-step adaptation strategy is called the CSR strategy. It is a modified order of the materials analysis identified by Henderson and Rovig (1977) and stands for Consequence-Stimulus-Response. It represents the order in which the teacher modifies an instructional material.

Step 1: The teacher changes the reinforcement tactic (C) using the assessment data collected daily to determine if the modification was successful. This step involves the least teacher effort and has the highest probability of gaining results.

Step 2: If Step 1 proves unsuccessful (the student appears to be working hard but not improving), the stimulus (S) properties of the materials themselves are modified, usually by providing an additional prompt or cue. Typically, this includes further instructions or demonstration and does not require excess time or effort.

Step 3: Finally, the response (R) the child makes in the materials is modified, usually by breaking down the tasks or improving the sequence of the program. Daily data is once again used to determine the effect of this modification.

A positive change in child performance should be observed within three days. If not, the next step of the CSR strategy should be initiated.

Each change in the instructional materials is made one at a time to ensure correct interpretation of the effect of the change on student performance. If several aspects of an instructional material were changed at the same time, it would not be possible to determine which component was responsible for the improvement or decline in student performance. By looking at one aspect at a time, the teacher can ascertain with relative certainty exactly which modifications are needed. In addition, the CSR strategy gives the teacher the advantage of beginning with the step that has the best chance of gaining a positive change in student performance. The final outcome of a child-based materials evaluation will be knowledge of the short- and long-term gains students are likely to make using a material in any given classroom. As stated earlier, continuous monitoring has the distinct advantage of allowing the teacher to determine not only what changes may be necessary, but how extensive the adaptations will need to be. (Self-Check 10-1 will give you practice relating consequence-stimulus response modifications to different instructional materials.)

HOW FEASIBLE IS IT FOR THE CLASSROOM TEACHER TO CONDUCT A CHILD-BASED MATERIALS EVALUATION?

The process of assessing the merits of an instructional material based on child performance data is relatively simple and straightforward. It can be accomplished with minor modification in classroom routine and with minimal disruption to ongoing education and training activities. Gaining the materials for short trial periods should not be difficult. Many materials can be ordered directly from the publisher on a tryout basis. Materials may be obtained through local and regional materials centers, publisher representatives, and even other teachers. The teacher should request two to three weeks to allow

Self-Check 10-1

Sample Form 1. Annual Performance Profile

Student ____________

Specific objectives	Placement* N/A	A	I	Evaluation dates	Comments

I. The student will be functionally independent in toileting provided he is physically capable of being trained.

Specific objectives	N/A	A	I	Evaluation dates	Comments
A. Indicates needs		√			
Maintains dry/unsoiled clothing			√		
Eliminates in toilet when taken			√		
Goes to toilet by self		√			
B. Closes bathroom door		√			
C. Sits on toilet		√			
D. Wipes self		√			
E. Flushes toilet			√		
F. 1. Washes hands		√			
2. Dries hands		√			
G. Arranges clothes		√			
H. (M) Uses urinal			√		

II. The student will be functionally independent in cleaning and grooming himself in a manner which allows him to perform optimally.

Specific objectives	N/A	A	I	Evaluation dates	Comments
A. Controls drooling			√		
B. Adjusts water temperature		√			
C. 1. Washes hands		√			
2. Washes face		√			

***N/A: Not applicable. Because of age of student or limitations of facility. A: Assistance. Student requires physical, gestural or verbal assistance to complete a task. I: Independence. The student anticipates the task (or responds to an initial verbal command, when applicable) and completes the task without and verbal cues, gestural prompts, or physical guidance.**

Instructions

A hypothetical situation is described and a checklist from *Teaching the Moderately and Severely Handicapped*, by M. Bender and P. Valletutti (1977), is shown above. Use the CSR adaptation strategy and state how this checklist might be modified to improve the performance of your students. The checklist is for assessing a student's performance before and/or after toilet training. The list could also be used as a daily performance record by the trainer. The goal is for the student to perform all of the steps at the independent level. The teacher has been working with the student for a number of weeks, praising all corrects. No progress has been noted at a number of steps. How can the teacher modify the steps (and assessment scale) so the student's response level will improve from the assistance level to independence?

Response

____

Compare your response to the sample response in Appendix A.

Source: Reprinted from *Teaching the Moderately and Severely Handicapped: Curriculum Objectives, Strategies and Activities* by M. bender and P. J. Valletutti with permission of the publisher. Copyright 1977, by University Park Press.

for ample time to evaluate the material. Some publishers go further than others with regard to trying out materials. Although many publishers do not guarantee their programs in this fashion, most are willing to provide their materials for a period of examination and tryout.

Once instructional materials are ordered and analyzed according to the process described here, the teacher selects the participant learners, designates a time and place for the teaching to occur, and implements the program according to publisher specifications. This is a simple process. However, the question of the feasibility of conducting a child-based materials evaluation in any classroom is probably best addressed by describing the overall process of child-based evaluation. Let us consider a hypothetical situation. Mrs. T, a teacher in a self-contained classroom for mildly to moderately handicapped learners, aged 9 to 15, is attempting to choose a mathematics program. She is interested in purchasing a program that could be used with all her children, either as the core remedial program or in a supplementary manner. During the process of preparing and implementing a CBME, Mrs. T will go through a number of steps. This process is described below.

To gain familiarity with available programs, Mrs. T spends several days reviewing materials catalogues and asking the opinions of other teachers. She listens carefully to the suggestions of other teachers, but has enough experience to know what worked for them, in their classroom with their children, may or may not work for her. She will not buy based on their recommendations alone.

Step 1. After some investigation she selects two programs to evaluate. Before ordering the programs on a trial basis, she checks the central storage room and discovers one of the programs. After some scrutiny she realizes that the program does not contain all of the features advertised. Achievement checks are at the end of large units and do not directly test the content of the units. The curriculum is also heavily weighted for teaching advanced mathematical concepts. She sees that it may require an inordinate amount of preparation to modify the program. She eliminates this program and orders the second on a trial basis.

Step 2. When the second program arrives, she reviews and analyzes the materials using the Materials Review Form provided in Chapter 2. Mrs. T approves of its detailed yet comprehensive units. She inspects the mastery tests to determine their adequacy and relationship to the units tested. The tests seem appropriate to the assessment of the skills being presented and require minimal time to administer and score. Mrs. T decides to proceed with a child-based materials evaluation.

Step 3. Mrs. T notes that her purpose for conducting a child-based materials evaluation is simply to determine if the program will effectively teach her children the skills it purports to teach.

Step 4. Mrs. T selects a unit from the beginning, middle, and end of the curriculum sequence. She thinks this unit is representative of the total program and adequate for the purpose of her CBME.

Step 5. Mrs. T has already decided that the mastery tests provided for each unit will be adequate for progress monitoring. Pre-posttest measures are appropriate tests given her stated purpose.

Step 6. She selects three students to work on each unit, students that have not yet come close to mastering the different skills.

Step 7. Mrs. T usually instructs in small groups or has her students work independently. She knows that she can conduct a child-based materials evaluation without changing her daily schedule. Her overall classroom-management program also will not need to be altered to accommodate her child-based evaluation.

Step 8. Once Mrs. T has considered how her daily schedule will be affected, she works out specific schedules for her children based on the time she estimates will be required each day. She also estimates that her total CBME should not exceed two weeks. She makes tentative instructional plans for the children following that two-week period.

Step 9. Mrs. T is now ready to implement the child-based evaluation. She uses the program's mastery posttest as a pretest to assess entry-level behavior and eliminate any children who may already have the skills. She then implements the program in accordance with publisher specifications.

Step 10a. Immediately after completing each respective unit, a student is posttested. Mrs. T carefully reviews all the data on each child and calculates average performances. She also considers the time required on each unit. She notes that all students passed the mastery posttest.

Step 10b. Mrs. T will not need to implement the CSR adaptation since the materials worked with her children.

Step 11. Mrs. T decides to purchase the program.

IS EXPENDING PRECIOUS TEACHING TIME TO CONDUCT A CHILD-BASED MATERIALS EVALUATION JUSTIFIABLE AND WORTH THE EFFORT?

In the example of a child-based materials evaluation just provided, the teacher was able to conduct the evaluation in approximately two weeks. Her daily schedule and teaching formats were not affected in this situation. Selected children were placed in units that taught skills they had not learned and these skills were mastered. In short, the use of the child-based materials was beneficial to the teacher, the students, and the school. The teacher gained clear information on whether the materials were effective and was able to make the decision to buy based on objective information on child performance. The evaluation would also allow her to set realistic goals given that she could now estimate the time that would be required daily and the number of days likely to be needed to master the different units. The students had learned a skill that was appropriate to their needs in mathematics without having to participate in a lengthy testing process. Their involvement led to positive, observable learner achievement.

A lot of money and teacher time was also saved by not selecting the other program. More money would not be required to purchase a "better" program at a later date; also extensive adaptation was not needed. These savings were clearly beneficial to all. Given the realities of most classrooms, a child-based materials evaluation can be productive, yet require minimal teacher preparation in return for numerous positive outcomes. This overview of child-based materials evaluation has shown that such an approach to the selection of instructional materials is highly pragmatic, feasible, and justifiable in terms of teacher effort, child time, and the taxpayer's money. This is the sequence of Mrs. T's activities and those generally followed when conducting a child-based materials evaluation:

1. Select material(s).
2. Conduct materials review and analysis.
3. State purpose of the CBME.
4. Select sample.
5. Select (or prepare) child progress measurement system.
6. Select students.
7. Assess overall classroom program.
8. Schedule each student.
9. Implement CBME.
10a. Assess performance data.
10b. Assess CSR adaptations.
11. Implement or reject material.

Some of these activities may be done simultaneously or in an order differing from the sequence presented. The main point to remember when doing a CBME is that each task must be completed by the teacher. The CBME Teacher Checklist is designed to assist the teacher through the overall process of evaluation. An example of the checklist, filled out by Mrs. T, is provided in Figure 10-1. As you can see, Mrs. T simply dated when tasks were accomplished and made notes relevant to completing each step in the process. Mrs. T used the CBME Teacher Checklist as an organizer for her work, to remind her of things she still needed to do, and as a record of when objectives were reached.

At each step in the process of conducting a child-based materials evaluation, teachers will be making decisions. For instance, after completing the materials

CHILD-BASED MATERIALS EVALUATION TEACHER CHECKLIST

Name of Program Math Program 8 / Ms. T

Sequence of Tasks	Comments	Date Accomplished
1 Select Material Program	Call/talk w/Ms. Herman	
	& Stein (each likes program)	Sept. 12
	Say it's very well sequenced	
2 Conduct a Materials Analysis	make additional copies	
	of form	Sept. 14
3 State Purpose of CBME		to evaluate
		effectiveness with class, all
		learners Sept. 14
4 Select Sample to Test	units of similar length	Sept. 14 Choose beginning,
	and increase in	middle, end; simple
	complexity	addition, coin recognition;
5 Select (or prepare) Child Measurement System		story problems mastery checks
		provided Sept. 14
6 Select Students	Unit A - H. Growe G. Steele	Sept. 15
	Unit B - M. Steele M. Holly	Unit C - F. Ted C. Caroll
	A. Caruthers B. Sharp	L. Byrd
7 Assess Overall Classroom Program	Classroom can continue as arranged & Scheduled	Sept. 15
	- no new B. mod.	
	plans seem necessary	
8 (Re) Schedule Each Student	F. Ted will need to have P.E. during	Sept. 15
	a.m.	
9 Implement CBME	Begin on Monday Field trip	Sept. 19
	on Friday - children	
	seem to like materials	
10a Assess Performance Data	all pass with	Oct. 1
	above 90% correct	
10b Assess CSR Adaptations	(Send reports home) →	Oct. 2
	No adaptations	Oct. 1
	necessary	
11 Implement or Reject Materials	Implement on Thursday -	Oct. 4
	pretesting, have Cindi	
	keep score	

Figure 10-1. Child-Based Materials Evaluation Teacher Checklist

analysis (Step 2), teachers must decide whether to stop or proceed with the evaluation. To make many decisions, teachers may be required to gain more detailed information on the material than is readily available. For example, the decision to implement an instructional material with a limited number of learners in the publisher-specified manner may require the teacher to construct his or her own mastery tests or daily probes. Later, to decide whether a material is adequate for the learners in their classroom, teachers will need a way to summarize and interpret child performance data. Still later, teachers may need further information on the adaptation process. A number of forms and guidelines to assist teachers at these and other tasks they may encounter during a CBME are provided in Appendex B (see Figures 10-1, 10-2, 10-3) and discussed later in this chapter.

The following sections of this chapter are aimed at helping the teacher resolve particular questions that may arise during the evaluation process. Each task in the evaluation process is reviewed and related issues discussed. The sequence of tasks presented is the same as that outlined earlier; however, more detailed discussion and examples are provided for a number of the tasks. Two additional self-check activities are provided to allow the reader an opportunity to apply the skills and information presented in this chapter.

CRITICAL DECISION POINTS IN A CHILD-BASED MATERIALS EVALUATION

At several points during your child-based materials evaluation you must make a decision to terminate or continue with the evaluation. The main points at which decisions must be made are: *Decision A*—during the preliminary preparation or selection phase; *Decision B*—when a limited number of materials are first chosen; *Decision C*—following the initial materials review; *Decision D*—before pretesting; *Decision E*—after posttesting the children; and *Decision F*—after each step in the CSR adaptation strategy (in those cases where it has been used).

Consider each of these phases and decision points briefly. First, during the preliminary assessment phase, the teacher is trying to acquaint herself as thoroughly as possible with all available materials. All resources are tapped. It is here that the teacher relies on her own experience and judgment, the opinions of other professionals, and published descriptions and evaluation of the material. Most teachers have little trouble eliminating materials. Next, the teacher orders or borrows one to three of the materials that seem most appropriate. At this time a Child-Based Materials-Evaluation Teacher Checklist (Figure 10-1) is begun for each material.

Once the materials are selected (Step 1 of the Checklist), the teacher will be ready to fill out a Materials Review Form (see Chapter 2). If the Materials Review Form does not provide strong evidence to suggest that the material is appropriate to the needs of the students, and has a high probability of benefiting the students, the teacher should proceed no further. The material is returned to the publisher and evaluation of another material continued. If no other options appear to be available, the teacher may need to develop his or her own material. Designing and developing effective instructional materials is a complex, lengthy process and probably should not be undertaken unless the teacher has thoroughly investigated all possible alternatives.

Having ascertained that a material is appropriate to the teacher's needs (before pretesting), careful consideration must be given to the specific purpose of each evaluation. The teacher must precisely identify the purpose of the CBME. This will save much time in the long run. If the material appears to be well sequenced, has been field tested on similar students, and teaches skills that are easily tested, the teacher has good reason to believe the materials will teach the skills purported. In such a circumstance the teacher's purpose will be to determine if the materials work with his or her students and a pre-posttest measure of child performance will suffice. Special students often do not make adequate progress in many marketed programs. Therefore, the teacher may feel that even though a material is basically well-designed and appropriate, it may not work well for handicapped learners. In this case the teacher anticipates that some modification will be necessary. He or she will need to discover exactly how to adapt a material to make it work best. In such instances daily monitoring of child performance will be required.

During the time when the materials are being tried out in the classroom and immediately following the posttest, the teacher will need to decide whether the materials (1) are effective and/or (2) need adaptation. To make an evaluation meaningful, the teacher must carefully assess individual child performance data as well as average performances. The Student Performance Summary Sheet (Figure 10-2) will help organize and interpret data on child performance. This sample Student Performance Summary Sheet contains information that Mrs. T might have collected on her children. Mrs. T monitored child performance using a posttest measure. However, this summary sheet may also be used for daily performance data.

It can be seen on Mrs. T's summary sheet that all students passed their mastery posttests (range = 92 = 100 percent correct with an overall average of 96.3 percent correct). Mrs. T recognizes that this is a significant gain considering the pretest performance of her students. She notes that it required three, eight, and six days for her three students to complete the sample addition facts unit; five, nine, and nine days to complete coin recognition; and four, three, and five days to master the story problem unit. The average number of days for her students to finish all three units was six.

Student Performance Summary Sheet

Program Math (B) Publisher ______ Date Initiated Sept. 12 Completed OCT. 4
Teacher Mrs. T Teaching Format Independent Seatwork

UNIT SAMPLED	CHILD NAME	LENGTH		SCORE			AVERAGE
		Aver. Session	Days to Complete	Pretest	Intervention	Posttest	
1 Simple Addition A	H. Growe	15 min.	3	20%	—	92%	Session & Days 14 min 6
	G. Steele	12 min.	6	32%	—	98%	Intervention NA
	M. Still	14 min.	8	8%	—	95%	Posttest 95%
2 Coin Recognition	M. Holly	13 min.	5	15%	—	100%	Session & Days 13 min 8
	A. Caruthers	13 min.	9	42%	—	92%	Intervention NA
	B. Sharp	12 min.	9	30%	—	95%	Posttest 96%
3 Story problems {4 basic Functions}	F. Ted	10 min.	4	25%	—	95%	Session & Days 11 min 4
	C. Caroll	13 min.	3	30%	—	100%	Intervention NA
	L. Byrd	10 min.	5	32%	—	98%	Posttest 98%
4 —							Session & Days ______
							Intervention ______
							Posttest ______
5 —							Session & Days ______
							Intervention ______
							Posttest ______
TOTALS		112	52				
OVERALL AVERAGE		12½ min	6 days	28.2%		96.3%	

Please Check:

Program Works ✓ Program Does Not Work ______ Use ✓ Do Not Use ______

Revise ______ Do Not Revise ______

Comments: 12 units × 6 = 72/5 = approx. 15 weeks of teaching in materials done daily.

Figure 10-2. *Student Performance Summary Sheet*

It can also be seen that each student required less than 15 minutes of interaction with the materials each day. Based on these data, Mrs. T predicts that this material will teach the skills claimed. She knows most of her students will require training on at least 12 units in this program. Since the students participating in the CBME required about 6 days per unit, Mrs. T estimates roughly that 15 weeks of instruction will be needed to teach 12 skill units (12 units × 6 days = approximately 15 weeks).

As noted, Mrs. T used the Student Performance Summary Sheet with pre-posttest data, but it may also be used with data that is collected each day. In that case you would enter average performances during the baseline and the trend or direction of the child's scores under "Pretest." For instance, if a child was being assessed on her sight word vocabulary and her scores were 6, 4, and 3 correct responses out of 30 possible, her "pretest" average would be 4.3 correct with "declining" written under the number (See Figure 10-3). Similarly, average scores and trends would be noted for "intervention" and "posttest." You can also see in Figure 10-3 that the word *frequency* has been entered across the section for scores. This indicates that the kind of data collected was number correct. Mrs. T used percent correct. Rate and duration measures could also be used, depending on the behaviors being taught and tested. Finally, after completing a summary sheet, the teacher would go to his or her materials inventory and compare the program being evaluated with other programs that were reviewed (see Chapter 2). By reviewing the materials inventory, the teacher may find other materials that will complement or supplement the material being evaluated. If so, the teacher may want to use both materials in his or her classroom.

If the data on daily child performance shows that the students' performance has leveled off below mastery criterion, is declining, or is increasing at a very slow rate, it may be necessary to modify the material. The CSR adaptation strategy should then be applied to provide a systematic, effective way of changing an instructional material. As a rule, the teacher should note a significant improvement within three to five days after an adaptation. If an improvement is not observed, it is time to change the next component of the CSR adaptation strategy. If improvement is still not forthcoming after the consequence, stimulus, and child response have been modified, teachers may conclude that the materials are not appropriate for their students or that they will require adaptations extending beyond the responsibilities and skills of most teachers. It is likely that modifications required to make a material work at this point would not be reasonable in terms of the efficient use of teacher time. Generally, a decision to reject the material should be made.

On the other hand, if a modification in an instructional material leads to substantial improvement in the student participants, it may be concluded that the change will be adequate to gain learning in the majority of students. If a mod-

	SCORE			
	Pretest	Inter-vention	Posttest	
	Frequency →			
	av. = 5/30 dropping	av. = 25/30 increasing	av. = 28/30 stable	

Figure 10-3. *Modification of the Scoring Section of the Summary Sheet*

ification in an instructional material leads to variable student performance levels, the teacher will need to assess carefully the conditions under which the students participated in the CBME. If the conditions are similar in all respects, the teacher should assess the children. He or she should review the baseline data for differences among the children and make anecdotal records of how the children differ in their skill repertoires and learning styles. Next, the teacher should try to identify which students will benefit maximally from the material and implement the program with those children rather than the entire group of learners.

As we have seen, child-based materials evaluation consists of 11 tasks or steps that must be completed by the teacher. At several points during the process of conducting a child-based materials evaluation, the teacher is required to make some critical decisions. The six major decision points, referred to as Decisions A-F, were described in the previous section. In addition to being thoroughly familiar with the overall child-based materials-evaluation process and knowing when and how to make decisions during that process, the teacher must also know how to prepare special materials, data-collection forms, and tests to assess student performance. The major supplementary materials that a teacher must prepare are discussed in the next portion of this text. Examples of various ways that teachers can accomplish these tasks most efficiently are presented.

Self-Check 10-2 provides a review of major issues related to the process of conducting a CBME. Read the hypothetical situation described and answer the questions below.

MATERIALS TEACHERS MAY NEED TO PREPARE FOR IMPLEMENTING A CBME

Two materials that teachers are often required to prepare when conducting a child-based materials evaluation are test or probe materials and forms for collecting and summarizing data. In addition, graphs for visually representing data are very important. Surprisingly, each preparation that may be required should take little time or effort for most teachers. Furthermore, many of the procedures, materials, and forms that have been prepared for other child-based materials evaluations or accompany the instructional material can be used with minor modification. Once graphs, summary sheets, and tests have been prepared and are judged to be adequate to meet the needs of the students, these materials can be used continuously throughout the course of later instruction.

Pre-Posttest Measures and Daily Probes

Some instructional materials may not have pre-posttest measures or procedures for monitoring daily child progress. Other materials may have performance measures, but these tests may not adequately assess the skills being taught. In either case it will be necessary for the teacher to construct a test or probe procedure that validly assesses child performance. Teachers must remember that they will most likely want a measurement system that *directly* assesses the concept or skill being taught. Test or probe construction will be relatively simple and require minimal effort on the part of teachers. For example, programs that do not have a system for monitoring child performance often have other materials that can be modified for testing. Many teachers have been highly successful adapting work sheets. By adding relevant problems or items and deleting irrelevant or misleading items, work sheets can be modified to assess child mastery successfully. Modified work sheets may be used as pre-posttest measures or during daily monitoring. If probes, or tests of child performance, are taken on a daily basis, it is important to keep the total time that the child is tested limited to a few minutes. It is also important to have a number of work sheets or probe items so the child does not simply memorize answers to the items being presented. For materials that do not have work sheets or other components that lend themselves to modification for testing purposes, simple flash-card procedures often suffice. Flash cards are an attractive alternative to testing child skills in that they allow for interaction between the teacher and the student. This gives the teacher opportunity to relate on a one-to-one basis with the student and to observe his or her progress first hand. Flash cards and work sheet monitoring tactics can often be supervised by an older student or any student specifically assigned that role. The tally sheet shown in Figure 10-4 is taken from Chapter 6. It shows modifications that have been made to create a test. Clearly, it contains enough items to sample the skill adequately, but not so many as to require a greal deal of time to complete.

For collecting daily data it is recommended that the teacher use a form similar to the Daily/Weekly Tally Sheet (Stowitschek, 1976), which allows for collection of various kinds of data across many different skills. You can modify this sheet to accommodate your particular situation in numerous ways. The Daily/Weekly Tally Sheet has a section for recording the response on each item and a section for summarizing student data on a daily or weekly basis. Figures 10-4, 10-5, and 10-6 present sample Daily/Weekly Tally Sheets that have been used to collect data on a number of different child behaviors.

Figure 10-4 shows how a teacher might collect information on the correct and incorrect responses of a child being tested on simple addition facts. The student's performance is summarized each day in total frequency correct and this in turn is converted to percent correct.

Figure 10-5 illustrates how a teacher might collect daily data on hand washing, a skill that has been task analyzed. Not only may child behavior be recorded in terms of the number of corrects and errors, but the level of assistance required from the teacher before the child performed each step is also entered. On Day 1 Bonnie erred on all but 1 step (Step 14). On 13 steps she required physical assistance, on 2 steps she needed a demonstration, and on 1 step she performed with verbal assistance only. The adaptation of the Daily/Weekly Tally Sheet in this case extended the utility of the sheet considerably without making it complicated. At the bottom of the form, the frequency and percent-

Self-Check 10-2

Instructions

Read the following hypothetical situation and answer the following questions.

Mr. B, an experienced teacher of exceptional children, has a self-contained classroom with nine moderately mentally retarded adolescents. All of his students need to acquire basic self-help skills such as brushing their teeth, selecting appropriate clothing, and eating in an acceptable manner. Ms. S, a newly graduated special education teacher, recommended to Mr. B that he use Project MORE Daily-Living Skills programs to teach his students. He takes her advice and orders the programs. Mr. B, however, understands the value of conducting a CBME and has ordered the programs on a trial basis. Soon 14 programs arrive and Mr. B looks them over one afternoon and begins pretesting all of his students the next day. Mr. B considers this pretesting to be the first phase of his CBME.

(For the readers' information, each daily-living skill program is presented in an individual manual with precise directions for teaching one self-help skill at a time in a one-to-one teaching situation. The publisher claims these programs have been field tested and will work if the teaching procedure is implemented correctly. Each program can be used independently of the others, includes a pre-posttest procedure, a daily monitoring system, and a specific description of the teaching strategy.)

Response

Place a check mark by the correct answer to each of the following questions—only one answer per question.

1. Mr. B made the correct decision when he ordered the Project MORE programs.

   _____ No, he should have at least looked for other possible programs.

   _____ Yes, he was an experienced teacher and knew there was nothing else available. Furthermore, the teacher that recommended the programs had just graduated from a very good college and had the latest information.

2. Mr. B made the correct decision when he began pretesting all the students.

   _____ No, he had not conducted a materials analysis, determined his precise purpose, or identified a sample of his students for the child-based materials evaluation.

   _____ Yes, he wanted to identify students who did not have the skill so it was appropriate to begin pretesting all of them. It would require a lot of time, but then he would know exactly which skills his students had.

3. If Mr. B was going to do a CBME, who should have participated?

   _____ All students who failed some of the 14 program pretests.

   _____ Several students who failed selected pretests.

   _____ One student who failed all of the pretests.

4. How many Daily-Living Skills programs should be tried?

   _____ All 14

   _____ Several

   _____ Only 1

5. If Mr. B were only interested in whether the programs worked with his students, what student measurement tactic should he use?

   _____ Continuous daily monitoring

   _____ Pre-posttest

   _____ Anecdotal records

Compare your response to the sample response in Appendix A.

DAILY/WEEKLY TALLY SHEET

Student Demetrius, A.

Task Addition, Math Facts

Item		3/21/78 cor.	3/21/78 inc.	3/22/78 cor.	3/22/78 inc.	3/23/78 cor.	3/23/78 inc.	3/24/78 cor.	3/24/78 inc.	cor.	inc.	item mastered	error type
Time (min.)													
1	4+2	✓		✓				✓					
2	3+1	✓		✓									
3	2+2	✓		✓									
4	0+3	✓		✓									
5	1+4	✓		✓									
6	5+0	✓		✓									
7	4+3	✓		✓									
8	5+4	✓		✓									
9	4+4	✓		✓									
10	3+2	✓		✓									
11	2+4		✓	✓				✓					
12	1+3	✓		✓				✓					
13	0+4	✓		✓				✓					
14	4+1	✓		✓				✓					
15	3+3	✓		✓				✓					
16	5+1	✓		✓					✓				
17	7+3	✓		✓				✓					
18	9+0	✓		✓				✓					
19	2+5	✓		✓				✓					
20	4+5	✓		✓				✓					
21	6+3	✓		✓					✓				
22	10+0	✓			✓			✓					
23	8+1	✓		✓				✓					
24	6+4		✓	✓				✓					
25	4+0	✓		✓				✓					
26	2+9	✓			✓			✓					
27	0+7	✓		✓				✓					
28	1+7	✓		✓				✓					
29	3+4	✓		✓				✓					
30	5+3	✓		✓				✓					
Total		28	2	28	2			28	2				
Percent		93		93				93					
Rate													

Percent Finder on reverse side of page.
Rate Finder on reverse side of page.

Figure 10-4. *Performance on Math Flash Cards Summarized for Evaluation Purposes*

Source: Reprinted from *Daily/Weekly Tally Sheets* by Joseph J. Stowitschek by permission of the author. Copyright 1976 by Joseph J. Stowitschek.

DAILY/WEEKLY TALLY SHEET

Student *Bonnie*

C = Demonstration

Task *washing hands*

Item	9/1 cor.	9/1 inc.	9/2 cor.	9/2 inc.	9/2 cor.	9/2 inc.	9/3 cor.	9/3 inc.	cor.	inc.	item mastered	error type
Time (min.)	8		7		4		5					
1 Grasp cold water faucet		D		D		C		A				
2 Turn on faucet		D		C		C		B				
3 Let go of faucet		D		D		D		B				
4 Wet hands		D	A		A		A					
5 Grasp soap		C		B	A		A					
6 Rub soap w/both hands		D		D		D		B				
7 Place soap on tray		D		D		C		D				
8 Rub front of hands		D		D		B	A					
9 Rub back of hands		D		D		D		B				
10 Rinse soap off		D		D		D		B				
11 Grasp cold water faucet		D		C		B		B				
12 Turn off faucet		D		C	A			B				
13 Let go of faucet		D		D		D		B				
14 Grasp towel (paper)	A			B	A		A					
15 Rub towel between hands		B		B		B		B				
16 Rub towel on back of hands		D		C		B		B				
17 Drop towel in wastebasket		C	A		A		A					
18												
19												
20												
21												
22												
23												
24												
25												
26												
27												
28												
29												
30												
Total	1	16	2	15	5	12	6	11				
Percent	6		12		29		35					
Rate	.1	2	.3	2.1	1.2	3	1.2	2.2				

Percent Finder on reverse side of page.
Rate Finder on reverse side of page.

Figure 10-5. *Evaluation of a Child's Progress Through a Hand-Washing Instruction Program*

Source: Reprinted from *Daily/Weekly Tally Sheets* by Joseph J. Stowitschek by permission of the author. Copyright 1976 by Joseph J. Stowitschek.

DAILY/WEEKLY TALLY SHEET

Student ________________

Task sight words

	Item	4/5	4/6	4/11	4/12	4/13	4/17	4/18	4/19	4/20	4/20	4/24	4/25	
	Time (min.)	1	1	1	1	1	1	1	1	1	1	item mastered	error type	
1	did		X			X	X	X		X		X		✓
2	new	X			X		X		X		X	X		X
3	no	X			X			✓	✓		✓	X		
4	now	X			X		X	X		X			X	X
5	our	✓			X		X		X		✓			X
6	pretty		X			X	X		X		X	X	X	
7	ride		✓			✓	✓		✓		✓		✓	✓
8	under		X			X		X		X		X		X
9	want		X			X	X	X		X			X	
10	well	X			✓		✓	✓		✓		✓		✓
11	went		X			X		X		X	✓		X	X
12	what		X			X			✓				X	✓
13	white	X			X		X			X	X		X	
14	again	X			X		X	X	X		X	X		
15	any		X			X	X	X	X		✓	X		X
16	could	X			X		X		X					X
17	every	X			X			X		X			X	X
18	give	X			X		X		✓		✓	✓		
19	her		X			✓	✓			✓			✓	✓
20	his		X			✓	✓	✓		✓		✓		✓
21	know	X			X		X	X	X		X		X	X
22	let		X			X	X	X		X			X	X
23	live		X			X		X		X			X	
24	once	X			X		X	X		X		X		
25	open		X			X	X	X	X		X		✓	✓
26	round	X			X				X		X	✓		
27	some	✓			X				✓		✓		✓	✓
28	take		X			X		X		X		X		X
29	thank	X			X			X		X		X		X
30	walk		X			X	X			X			✓	O
	Total													
	Correct	2	2		1	3	4	4	5	4	8	7	8	11
	Percent	8%	8%		5%	14%	17%	17%	23%	15%	35%		29%	40%
	Rate	2/M	2/M		1/M	3/M	4/MM	4/MM	5/M	4/M	8/M	7/M	6/M	11/M

Percent Finder on reverse side of page.
Rate Finder on reverse side of page.

Figure 10-6. *Summary of a Child's Progress in an Oral Reading Portion of a Program*

Source: Reprinted from *Daily/Weekly Tally Sheets* by Joseph J. Stowitschek by permission of the author.

Self-Check 10-3

OPEN ENDED

Instructions

Consider this hypothetical situation.

You are a teacher in a self-contained classroom for nine children, aged 8-11, with mild learning disabilities. You need to purchase a program to teach coin recognition and functional use of money. Go to a curriculum laboratory, materials center, or other resource and select an instructional material to teach coin recognition and functional use of money. Then, given the steps below, conduct a child-based materials evaluation to determine if the material you are reviewing will lead to the acquisition of coin-recognition skills and teach functional use of money to your students.

1. Select materials.
2. Complete a Materials Review Form.
3. State your purpose.
4. Select samples.
5. Select (or prepare) a child progress monitoring system.
6. Select students.
7. Assess overall classroom program (that of the teacher whose class you are conducting this CBME in).
8. Schedule each student.
9. Implement a CBME.
10. Assess performance data.
11. Accept or reject materials.

No sample response is provided.

age of correct responses were tallied daily. In addition, the rate of responding was also calculated. Rate data allow for finer analysis, analysis of performance trends, and better day-by-day comparison of student progress. The advantages of rate data are presented in Chapter 6.

Figure 10-6 presents daily data on Chris's labelling of sight words. Thirty sight words were tested daily with correct and incorrect words noted individually. Thus words causing difficulty were identified. Summaries of the data include percent and rate correct and incorrect.

CONCLUSION

Child-based materials evaluation is a process that has great potential for determining how successful an instructional material is likely to be with any group of handicapped individuals. It is a process that may be implemented in the classroom with little disruption or additional work and yields numerous positive outcomes in terms of money saved, child learning, and conservation of teacher time and effort. (Self-Check 10-3 follows. Please complete it before proceeding to Chapter 11.)

CHAPTER 11

Specialized Applications of Materials Management and Adaptation

Objectives

1. Identify some of the "extraordinary" instructional needs children with severe handicapping conditions may have that affect instructional materials management and adaptation.
- What is the most general instructional goal for severely handicapped persons? For other distinct populations?
- Why is continuous data collection so critical when using materials with severely impaired children?
- How might a classroom be organized to accommodate teaching daily living skills?

2. State why special populations of students generally require nontraditional instructional materials.
- What is meant by a nontraditional instructional material?
- Why are materials for severely handicapped students often teacher directed?
- Give an example of an overall system of collecting child performance data on nontraditional instructional materials.

3. State two ways an instructional material might be adapted to facilitate training prerequisite skills.
- What are two of the most common prerequisite behaviors needed for severely handicapped persons to benefit from training?
- What are some common adaptations made in instructional materials to be directed towards preschoolers? Adolescents?
- What is meant by fading instructional cues?
- Why are instructional materials that rely on chaining procedures likely to be effective with young children?
- How can task analysis and physical guidance be combined to promote motor-skill development?

Previous chapters have addressed a variety of issues pertaining to the use of instructional materials with special learners. To this point, discussion of topics related to selection, management, and adaptation of instructional materials has not centered on categories of exceptionality. Diagnostic labels have not served as a pivotal point for examining instructional materials for reasons previously stated (see Chapter 1). The primary reason a cross-categorical approach has been advocated throughout this text is that diagnostic labels seldom differentiate one exceptional learner from another (Hallahan & Kaufman, 1978). Diagnostic labels such as learning disabled or mentally retarded do little to aid a teacher trying to find instructional materials to match the learning needs of his or her students. Nonetheless, it would be foolhardy to ignore common characteristics that children with certain handicapping conditions often display. By this time it should be clear that all decisions regarding instructional-materials selection, management, and adaptation must be made in light of the students to be served. Consequently, it would also seem reasonable that children with similar yet distinct learning needs could be grouped together and special management and adaptation procedures designed.

Children with sensory deficits provide a good illustration of how a group of students with similar learning characteristics may benefit from and often require materials that have been adapted to meet their unique needs. Regardless of the nature or degree of their sensory impairment(s), these children usually will not profit sufficiently from instructional materials presented in a conventional manner. As a rule most instructional materials will have to be modified, particularly with regard to the mode of presentation. (Special training is not necessary for anyone, teacher or lay person, to understand that a child with a severe visual or hearing impairment will need to have instructions, for example, presented through the functional sensory channel(s).)

Modifications in instructional materials must allow for learning to occur through the most intact channel(s) and for development of any residual capacities in the deficit channel(s). With special populations, materials modifications often not only include the mode of presenting stimulus items, but the child's response mode as well. In short, at the onset of instruction, the interaction between child and material may have to be altered in several ways for learning to occur. Moreover, basic alterations are likely to be needed for entire populations exhibiting certain characteristics, in this case sensory impairments, to benefit maximally from instruction.

In addition to children with sensory deficits, other groups of exceptional learners exhibit common characteristics or common learning needs. Thus in some instances it is advantageous for instructional-materials considerations to be viewed in light of groups of students with special needs. Consideration of special learner needs is particularly relevant with regard to instructional-materials *management* and *adaptation* issues. The purpose of this chapter is to discuss factors related to special applications of instructional-materials management and adaptation that were not covered earlier. To attempt an exhaustive review of special topics related to materials management and adaptation is not within the scope of this chapter. Our intent is to demonstrate through illustration and discussion how teachers can plan to account for three major factors—special handicapping conditions, special curriculum content areas, and age—and thereby set up effective, relevant learning environments. These illustrations relate special issues and procedures that fit specific categories of exceptionality, age levels, and content areas; however, the points discussed are generalizable to situations other than the examples presented herein.

To help the reader conceptualize how students may be grouped and special management and adaptation considerations examined, you are asked to visualize a three-dimensional matrix. Along the left side of the matrix the label "Handicapping Conditions" is printed. Along the top of the matrix "Curriculum Content Areas" is noted, and along the third dimension "Age" is written. Each of the sides is divided into sections with "Handicapping Conditions" consisting of learning-behavior disorders, mild to moderate mental retardation, sensory impairments, physical disabilities, severe and profound mental retardation, and multiple handicaps. The section for special "Curriculum Content Areas" is comprised of preacademic skills, academics, gross and fine motor skills, language, social skills, daily-living skills, and vocational skills. Special "Age" groups include infants, preschoolers, school-aged children, adolescents, and adults. In all, the matrix is comprised of six categories of handicapping conditions, seven categories of curriculum content areas, and five age groupings. It is conceivable that a teacher may have students falling into a cell in this matrix that represents any combination of the three major areas. In reality, teachers will be required to adjust their instructional-materials management plans and adapt materials to meet learner needs represented by many of these cells.

LEARNER CHARACTERISTICS: INSTRUCTIONAL GOALS

Teachers faced with the challenge of creating meaningful and effective learning environments for students with special needs, needs that cannot be met by direct application of instructional materials in the intended or conventional manner, must take into account the "extraordinary" needs of their students. First, the ultimate goal of instruction for all special populations—severely mentally retarded, autistic, severely visually or hearing impaired, and multiple handicapped—is basically the same. That is, the main educational goal is to bring these students rapidly to as high a level of functioning as we can. Often this goal is related to special, nontraditional curricular areas. Rather than targeting reading comprehension or division computations, the goal of instruction may be to expand basic, daily-living skills, develop simple expressive language repertoires (perhaps using nonoral language systems), and build acceptable social behaviors. In short, these students lack behaviors that are appropriate *and* functional in their everyday and future environments. Second, to reach this ultimate goal, teachers will need to employ instructional materials that not only facilitate the *acquisition* of needed skills but subsequently promote *maintenance, generalization,* and *application* of the skills (Haring & Pious, 1976).

Haring and Bricker (1976) suggested that instructional materials for severely limited populations will need to meet several criteria to be effective. Three of the criteria they list are especially critical. These criteria include the need for: (1) very systematic sequencing of the instructional material, beginning with the most primitive skills and followed by controlled introduction and training of more and more advanced skills, (2) a *direct* and concisely stated linkage between the instructional material and objective measures of student progress, and (3) precise behavioral descriptions of the *objectives, procedures,* and *criterion performance* levels. For these special populations, the need for a close tie between curriculum content and direct, continuous measurement is much greater than that ordinarily needed with mildly to moderately handicapped students. (Inferential and intermittent assessment of child progress may be adequate and preferred with children exhibiting much greater skill repertoires.)

Teachers working with more severely handicapped populations—children with sensory impairments or other distinct instructional needs—must have skill applying specific knowledge of behavioral principles in an adaptive, flexible manner on a daily basis. Materials and methods must be more intricately and precisely correlated than in other teaching circumstances. As Haring and Bricker (1976) have stated with regard to teaching severely handicapped persons, "Curriculum materials, no matter how excellent, cannot completely counter the effects of poor presentation by instructors who do not use behavioral principles" (p. 27). Consequently, in their effort to manage and adapt materials, teachers will need to (a) very carefully evaluate primary curricular goals for each student to ascertain their relevance and functionality, (b) critically assess each instructional material and the teaching and evaluation methods that will accompany them, and (c) objectively conduct a self-evaluation of their own level of competence, applying behavior principles and assessing student performance data. Brown (1975), Siegel (1972) and many others have discussed the variety of skills teachers must possess to simply implement much less adapt materials so effective teaching will occur. Teacher training and competence are factors that cannot be overlooked when discussing successful adaptations for special populations.

As mentioned, the first consideration when preparing to teach distinct populations such as the severely handicapped or very young children is the goal of instruction. For most special students, goals will be quite utilitarian. The materials and methods used should lead directly to functional skill development (LeBlanc, Etzel, & Domash, 1978), all others should be given a low priority status.

Once goals have been established relevant behavioral objectives are defined. During the process of writing behavioral objectives teachers will need to (a) identify instructional materials to meet nontraditional objectives and (b) organize the classroom (or other teaching areas) to accommodate management of materials and delivery of instruction.

Nontraditional Instructional Materials

Since the skills to be taught may include sign reading, toilet training, personal hygiene, household management, leisure-time skills, and vocational skills, the instructional materials used to teach these skills may often be nontraditional. *Nontraditional materials* are materials used directly to teach skills that may not be within the range of conventional educational objectives. Nontraditional materials often consist of materials that are used in the absence of available published materials. Instructional materials with full scope and sequence skill programming for severely handicapped students have not been developed for many of the same reasons materials were not developed for the mildly-to-moderately handicapped in the past. Until recently it was believed that these children were educationally untrainable and would not benefit from instruction. More recently the high cost of designing and testing finely programmed materials for relatively low-incidence populations has hampered materials development. Such activity simply has not been viewed as economically feasible. LeBlanc, Etzel, and Domash (1978)refer to *alternative* teaching materials that might be used to guide young children to functional competence in their environment and even towards creative responding. Alternative materials might include shoes and lacing boards for preschoolers (or older students), if the instructional goal is for the student to learn to tie his or her shoes independently.

A feature of most published instructional materials for special populations such as the multiple handicapped or language-delayed preschooler is that these materials are often directed to and used primarily by the agent delivering instruction, for example, the teacher, parent, or paraprofessional. Thus rather than the traditional teacher's guide and accompanying materials with which students are intended to interact, many instructional materials guide adult instructors through a series of sequenced activities. As with other instructional material, the teacher must be careful to determine whether the sequence of activities and teaching strategies have been field tested. Without information on field testing the teacher will be unable to predict whether using the materials in the suggested fashion will lead to acquisition and maintenance of the desired skills.

Instructional materials are presented in this nontraditional teacher-directed form for several reasons. The primary reason the instructor or trainer interacts with the published material and not the child relates to the fact that materials, method, and measurement must be closely aligned for maximal learning to occur. Every effort is made to ensure correct procedural implementation of specified learning activities. Much detail is directed to the manner in which teaching should be conducted, data collected, and progress assessed. Thus instructional materials often resemble teacher's manuals or textbooks (e.g., *Language Acquisition Program for the Severely Retarded*, Kent, 1974). Further instructional goals within these materials focus on developing functional skills. Use of common materials and interaction with persons encountered in the students' everyday lives is desired. Acquisition of functional, productive, environmental interaction is promoted by including real materials and persons from the student's current and future environments. In addition, by using common materials and different people during training, generalization of functional skills is actually being promoted during the initial stages of learning. Another important factor is that teaching toward nontraditional goals often requires one-to-one instruction with the instructor providing physical guidance or full demonstrations. It would be extremely difficult to provide such interventions through programmed materials alone. Consequently, the trainer is instructed how to provide needed antecedent cues and subsequent corrective measures that specifically and immediately relate to each child response. Not only is this efficient teaching, the cost of developing materials for trainer use is less prohibitive than those for child use.

Sample Daily-Living Skills Materials.

Project MORE's (Lent & McLean, 1976) *Daily Living Skills Curriculum* is a series of individual skill-training packages. It represents an example of a trainer-directed instructional material and includes standard features of such instructional materials. Each package provides the teacher or paraprofessional with a specific strategy for giving instructions, arranging and presenting all materials, and administering corrective procedures. Specific motivational techniques as well as a system for keeping records of daily performance and assessing student progress by graphic display are also delineated.

Baker and Heifetz (1976) similarly developed a series of instructional materials in manual format. These materials likewise focus on nontraditional curricular content areas. The manuals are designed to be used by teachers or parents and lead them through the process of developing retarded children's self-help and toileting skills, speech and language skills, and general behavior and play skills. *Steps to Independence,* instructional materials based on Baker and Heifetz's original work, is now commercially available. It focuses on training self-help and toileting skills and may be used with young children, adolescents, and even adults.

Sample Language-Development Materials

Horstmeir, MacDonald, and Gillette (1975) developed instructional materials in a format similar to the above-mentioned materials. Their materials are also designed to be used by parents and professionals. One package, *READY, SET, GO—Talk to Me!* is intended to teach prelanguage skills and initial verbal communication. In the preface the authors stated that the purpose of this program is to help the child deal with his world—a simple, utilitarian goal. The means by which this is to be achieved is by structuring his "natural environment" so training includes common materials and the most important people in the child's life as teachers. Again, the user of the published instructional material is an adult, not the target learner. Further, the content of this program is different from earlier language-training programs. *READY, SET, GO—Talk to Me!* emphasizes the *semantics* (meaning) of language and it's social nature rather than the development of syntax. As in the other instructional materials directed to the trainer, it includes general and specific instructions regarding implementation of the training procedures and assessment system. In addition, much of this prescriptive manual is diagnostic. A large portion of the manual is directed toward assessment of prerequisite skills and gives suggestions for their development. Prerequisites include skills such as attending to people and tasks, functional play with objects, and the ability to imitate motor movements. Receptive language is also assessed (as in more traditional language-training programs and tests) along with the child's ability to imitate sounds, single words, and word combinations. A unique and impressive component of this program, which was developed in the early 1970s, is its emphasis on generalized use of each skill the child has acquired to his or her everyday setting. The instructional manual also includes provisions for monitoring and training generalized skill usage, a vital program element that is often omitted or only tangentially referred to in many instructional materials.

CLASSROOM ORGANIZATION AND MANAGEMENT OF NONTRADITIONAL MATERIALS

Ecological or physical arrangement of the learning environment may contribute to or distract from successful use of instructional materials. Factors such as the presence or absence of teachers, scheduling of activities, display and accessibility of materials, variety and durability of materials, arrangement of furniture, number of centers, availability of individual and group space, lighting, and noise levels must be taken into account in any learning environment. However, these factors take on additional relevance when the educational goals and instructional materials are nontraditional. Arrangement of the physical space and general ecology have broader significance in such circumstances since modification of the classroom is often preliminary to student attainment of nontraditional instructional objectives. Modification of the classroom for delivery of instruction and skill practice beyond classroom walls is almost always perfunctory for the child to develop functional skill usage in applied contexts.

Engineering classrooms to accommodate nontraditional materials and instruction—materials such as cooking utensils, dishpan and sink, housekeeping equipment, and painting and carpentry tools—will eventually lead to the existence of varied model classrooms. As research becomes more directed toward the ecological aspects of learning, it is likely that what is now considered nontraditional will become standard classroom equipment, instructional materials, and arrangements of space and time. Scheduling of teaching activities and materials usage in the classroom is also a critical variable affecting skill transfer. Schedules should allow the way given skills are taught in the classroom to correspond with when and how they are used outside the classroom. Behavior such as hand washing, for instance, can be strengthened and sustained by arranging for students to wash their hands at different times and in various locations. That is, singling out appropriate times (such as after using paints, before meals, and after toileting) for training and practicing hand washing will increase the likelihood of the skill becoming a functional behavior outside of the classroom. Daily use of materials should also provide numerous opportunities for maximizing spontaneous use of each skill being taught.

In addition, the layout of the classroom can be made to approximate settings in which a child would be expected independently to engage in the target behavior, for example a bathroom or kitchen area. These simulated environments may be constructed on a temporary or permanent basis. When arranging a classroom to contain numerous learning centers, teachers should consider the flow of the classroom traffic. Wheel chairs, access to handrails or other means of support must be considered for students with mobility difficulties. Areas that are more remote or less accessible should be used for initial skill-acquisition training or quiet independent work. Cloistered and open space should be created and used for various group training activities. Instructional materials should always be accessible and stored as close to the training area as possible.

Management of nontraditional materials for delivery of individualized instruction, in short, is an issue of extreme importance to the teacher. Generally, the teacher should train students to locate and collect needed materials before skill-training sessions. Subsequent putting away of materials by students should also be a goal of magnitude equal to correct use of the material. Whenever possible, children should be given the responsibility of obtaining and setting up materials, for example, going to storage areas and singling out from various containers the laundry detergent or locating appropriate equipment for gross motor exercises and placing it in predetermined areas. In this the way the teacher is relieved of the task of distributing or setting up materials. Further, students are provided an opportunity to both assume responsibility and engage in those behaviors that naturally precede use of materials.

Generally, instructional manuals for the teacher or paraprofessional will not have guidelines or specific task analyses to assist the teacher in training helping behaviors that typically precede or follow use of a given material. Consequently, teachers will have to conduct their own task analysis, teaching, and data-collection activities. Often the teacher can adjust the strategies and data-collection systems provided in the trainer's manual for teaching the core skill. Thus continuity between training antecedent or preparatory behaviors, the core skill, and follow-through behaviors is established. Such continuity will benefit the teacher and student and should be attempted whenever possible.

Likewise, a useful purpose is served when the teacher organizes a schedule whereby materials are used or put in storage. Deviation from established schedules or lack of adherence to designated time periods should lead to consequences similar to those one would experience outside of the classroom. For example, if a student did not take pudding that was cooking off the stove when a timer rang, he should be responsible for cleaning the pan, utensils, and stove. That student should also be responsible for determining (with the help of the teacher) if a second attempt is possible or desirable at that time. If so, all needed materials should again be gathered and arranged before the core activity, preparing pudding, begins.

At this time the reader is asked to complete Self-Check 11-1.

MANAGING PERFORMANCE DATA

Another management issue to take into account when using nontraditional materials is the manner in which performance data are obtained within or

Self-Check 11-1

Instructions

Complete the following fill-in-the-blank questions.

1. Name three major factors that affect instructional materials management and adaptation.

2. What is the ultimate educational goal for all special populations?

3. Why are many nontraditional instructional materials directed towards the trainer?

Response

1. ____

   ____

   ____

2. ____

   ____

   ____

3. ____

   ____

   ____

across various curricular areas on individual children and groups of children. Since measurement and evaluation play such an important part in teaching these populations, it is clear that evaluation of instructional materials and teaching strategies across a number of skills could be time consuming. The task of monitoring the impact of selected programs and managing overall data collection can be simplified, however. Sasser (1978) for example, modified the Project MORE (Lent & McLean, 1976) daily living skill evaluation system to assess the performance of severely limited youngsters across the areas of self-help, communication, motor development, prevocational skills, and preacademic-academic skills. His system allowed him to obtain reliable data in several performance areas for each student. Little time was required to maintain this system. The teacher's aide, student teachers, and other classroom volunteers were able to learn to use the system and reliably record student performance data.

To understand Sasser's (1978) data-management system, it is helpful to be acquainted with Project MORE's recording procedure. In this procedure the level of assistance the student requires at each step in training of the task-analyzed skill is recorded. Four levels of teacher assistance are possible at any step in the instructional sequence. These include:

1. No help (e.g., "I want you to wash your hair by yourself. Do the best you can"). Coded *A* on data sheet.
2. Verbal help (e.g., "Turn the cold water on"). Coded *B* on data sheet.
3. Demonstration (e.g., Trainer turns water on and tells the student how to perform the step). Coded *C* on data sheet.
4. Physical help (e.g., Trainer guides the student's hands and tells the student how to perform the step). Coded *D* on data sheet (Sasser, 1978).

At each step the student begins at the no-help or independent level of assistance. By following this instructional sequence, a student receives the least teacher assistance needed to perform the desired behavior. In evaluating student performance, the teacher records the level of teacher assistance required to complete a desired behavior. The letters A, B, C, or D concurrently show both a correct student response and the kind of teacher response needed. Figure 11-1 shows Sasser's (1978) modified data-collection form. Rather than listing a sequence of subtasks of a single task, such as hand washing, along the left-hand column, different skills are entered. In addition, Sasser (1978) has used numerical notations above the code for physical assistance (D) to differentiate further the types of student responding. D_1 is used to denote a slight physical prompt, D_2 represents a total physical prompt, and D_3 indicates that the student resisted being prompted. These two modifications make data collection and overall management of materials much easier for the teacher. The system can

Student Peter S. Days

TASKS	9/26	9/27	9/28	9/29	9/30	10/3	10/4	10/5	10/6	10/7	10/10
1 Trace name	D^2	D^2	D^2	D^2	D^1	D^1	D^2	D^1	D^1	D^2	D^1
2 peg pattern #11	C	D^1	D^1	C	C	C	B	B	B	A	A
3 numerals to sets	C	C	C	C	C	B	C	B	B	C	C
4 sort food cards	D^1	C	D^1	C	C	C	C	C	C	B	B
5											
6											
7											
8											
9											
10											
11											
12											

Figure 11-1. *A Teacher-Modified Data Form Used to List Several Skills Where Daily Summary Data Is Recorded*

Source: Reprinted from "Adapting Packaged Measurement Systems to Monitor the Progress of Severely Handicapped Persons" by R. Sasser, in the *Journal of Special Education Technology*, with permission of the editor. Copyright 1978 by the Association for Special Education Technology.

be used with students in one-to-one training, small groups, or independent work. If students are stationed at individual cubicles with a number of different tasks, for instance, the teacher and aide may float from student to student and assess their performance on each task assigned for that day. If physical assistance were required on a specific puzzle or other manipulative for a number of days in a row, this would indicate that the material may be too complex or unmanageable (in the case of physically disabled children) and needs to be modified or replaced before learning of the task or concept will occur efficiently.

SPECIAL ADAPTATION CONSIDERATIONS

Numerous authors have noted programming techniques that may be applied to instructional materials to enhance their effectiveness with various handicapped populations (Hayden, McGuinnes, & Dimtriev, 1976; Haring & Bricker, 1976; LeBlanc, Etzel & Domash, 1978; and Schilmoeller & Etzel, 1977). The techniques most frequently cited and instructional materials features most highly acclaimed include: (a) employing frequent and intense stimuli, (b) using shaping and chaining procedures, (c) using cuing and priming procedures to evoke responses that have been established earlier, (d) providing for imitative responding and immediate reinforcement or corrective feedback, (e) providing multiple modality input and alternative-response mode training, (f) using errorless learning procedures, (g) providing for delivery of simple, precise instructions, and (h) sequencing of material from simplest to most complex. When an instructional material requires modifications beyond the adaptation process discussed earlier in this text, it is likely that one of the aforementioned techniques will need to be employed. The number of days the CRS adaptation strategy (see Chapter 8) is applied to a population of students with severe handicaps will need to be increased since learning will be expected to occur in smaller units and generally require more time.

Before giving illustrations of a number of the adaptation techniques just listed, several additional factors that impinge on the success of instructional materials and the decision to adapt are presented. First, as Carrier and Peak (1975) have noted, in many instances it will be mandatory to prepare the student for training. The student may need, for instance, to sit in a chair and attend to specific stimuli. Reinforcers will need to have been identified before initiating training. Skills such as sitting and attending may be considered fundamental prerequisites to meaningful interaction with instructional materials.

Students displaying high-frequency, stereotypic, self-abusive, violent or other incompatible behavior will require intervention on these behaviors before and concurrent with being trained to use various instructional materials. Adaptation of materials should not be undertaken until satisfactory control over student behavior is achieved. Only after the trainer has adequate control over student behavior can student performance data on specific skills be interpreted in relation to the instructional material and adaptation decisions made. With many students, particularly young children, sensory impaired and multiple handicapped, it may also be necessary to teach the child a functional response topography, for example, pointing, picking up symbols or eye movements, before teaching the target concepts or tasks. If upon examination of the instructional material to be used it is determined that imitative responding is required, the teacher will need to be sure the child has imitation skills. If the child does not imitate, such skills will need to be developed or materials that shape behavior through successive approximations employed instead.

Language-Training Adaptations

Non-SLIP (Non-Speech Language Initiation Program) designed by Carrier and Peak (1975) is intended to teach nonverbal and severely limited students a functional language system. Non-SLIP employs visual symbols, plastic chips, in the language-learning process. The basic response topography the child will need is to pick up and place symbols one at a time on a tray. Demonstration or gestural prompts usually are sufficient to train this behavior. However, Non-SLIP is exemplary in that it also includes a program designed to handshape this basic motor response. Initially children learn to sequence the plastic chips based on color, number cues, and the shape of the chips. Later sequencing is tied to grammatical sequence. Again, the authors have designed their instructional program to maximize successful responding and minimize errors. The instructional materials are highly dependent on student visual-discrimination skills. However, simple adaptation of the chips, for example, replacing color cues with textured cues, should make this program useful for visually impaired children. In addition, modifications can be made for students with motor handicaps. Carrier and Peak (1975) suggest that such students slide the chips on the table rather than pick them up and place them on the tray.

Preschool Curriculum Adaptations

Of the list of programming techniques that may be used to improve learner performance in relation to instructional materials, the delivery of simple, clear instruction is particularly critical for young exceptional learners. It is important that minimal detail be contained in all directions. For instance, when using a phonics approach to teaching initial reading, learning occurs rapidly if the sound of the letter is presented concurrently with the letter and a simple instruction, "This is 'r', say 'r-r-r'." If the teacher instructs, "This is the letter 'r', it makes the 'r-r-r' sound as in 'rabbit'. Okay, point to the word 'rabbit' and say the 'r' sound," he is likely to be complicating the learning task. By reducing instruction length and complexity, the number of trials that can be presented in a given time is also increased. More appropriate practice may increase rate of acquisition.

Similarly, if work sheets are used to teach a skill or provide practice for the child to respond motorically, for example, by printing, crossing out, or pointing to the answer, it may be necessary to modify them to allow for high rates of correct responding. Suggestions for modifying work sheets or other instructional materials for young learners and severely mentally retarded persons include: (a) eliminating all items not directly related to the skill being taught, (b) eliminating all items that are visually complex, unclear, or confusing, (c) reducing the number of stimulus items, and (d) intensifying the stimulus items by making them larger, adding color, and systematically presenting repetitions of the same items. Without exception, complete demonstrations on sample items or extra work sheets should be provided. The teacher should have the child respond alone. Always be sure the child knows what is expected before allowing him or her to begin making independent responses. Further, the time children engage in work-sheet activity should be carefully monitored and increased slowly. When work sheets are present, children should be attending to them and working appropriately on them. Provision should be made for giving feedback to each child as soon as possible on his or her performance. Some teachers have used a "flag system" to manage giving rewards and corrective feedback on work sheets. When children complete a work sheet, they flip up a flag that is attached to their desk. This signals the teacher to check their work. One adult moving about the room is much less disruptive than having the children file past the teacher's desk.

Self-Help and Motor-Skill Development

Often instructional materials and programs designed to promote self-help skills and/or motor development use trainer models as a primary teaching tactic. If this tactic is not successful, the teacher may modify his or her approach without changing the instructional material and find that children will now acquire the desired behaviors. The first modification should be to present slow, exaggerated demonstrations. For children with ambulatory difficulties, tactics such as this are very beneficial. (Slow, exaggerated demonstrations and emphasis on desired sounds or words in oral expressive-language training or signs in manual-communication systems are also effective.) If such demonstrations are not successful, the child should be physically guided through the sequence of activities. Often it is easier for a child, for example, to learn to alternate feet when climbing steps if the teacher holds the child by the ankle and physically guides him or her rather than if the teacher demonstrates correct stair climbing. Color strips can be taped to the stairs and the child's shoes and serve as cues. These prompts can be removed slowly, first from one shoe and step and then the next.

Adapting Learner Responses

LeBlanc and her associates (1978) describe a set of instructional materials designed to teach addition calculations with sums of five where the child's response was adapted for children with fine motor problems. Rather than place Xs at designated places in relation to simple addition facts, these children were given stamps and an ink pad to record their answers. Consequently, arithmetic learning was not delayed. Consideration of modifying the nature of a child's response is very critical when teaching young learners. It is essential that all children acquire the basic skills that will be the building blocks of more complex learning as early as possible. Deferring cognitive or language-skill development because of learner difficulties in conventional modes of responding is unacceptable regardless of the student's age or functioning level.

Cuing Learner Responses

Verbal response or motor responses or both may be added to cue children to perform more difficult behaviors. LeBlanc and her associates (1978) gave examples of how additional responses may be used by a child to cue correct numeral labeling and number writing. To enhance one set of instructional materials aimed at writing numerals, for instance, children were taught to say phrases that cued each stroke in making a numeral. When drawing the numeral 2, for example, the child was taught to say, "Hook, shoe, two." In naming numerals children were taught to say words that began with the same initial sound as the numeral being learned. In addition, they were taught to emit a motor response to correspond with the cue word. Although these modifications are clearly appropriate for young children, mnemonic devices and motor responses are also effective with older populations.

Please take Self-Check 11-2 at this time.

ERRORLESS LEARNING PROCEDURES

Schilmoeller and Etzel (1977) reviewed procedures that have been used by various researchers to promote essentially errorless learning. The procedures they discussed all have potential utility, although each is not directly and immediately applicable, for teachers adapting instructional materials. Most instructional materials provide for learning to occur by the process of trial and error. Instructions or demonstrations of how a task is to be performed are given and students practice for varying amounts of time on the concepts or discriminations being trained. Hopefully, after some time practicing, student correct responding is reinforced and increases and errors are eliminated. Trial and error learning is taking place in instructional materials that provide exercises, for example, where numbers are placed in a column along the left-hand side of a page, and children are instructed to draw lines to pictures of groups of objects in a column on the right-hand side. The problem with instructional materials that use trial and error learning is that even when careful demonstrations of desired responses are presented and when the work sheet meets all the general criteria with regard to a limited number of stimulus items, clarity of visual depictions, and so on, there will be occasions when children simply do not learn. In such instances it will be necessary for the teacher to reconstruct or supplement the instructional material so learning can occur in as much of an errorless fashion as possible.

Self-Check 11-2

Instructions

Consider this hypothetical situation. You are a teacher of moderately to severely delayed young children. You are teaching them to discriminate among the primary colors. The instructional materials you have available for teaching colors present four colors—red, green, blue, and yellow—at the top of a page in the children's individual workbooks. They are instructed to draw lines from the colors to the printed words *RED, BLUE, GREEN,* and *YELLOW*, each of which are printed several times in random placement on the bottom of the page. State three ways that these materials might be modified to facilitate acquisition of the desired behavior.

Response

Stimulus Fading, Stimulus Superimposition, and Stimulus Shaping

Three procedures discussed by Schilmoeller and Etzel (1977) are stimulus fading, stimulus superimposition, and stimulus shaping. As indicated earlier, these procedures may not be useful for a teacher if an entire sequence of instructional materials is in need of adaptation. These procedures are, however, relevant and may be highly beneficial for assisting learners through "rough spots" or in the acquisition of skills prerequisite to entry into a published instructional-materials sequence. The authors noted that successful use of these procedures in materials modification is dependent on the programmer's (teacher's) choice of the right stimulus to emphasize at any given time.

LeBlanc and her associates (1978) described instructional materials that employ various errorless learning techniques. Their examples show how a material might be adapted to help some learners bridge the gaps found in many instructional materials or those that appear because of individual student learning histories. One instructional material was designed to help children with poor motor control write color words, for example, *red*. The program begins with having the child trace a complete model of the first letter in the word. Subsequent tracings have fewer and fewer portions of the model letter available. Finally the child is drawing the entire letter from memory. Once the first letter has been learned and the second letter is being taught, the child is still required to write the first letter before tracing the second letter. This second letter's model is then faded slowly. In essence, the materials are using fading and chaining techniques to help the child remember what was learned (the first letter) and to establish learned responses as cues for subsequent responding (the second and third letters). At the end of the program the child reads the entire word. In this way prior learning was reinforced, new learning introduced, and mastery performance achieved. Stimulus cues, full letters, were faded gradually as the primary adaptation in this material. Clearly, other similar responses could be modified in this manner.

Imposing one stimulus over another and then fading that stimulus out across time or trials is another way to adapt instructional materials that are resulting in high rates of errors. One example modification of an instructional material designed to teach spatial relationships (e.g., behind, front, side, top, and back) is to cue position with a light or buzzer. Gradually the intensity of the buzzer is faded until the child is responding without reliance on the secondary cue.

Stimulus-shaping procedures have also been used to teach responses that were not learned in conventional or very well-sequenced materials. LeBlanc and her associates (1978) described a procedure used to teach students who have difficulty blending sounds to make words. Blending was taught by using words already known to the student. The method entailed starting with a picture of an object to which the word refers and gradually transforming this picture into the word. The procedure involved use of flash cards and training one word at a time but included words that were untrained or partially trained as a mechanism for aiding memory of the blends.

In all, materials based on trial and error learning may often result in high rates of errors for certain populations or may simply not meet the learning requirements of certain students at specific points in the program. A first level of modification that the teacher can apply is to break down the learning units or steps in the instructional material further or rearrange their sequence to be sure that basic skills are introduced before more complex skills. At this time the teacher will also be reevaluating the teaching strategy being used and determine if more exaggerated demonstration or physical assistance may be needed. If these modifications are not adequate, that is, do not result in improved child performance, it will be necessary to add supporting clues to assist the child in making successful responses. Programming materials, arranging the stimuli to maximize correct responding, can be achieved in a number of ways. Stimulus fading, stimulus superimposition, and stimulus shaping represent three prominent procedures. The major disadvantage of modifying materials to include heavy stimulus cues is that they typically require a relatively substantial amount of time to prepare.

NONTRADITIONAL INSTRUCTIONAL MATERIALS AND ADAPTATIONS FOR ADOLESCENTS

Secondary-level education objectives for handicapped learners often reflect a heightened level of concern for developing skills so students can function beyond the classroom. Emphasis is placed on increasing their ability to function as adolescents and their potential to function as adults. For the more severely handicapped, goals and instructional materials will remain focused on teaching self-help and survival skills, language skills, reducing self-injurious or stereotypic behavior, and developing some potentially marketable vocational skills. For less handicapped students, instructional materials will be geared toward developing appropriate social behavior, useful vocational skills, basic academic skills, and leisure-time and recreational behaviors.

Most instructional materials that are available for use in teaching functional academics to adolescent populations are deficient in a number of ways (Wiederholt & McNutt, 1977). The main features of materials that may require adaptation (adaptation that is critical to the adolescent learner) include: (a) the relevance of the instructional material to the student's life, (b) the readability level and language of the instructional material, (c) prerequisites that may be required for students to use the materials successfully, and (d) how intrinsically motivating the materials are or how extrinsically to foster interest in the materials.

With regard to relevance of the material used with adolescent populations, it should be remembered that occupational skill-training and social-leisure time skills have particular importance to these students. Efforts to supplement materials so they relate to these areas or provide training in situations that may be considered beyond the traditional classroom setting are recommended.

The readability level of materials has been discussed by numerous authors as a major factor impeding successful acquisition of numerous skills by handicapped teenagers. The readability level of materials should always be assessed. W. H. Miller (1973) suggested that if a student can supply about 45 percent of the words in a passage that has had the *n*th word arbitrarily omitted, that student is in material at his or her instructional level. C. H. McLaughlin (1969) devised a readability formula referred to as SMOG. His formula is based on an expectancy of 90 to 100 percent accuracy in comprehension. Setting the level this high ensures that students will be gaining from the content and concepts presented in the materials and not struggling to understand the words and grammatical structure of sentences. When difficult words are impeding understanding of the content of printed material, teachers might provide preview lists of words and understandable synonyms for students. In some instances words and even sentences can be stricken from material without sacrificing meaning. Preliminary oral reading of difficult passages by the teacher or tape recordings of passages should also assist the student having difficulty understanding printed materials. Software programs for rapidly calculating readability are now available for use in microcomputers such as those sold by Radio Shack.

The language of instructional materials used with adolescents, young children, preschoolers, or adults must be appropriate to their age. Although many academic skill-training and language-training programs are available for younger students, few are designed to be used with teenagers or adults if their language and instructional cues are assessed. One teacher, pleased with student performance in Distar Reading materials (Englemann & Bruner, 1974), decided to adapt these materials for use with students in a junior high school class for educable mentally retarded (EMR) children. First, the language used by the teacher to direct the students was changed. The address of "children" was eliminated and "group" was sometimes used instead. Rather than saying, "my turn" and "your turn," the teacher used "Listen to me now," or "Now listen." In Distar three rules for children include sit tall, "Look at the big book," and "Talk big." The language of these rules was adjusted. Students were requested to sit up straight and not allowed to support their heads with anything other than their necks. They were requested to speak loudly and clearly. The students accepted and followed these requests as rules. With regard to rules and other information, the teacher typically explained things more thoroughly to the students and expected them to understand the reasons they might be asked to do something or be the focus of the teacher's attention. For example, the teacher explained that if she did not see a student reading a word (looking at the word on signal and responding on time), it made her think that the student did not know the word. The teacher felt that explanations such as this were important to the students. However she emphasized that for the most part, little time was consumed with lengthy explanations or discussion.*

A word of caution to teachers is that although materials may be advertised to be high-interest, low-vocabulary material or have language appropriate for certain ages or be written at a certain reading level, publishers are often inaccurate in their description of educational materials and readability levels (Lavely, Lowe, & Fallman, 1975).

One final area of concern to the teacher adapting instructional materials for any exceptional learner is that needed prerequisites are clearly stated so materials and procedures for building entry-level skills can be designed by the teacher. Preferably, the published materials themselves will soon be designed to teach certain prerequisite behaviors or give the teacher suggestions how to approach that task.

Sequenced Materials Use and Their Management

Independent use of instructional materials is important for students of any age level; however, it should be stressed increasingly with older students. Instructional materials, work sheets, manipulatives, or games can be placed in order of difficulty along shelves in the classroom and used by students totally independent of the teacher. When an unexpectedly high frequency of errors occurs with any student or a number of students, the teacher can modify the sequence of materials by providing additional exercises or by changing the practice conditions.

Social-Skill Training

In addition to general language development, social skills include initiating and responding behaviors such as sharing, learning from others, and following suggestions (LeBlanc, Etzel, & Domash, 1978). As students grow older, they are expected to exhibit greater social sensitivity and more complex, socially appropriate behavior. Although social-skill development has been identified as a primary educational goal, instructional materials designed to promote social learning generally entail teaching global behavior patterns. As such, these materials are not sufficient to meet many of the demands that severely handi-

*Thanks is extended to Donna Bryington for her recommendations with regard to modifying Distar Reading.

capped students place on instructional materials and therefore are not thoroughly reviewed here. Three instructional programs that may be of interest to the reader are DUSO (Developing Understanding of Self and Others), which is published by American Guidance Service; the *Social-Control Curriculum*, published by Charles E. Merrill; and the *Social Learning Curriculum*, published by Hubbard Scientific. Each includes a wide range of social skill training areas and a number of instructional formats.

Perceptual-Psycholinguistic-Training Materials

A great deal of material has been developed to correspond with theories about perceptual development and psycholinguistic approaches to teaching handicapped learners. These materials have not been presented in the context of this discussion primarily because little data exists to support their effect on basic living skills of severely limited students. Generally, these materials are evaluated using indirect and infrequent measurement procedures. A first step in modifying of instructional materials designed to adhere to these theories would include construction of direct behavior-measurement systems. Many of these materials are sequenced, based on developmental literature. Therefore, fleshing out content may not be an overwhelming task if the sequences based on normative data prove to be as utilitarian as skill sequencing based on task analyses. At this point there is minimal evidence to suggest that normative data will be more productive in constructing instructional materials than task analytic approaches.

Please take time to read and complete Self-Check 11-3.

Materials Resources for Children with Sensory and/or Physical Impairments

There are numerous materials adaptation requirements and special considerations for children with sensory and/or physical impairments. Adequate treatment of these requirements and considerations would constitute the preparation of another book. Some current resources which provide information on the selection, adaptation and evaluation of materials for these groups of children include the following:

1. *Education of the Visually Handicapped*—a publication of the Association for the Education of the Visually Handicapped.
2. *American Annals of the Deaf* and *Volta Review*—publications relating to problems and education of hearing impaired persons.
3. Calovini, G. *The Principal Looks at Classes for the Physically Handicapped.* Reston, Virginia: The Council for Exceptional Children, 1969.

Self-Check 11-3

OPEN ENDED

Instructions

The instructional material that you have been using to teach a severely retarded adolescent has successfully taught him a vocabulary of 20 survival sight words. Your student has been unable to learn the word *exit*. Design a simple program using a stimulus-fading, stimulus-superimposition, *or* stimulus-shaping procedure to teach him *exit*.

References

Adamson, G., Shrago, M.S., & Van Etten, G. *Basic educational skills inventory*. Rolling Hills Estates, Calif.: B.L. Winch & Associates, 1972.

Anderson, R.M., Greer, J.G., & Odle, S.J. *Individualizing educational materials for special children in the mainstream*. Baltimore: University Park Press, 1978.

Armstrong, J. A model for materials development and evaluation. *Exceptional Children*, 1971, *38*, 327-334.

Ashcroft, S.C. Research and evaluation: New directions. *Journal of Special Education Technology*, 1979, *2*(4), 3-6.

Baker, B., & Heifetz, L. The read project: Teaching manuals for parents of retarded children. In T. Tjossem (Ed.), *Intervention strategies for high risk infants and young children*. Baltimore: University Park Press, 1976.

Bender, M., & Valletutti, P. *Teaching the moderately and severely handicapped*. Baltimore: University Park Press, 1977.

Berman, A. LD resource materials: The great ripoff. *Journal of Learning Disabilities*, 1977, *10*(5), 261-263.

Bliel, G. Evaluating educational materials. *Journal of Learning Disabilities*, 1975, *8*(1), 12-19.

Boland, A. Instructional materialism—Or how to select the things you need. *Teaching Exceptional Children*, Summer, 1976, pp. 156-158.

Brown, V. A basic Q-sheet for analyzing and comparing curriculum materials and proposals. *Journal of Learning Disabilities*, 1975, *8*(7), 409-416.

Buchanan, C.D. *Spelling*. Palo Alto, Calif.: Sullivan Associates, 1972.

Burney, J., & Shores, R. E. Effects of a precision planning technique on the arithmetic performance of mentally retarded children. *Journal of Special Education Technology*, 1979, *2*(3), 16-25.

Carrier, J., & Peak, T. *Non-SLIP: Non Speech Language Initiation Program*. Lawrence, Kan.: H&H Enterprises, Inc., 1975.

A consumer's union for education can tell you when your district is being gypped. *American School Board Journal*, 1975, 38-40.

Cooper, J.O. *Measurement and analysis of behavioral techniques*. Columbus, Ohio: Charles E. Merrill, 1974.

Cox, L.S. Diagnosing and remediating systematic errors in addition and subtraction computations. *The Arithmetic Teacher*, 1975, *22*, 151-157.

Crutcher, C., & Hofmeister, A. Effective objectives and monitoring. *Teaching Exceptional Children*, 1975, *7*(3), 78-80.

Englemann, S. *Preventing failure in the primary grades*. Chicago: Science Research Associates, 1970.

Englemann, S., & Bruner, E. *DISTAR—Reading I* (2nd ed.). Chicago: Science Research Associates, 1974.

Ensminger, E.E. A proposed model for selecting, modifying or developing instructional materials for handicapped children. *Focus on Exceptional Children*, 1970, *1*(9), 1-9.

Erickson, D.K. Forward. *Instructional programming for the handicapped student*, unknown source.

Free and Inexpensive Learning Materials. Nashville: George Peabody College for Teachers, 1975.

Fuchs, V.E. The realities of commercial marketing for special education. *Journal of Special Education Technology*, 1979, *2*(4), 16-20.

Gast, D.L., & Nelson, G.M. Time out in the classroom: Implications for special education. *Exceptional Children*, 1977, *43*, 461-464.

Guess, D., Sailor, W., Keogh, B., & Baer, D. Language development programs for severely handicapped children. In N. Haring & L.J. Brown (Eds.), *Teaching the severely handicapped* (Vol. 1), New York: Grune and Stratton, 1976, pp. 301-324.

Hall, R.V. *Managing behavior, part I*. Lawrence, Kansas: H&H Enterprises, 1971.

Hallahan, D.P., & Kauffman, J.M. *Exceptional children: Introduction to special education*. Englewood Cliffs, N. J.: Prentice-Hall, 1978.

Haring, N., & Bateman, B. *Teaching the learning disabled child*. Englewood Cliffs, N. J.: Prentice-Hall, 1977.

Haring, N., & Bricker, D. Overview of comprehensive services for the severely/profoundly handicapped. In N.G. Haring and L.J. Brown (Eds.), *Teaching the severely handicapped* (Vol. I), New York: Grune and Stratton, 1976.

Haring, N., & Eaton, M.D. Systematic instructional procedures: An instructional hierarchy. In N. Haring, T.C. Lovitt, M.D. Eaton, & C.L. Hansen, *The fourth r: Research in the classroom*. Columbus, Ohio: Charles E. Merrill, 1978.

Haring, N., & Gentry, N.D. Direct and individualized instructional procedures. In N. Haring & R.L. Schiefelbusch (Eds.), *Teaching Special Children*. New York: McGraw-Hill, 1976.

Haring, N., & Pious, C. Future directions in work with severely and profoundly handicapped persons: An overview. In N. Haring & L.J. Brown (Eds.), *Teaching the severely handicapped* (Vol. 1). New York: Grune and Stratton, 1976.

Haubrick, P.A., & Shores, R.E. The interrelationships of controlling attending behavior and academic achievement of emotionally disturbed children. *Exceptional Children*, 1976, *42*, 337-338.

Hayden, A., McGinnes, G., & Dimtriev, V. Early and continuous intervention strategies for severely handicapped infants and very young children. In N. Haring & L.J. Brown (Eds.), *Teaching the severely handicapped* (Vol. 1). New York: Grune and Stratton, 1976.

Henderson, H., & Rovig, T. Evaluating, selecting and adapting instructional materials: A critical teacher competency. *NSPI Journal*, July 1977, 18-23.

Hewett, F. *The emotionally disturbed child in the classroom*. Boston: Allyn and Bacon, 1968.

Hewett, F. An approach to planning. In J. Blacklow (Ed.), *Environmental design: New relevance for special education*. Reston, Va.: Council for Exceptional Children, 1971.

Hofmeister, A. *Diagnostic arithmetic test*. Logan, Utah: Utah State University, 1972.

Hofmeister, A. *Independent drill for mastery*. Niles, Ill.: Developmental Learning Materials, 1979.

Hofmeister, A. Personal communication, 1978.

Hofmeister, A. Programmed instruction revisited: Implications for educating the retarded. *Education and Training of the Mentally Retarded*, 1971, *6*(4), 172-176.

Hofmeister, A. Selecting and modifying programmed materials. *Teaching Exceptional Children*, 1969, *2*(1), 38-42.

Homme, L., & Tosti, D. *Behavior technology: Motivation and contingency management*. San Rafael, Calif.: Individual Learning Systems, 1971.

Horstmeir, D., MacDonald, J., & Gillette, Y. *READY, SET, GO—Talk to me!* Columbus: The Nisonger Center, The Ohio State University, 1975.

Howell, K., Kaplan, J.S., & O'Connell, C.Y. *Evaluating exceptional children: A task analysis approach*. Columbus, Ohio: Charles E. Merrill, 1979.

Indepth Report #48; *Evaluating kits for early learning*. New York: Educational Products Information Exchange Institute, 1973.

Kent, L. *Language acquisition program for the severely retarded*. Champaign, Ill.: Research Press, 1974.

Komoski, P.K. What's happening on the educational materials scene? *EPIE*gram (Newsletter published by Educational Products Information Exchange), February, 15, 1973.

Lavely, C., Lowe, A.J., & Fallman, J. Actual reading levels of EMR materials. *Education and Training of the Mentally Retarded*, 1975, *10*, 271-275.

LeBlanc, J., Etzel, B., & Domash, M. A functional curriculum for early intervention. In E. Allen, V. Holm, & R. Schiefelbusch (Eds.), *Early intervention—A team approach*. Baltimore: University Park Press, 1978.

Lent, J., & McLean, B. The trainable retarded: The technology of teaching. In N. Haring & R.L. Schiefelbusch (Eds.), *Teaching special children*. New York: McGraw-Hill, 1976.

Lovitt, T.C. *Inspite of my resistance. . . I've learned from children*. Columbus, Ohio: Charles E. Merrill, 1977.

Lovitt, T.C., & Hansen, C.L. Use of contingent skipping and drilling to improve oral reading and comprehension. *Journal of Learning Disabilities*, 1976, *9*, 481-487.

Martin, E.W. The regional resource center strategy: Six men in search of an elephant. In *State of the art: Diagnosis and treatment*, Reston, Va.: National Resource Center Conference, 1974.

McLaughlin, C.H. SMOG grading—A new readability formula. *Journal of Reading*, 1969, *12*, 639-646.

Menhusen, B., McGonigel, M., Alexander, L., Smith, D., Tremblay, A., Caruthers, M., Griffin, L., Grafton, S., & McClure, C. Media materials center for the severely handicapped. *Journal of Special Education Technology*, 1978, *1*(2), 5-12.

Miller, W.H. *Diagnosis and correction of reading disabilities in secondary schools*. New York: Center for Applied Research in Education, 1973.

Morrissey, P. *A guide for teachers: How to set up a peer tutoring system in your classroom*. LD Series No. 4. Bloomington, Ind.: Center for Innovation in Teaching the Handicapped, Indiana University, no date.

Popham, J., & Baker, E. *Systematic instruction*. Englewood Cliffs, N.J.: Prentice-Hall, 1970.

Rosen, T. Personal communication, 1973.

Rude, C.R. Trends and priorities in inservice training. *Exceptional Children*, 1978, *45*(3), 172-176.

Sasser, R. Adapting packaged measurement systems to monitor the classroom performance of handicapped persons. *Journal of Special Education Technology*, 1978, *1*(1), 51-57.

Schilmoeller, K., & Etzel, B. An experimental analysis of criterion-related and noncriterion-related cues in "errorless" stimulus control procedures. In B. Etzel, J. LeBlanc, & D. Baer (Eds.), *New developments in behavioral research*. Hillsdale, N.J.: Lawrence Erlbaum Associates, 1977.

Shores, R.E. Personal communication, 1979.

Shores, R.E., & Haubrick, P.A. Effects of cubicles in educating emotionally disturbed children. *Exceptional Children*, 1969, *36*, 21-24.

Shores, R.E., & Stowitschek, J. *InSTEP final report*. Nashville: George Peabody College for Teachers, 1975.

Siegel, E. Task analysis and effective teaching. *Journal of Learning Disabilities,* 1972, 5(10). 519-532.

Smith, R.M., Neisworth, J.T., & Greer, J.G. *Evaluating educational environments.* Columbus, Ohio: Charles E. Merrill, 1978.

Standard criteria for the selection and evaluation of instructional material. Columbus, Ohio: Ohio State University, 1977.

Starlin, C. Evaluating progress toward reading proficiency. In B. Batemen (Ed.), *Learning disorders* (Vol. 4). Seattle: Special Child Publications, 1971.

Stowitschek, C., & Stowitschek, J. Evaluating handwriting performance: The student helps the teacher. *Journal of Learning Disabilities,* 1979, *12*(3), 203-205.

Stowitschek, J. *Daily/weekly tally sheet.* Special Education Instructional Development, Nashville: The Peabody College for Teachers, 1976.

Taylor, F., Artuso, A., Soloway, M., Hewett, F., Quay, H., & Stillwell, R. The learning center plan. In *Focus on Exceptional Children,* May, 1972.

Tiegs, E.W., & Clark, W.W. *The California achievement tests.* Monterey, Calif.: CTB/McGraw-Hill, Inc., 1970.

Tiemann, P.W., & Markle, S.M. Teacher and technology-as-media or technology-as-system: Implications of "to improve learning" for teacher training. *Educational Technology,* 1973, *12*(8), 7-10.

Walker, H. Engineered learning project. North Western RMC/IMC, University of Oregon, 1970.

Wallace, G., & Larson, S. *Educational assessment of learning problems: Testing for teaching.* Boston: Allyn and Bacon, 1978.

White, O.R., & Liberty, K.A. Behavioral assessment and precise educational measurement. In N. Haring & R.L. Schiefelbusch (Eds.), *Teaching special children.* New York: McGraw-Hill, 1976.

Wiederholt, J., & McNutt, G. Evaluating materials for handicapped adolescents. *Journal of Learning Disabilities,* 1977, *10*(3), 11-19.

Young, J. *Precision teaching.* Provo, Utah: Brigham Young University Press, 1972.

APPENDIX A

Sample Responses to Self-Check Exercises

CHAPTER 1

Self-Check 1-1

1. Use as a model and make my own materials.
2. If body-parts recognition is the only skill of interest, use the child's body or the teacher's body.

Self-Check 1-2

1. Have another student read the directions to the nonreader.
2. Add a demonstration example to the material.
3. Add a pictorial diagram.

Self-Check 1-3

1. Color-code each column.
2. Choose beads of different sizes or textures.
3. Increase the thickness of the rod (upon which the beads slide) so they are more difficult to move if accidentally bumped.
4. Use clothes pins to hold the beads in place.
5. Secure the abacus on the table top to prevent sliding.
6. "Braille" the place values.
7. Attach pictorial directions (e.g., signs) for deaf users who are nonreaders.
8. Attach written directions.
9. Prepare permanent demonstrations of its use (e.g., Polaroid snapshots).

CHAPTER 2

Self-Check 2-1

Objectives: OK
Sequence: OK
Redirect: Whole-book recycling instead of smaller steps

Initial Assessment: OK
Progress Monitoring: Pass-no pass on the whole book and not by individual reading tests
Mastery Assessment: OK
Appropriate Practice: Must supplement on oral reading
Reinforcement: OK (feedback on correctness of answers)
Prompting: OK

Self-Check 2-2

Title: Oregon Math Workbooks
Publisher: Oregon Math
Level: Grades 1-3 (est.)
Scope: Across skills
Brief Description: Test-practice-test on computation skills
Costs—Initial cost: $119.90 (for both parts)
—Per student: $12.00 (for 10 students)
—Replacement cost: $4.95 (record book)
—Portion consumable: 75 percent (est.)
—Portion reusable: 25 percent
—Initial cost low? No
—Replacement cost low? Moderate
—Hidden costs? No
Preparation: Initial preparation—little?
Daily preparation—10-15 min.?
Preparing materials—none?
Physical Characteristics: No media required
No duplication required
No extra materials required
Visual sensory mode
Safety—?
Durability—softback paper materials
Time Involved: A. Entire year
B. Teacher—30 minutes
Learner—30–50 minutes
Other: Written response
Prerequisite—basic numeration skills

Self-Check 2-3

1. *Objectives:* Not stated (in catalogue)
2. *Sequence:* Not determinable (seems highly sequenced)
3. *Redirection:* Can't determine from catalogue
4. *Initial Assessment:* Can't determine

5. *Progress Assessment:* Can't determine
6. *Mastery Assessment:* Can't determine
7. *Appropriate Practice:* All work seems appropriate to the purpose
8. *Reinforcement:* Specific instructions, according to the catalogue
9. *Prompting:* Highly prompted, fading of prompts
10. *Amount of adaptation required:* Possibly up to five of the characteristics, particularly measurement if none is provided

CHAPTER 3

Self-Check 3-1

Instructional Characteristics: My reading instruction time is 35 minutes per day. How can I use your materials to individualize better?

Validity—What student population was it field tested on?

Can I try out the program with my students (for, say, 30 days) before I buy it?

Service: Do you provide any teacher training in the program's use?

What will you do if the machine breaks down?

Cost: Aside from the purchase price, what is the yearly replacement price and how long can I expect the materials to last?

Media/Materials: Is there any way I can use the media already in the school?

Do you have a rental option on the media?

Self-Check 3-2

7. *Appropriate practice:* All work is appropriate (as long as the students don't "scrub" to get the gray line).
8. *Reinforcement:* Specific instructions—students may get immediate reinforcement from seeing that their writing is correct.
9. *Prompting:* Fading of prompts.
10. Amount of adaptation required: Can't determine.

Format: Self-instructional, drill and practice, possibly for one-to-one tutorial use.

Are you willing to say from this information that the materials are appropriate for a basic handwriting prescription? No—can't determine.

CHAPTER 4

Self-Check 4-1

1. Materials may be placed into instructional- or core-materials, drill- and practice-materials, test-materials, and free-play materials categories.
2. Instructional materials should receive the higher purchasing priority.

3. Diagnostic tests are ill-advised, particularly if the teacher's budget is limited, since their results or scores often do not relate directly to instruction and they often require considerable time to administer and expense to purchase.
4. Three major needs that a classroom teacher must assess to determine overall needs before setting up a classroom include the students' needs, the teacher's needs, and classroom space and equipment.

True and False Answers
1. True
2. False
3. False
4. True
5. True

Self-Check 4-2

A. The first letter is a good plan for help but it is hard to tell precisely what the teacher is requesting. Further, it is unlikely the publisher will give blanket permission to copy all materials (negative publisher response predicted).
B. This letter contains a precise statement of the teacher's need and purpose for requesting permission to duplicate. It also seems that there will be potential benefits to the publisher if they grant permission (positive publisher response predicted).
C. In this letter the teacher very clearly articulates precise needs, specific purposes, and how the duplicated material will be used. It would also appear to have long-range benefits to the publisher (positive publisher response predicted).

CHAPTER 5

Self-Check 5-1

Johnny: Accuracy, some error allowance
Jason: Review, no error allowance
Gessell: Speed, no error allowance
Beverly: Consistency, no error allowance
Julie: Accuracy, some error allowance
Robin: Accuracy, no error allowance

Self-Check 5-2

Student: Daniel T.
Skill Area: Reading
Long Range Goal: Student will be able to master each of the reading subskills

INSTRUCTIONAL OBJECTIVES

A. **OBJECTIVE** *Entry Date* 4/3 *Eval. Date* 5/12	Dropped	More Time Needed	Progress to Continue	Objec. Met
WILL BE ABLE TO: Match letters of the alphabet				X
	Comment: 4/3—mastered 5/12—mastery retained			
B. 4/3 5/12				
WILL BE ABLE TO: Match upper to lower case letters		X		
	Comment: 4/14 — mastered — 79% retention			
C. 4/3 5/12				
WILL BE ABLE TO: Orally identify the lower case letters				X
	Comment: 4/16 — mastered 5/12 — mastery retained			
D. 4/3 5/12				
WILL BE ABLE TO: Identify upper case letters				X
	Comment: 4/16 — mastered 5/12 — mastery retained			
E. 4/3 5/12				
WILL BE ABLE TO: Name long vowel sounds			X	
	Comment: mastery never met—16 percent			

Self-Check 5-3

	Test Part/Page	Criterion/Items
Identify beginning sounds	Part I Pg 2 Item # — 1–10	9/10
Identify ending sounds	Part I Pg 2 Row — right column Item # — 1–10	9/10
Match capital letters	Part I Pg 3 Row — Top Half Item # — 1–4, 9–12	7/8

Match lower case letters	Part I Pg 3 Row — Top Half Item # — 5–8, 13–15	6/7
Identify same words	Part I Pg 3 Row — Bottom Half Item # — 3, 7, 8, 10	4/4
Identify different words	Part I Pg 3 Row — Bottom Half Item # — 1–6, 9	5/6

CHAPTER 6

Self-Check 6-1

1. Pinpoint Diagnosis
2. Daily/Weekly Progress Assessment
3. Skill-Deficit Identification
4. Global Achievement

Self-Check 6-2

1. Well, we'll, we're west, wet
2. Five
3. Wells, went, what, West
4. When, which, while, whine, whip

Self-Check 6-3

1. Come—unlearned
3. Dome—mislearned
5. Here—chance
7. Like—unlearned
9. Play—mislearned
11. Not—mislearned
13. Had—chance
15. Let—unlearned

CHAPTER 7

Self-Check 7-1

A. *Set up* Obtain correct response sheet—teacher—one min. (est.)
Locate player at cassette tape—pupil—two min.
Set up player, plug in ear phones—pupil—one min.
Find starting point in tape—pupil—one min.

B. *Operation* Complete taped unit—pupil—3-5 min.
Check answers with answer card—both—two min.
Restudy or complete unit—pupil, until end of period.

Self-Check 7-2

I. a. c a t
b. c a k _
c. t r e _

II. a. g _ _ _
b. r _ _
c. r _ _

III. a. _ _ _ _
b. _ _ _
c. _ _ _ _ _

IV. a. ____________
b. ____________
c. ____________

Self-Check 7-3

	Mastery Required	*Prerequisite Skill Required*
1.	yes	Recognize numbers
2.	no	#1 plus read from left to right
3.	no	#1 plus read from left to right
4.	no	#1 plus read from left to right
5.	no	#1 plus read from left to right
6.	no	#1
7.	no	#1 plus make a C or √ mark (for correct problems)
8.	no	#1 plus make a check mark

CHAPTER 8

Self-Check 8-1

Sample Response

1. False
2. True
3. True
4. True
5. False
6. True

1. Yes, there is hope of reaching the point that the majority of instructional materials are field tested. Teachers can assist by asking for field-test data on all materials and letting it be known they will only buy validated material in the future.
2. The advertisement for Sounder is unique because it offers a performance warranty.
3. Teacher creativity might interfere with the predictableness of student gains when he or she is using validated instructional materials because modifications away from validated usage might actually decrease student performance outcomes.

Self-Check 8-2

The development and field-test information that is available on PEEK should be checked on the Field-Test Results section of the Materials Analysis Form and include "one-group field tests" (as closest fit). Field testing is not clearly discussed in the advertisement and should be followed with a question mark and further inquiry. Categories 1–3 may also be checked and followed by a question mark. It would seem expert appraisal, publisher testimonials, and teacher testimonials were all part of the long, early development and revision phase. Category 6 is not checked because there is no indication that individual learner's verification was used to evaluate the effect of the material.

Self-Check 8-3

1. Yes, the rationale is clearly stated.
2. Yes, the population is clearly stated.
3. Yes, there is evidence of revision based on evaluation data; further information would be needed.
4. No, the types of assessment instruments used are not given.

CHAPTER 9

Self-Check 9-1

__X__ (A-Obj) Objectives— Need to specify the pupil response.

__?__ (A-Seq) Sequence— May want to rearrange the sets to match with levels of difficulty.

__?__ (A-Cont) Content— The number of words per card may be too many—cover up some of the words at first and then increase the number used in the game as the learners improve.

Self-Check 9-2

__X__ (B-Pre) Preassessment—Use of preassessment would help to identify words already learned.

__X__ (B-Prog) Progress Assessment—Use of a daily tally sheet would help select words for the next day's game.

__?__ (B-Vis) Visual Display—May want to have pupils keep a progress chart on daily results.

__X__ (B-Crit) Mastery Criteria—Need to specify performance criteria (e.g., three successive corrects per word).

__X__ (C-Prac) Practice—Probably need to have learners call out the words shown on flash cards before they place the marker on the game card.

__?__ (C-Dir) Learner Directions—May need to model or prompt learners on first game.

__?__ (C-Prog)—May have to use a partial model as a prompt on some words (e.g., for *there*, say, "Look for *th*").

__?__ (Teacher Activity)—To ensure that slow learners win, the teacher may want to be a participant (and lose sometimes).

__?__ (C-Reinf) Reinforcement—May want to set up a group contingency where a team wins.

__?__ (C-Redir)—Need to provide backup instruction for words missed in game.

CHAPTER 10

Self-Check 10-1

Sample Response: This student has required assistance on steps A, B, C, D, F, and G. First, the teacher would focus on critical steps, for example, A–D, and then further task analyze these steps. Alternative reinforcers should be identified and used; B could be omitted temporarily.

Self-Check 10-2

Sample Response:

1. No, he should have at least looked for other possible programs.
2. No, he had not conducted a materials analysis, determined his precise purpose, or identified a sample of his students for the child-based materials evaluation.
3. Several students who failed selected pretests.
4. Several.
5. Pre-posttest

CHAPTER 11

Self-Check 11-1

Sample Response:

1. Handicapping conditions; curriculum content areas; age.
2. Developing functional skills that students use appropriately in applied settings.
3. Because of functional, nontraditional training goals and use of common materials. Because materials, measurement, and methods must be so closely tied, emphasis is on the person training. Because cost may be prohibitive with regard to child-directed materials.

Self-Check 11-2

Sample Response:

1. Resequence the material to consist of a number of work pages.
2. Omit words and have students match colors.
3. Decrease the number of stimuli at the bottom of the page.

APPENDIX B
Blank Forms

MATERIALS INVENTORY FORM

Subject Area ______________________

Curriculum Sequence	Material #1	Location	Material #2	Location	Material #3	Location	Analysis Showed Them Useful?	Material Pinpoint Need?

MATERIALS REVIEW FORM

Title ________ Subject ________ Date Reviewed ________

Publisher ________ Level ________ Scope: Comprehensive ____

Address ________ Across Skills ____

Brief Description ________ Single Skill ____

Costs: (See Chapter 4)

Initial cost ____
cost per student ____

Comment (Are the cost factors within reason?)

Replacement cost ____
portion consumable (%) ____ ________
portion reusable (%) ____ ________

Initial cost low? ____ ________

Replacement cost low? ____ ________

Hidden costs? ____ ________

Time Involved:

(A) Time to complete in program (estimated)
weeks ____ days ____

(B) Daily time required
of teacher ____ of learner ____

Comment ________

____

Other:

Response(s) required in the material ________

Prerequisites required ________

Student ability to use media equipment ________

Comment (prohibitive learner prerequisite?) ________

____

Preparation:

Initial preparation/training involved ________

Daily preparation involved ________

Preparing materials ________

Comment (Are you willing to expend the effort required?)

____

____

Physical Characteristics:

(A) Media/hardware required..... ____
available.................. ____
obtainable................. ____
non-obtainable............. ____
alternatives?.............. ____
service warranty?.......... ____
local service?............. ____
can get on loan?........... ____
requires special training? ____

(B) Duplication required........ ____
mimeo...................... ____
xerox...................... ____

(C) Extra materials required.... ____
locate..................... ____
make....................... ____

(D) Sensory mode required
visual..................... ____
auditory................... ____
tactual.................... ____
olfactory/gustatory........ ____

(E) Safety
toxic...................... ____
non-toxic.................. ____

(F) Durability of manipulatives
durable.................... ____
non-durable................ ____

Comment (Are there prohibititive physical characteristics?) ________

____

____

____

____

____

MATERIALS REVIEW FORM (cont'd.)

Instructional Characteristics:

Format

	Self Instruction	One to One Tutoral	Small Group	Group
Initial Instruction	___	___	___	___
Drill and Practice	___	___	___	___
Enrichment	___	___	___	___

Comment ______________________________

Planning

1. Objectives: specific___ general___ not stated___
   Comment ______________________________
   (Do the stated or implied objectives match your intent for the materials?)

2. Sequence: complete___ gaps___ not determinable___
   Comment ______________________________
   (Is the sequence thorough and in logical order?)

3. Redirection: can recycle___ can vary instruction___
   no redirection specified___
   Comment ______________________________

Measurement

4. Initial assessment: placement___ pretest___
   no initial assessment___
   Comment ______________________________

5. Progress assessment: daily___ weekly___
   summary chart or graph___ none specified___
   Comment ______________________________

6. Mastery assessment: same as initial assessment ___
   same as progress assessment ___
   new assessment ___
   no mastery assessment ___
   Comment ______________________________
   (Are you going to have to supply another assessment?)

Direct Teaching

7. Appropriate practice: all pupil work is appropriate ___
   some pupil work is appropriate___
   no pupil work is appropriate ___
   Comment ______________________________

8. Reinforcement: general instructions ___
   specific instructions___
   none specified ___
   Comment ______________________________
   (Are you going to have to design and implement your own reinforcement?)

9. Prompting: errorless responding possible___
   fading of prompts ___
   no prompts provided ___
   Comment ______________________________

10. Amount of adaptation required (number of characteristics)___

Field Test Results:

Subjective
1 expert appraisal...............___
2 publisher testimonials.........___
3 teacher testimonials...........___
4 marketing research.............___
5 no field tests reported........___
6 individual learner verification___
7 one group field tests (pre--post-tests).............___
8 controlled study comparing one material to another........___
9 controlled study comparing material to objectives (validation research)..........___

Objective
10 performance warranty...........___

WILLIAMSON COUNTY SCHOOLS
PUBLIC SERVICES DEPARTMENT

INDIVIDUALIZED EDUCATION PROGRAM — TOTAL SERVICE PLAN

STUDENT ______________________________

SKILL AREA ____________________________

LONG RANGE GOAL: ____

____

INSTRUCTIONAL OBJECTIVES:

Objective	DROPPED	MORE TIME NEEDED	PROGRESS TO CONTINUE	OBJEC. MET
A. OBJECTIVE ENTRY DATE: EVAL. DATE WILL BE ABLE TO:				
	COMMENT:			
B. OBJECTIVE ENTRY DATE: EVAL. DATE WILL BE ABLE TO:				
	COMMENT:			
C. OBJECTIVE ENTRY DATE: EVAL. DATE WILL BE ABLE TO:				
	COMMENT:			
D. OBJECTIVE ENTRY DATE: EVAL. DATE WILL BE ABLE TO:				
	COMMENT:			
E. OBJECTIVE ENTRY DATE: EVAL. DATE WILL BE ABLE TO:				
	COMMENT:			

Test Adaptation Results

Skill List									
Test Part/Page	Part____ Pg____ Row____ Item#____	Part____ Pg____ Row____ Item#____	Part____ Pg____ Row____ Item#____	Part____ Pg____ Row____ Item#____	Part____ Pg____ Row____ Item#____	Part____ Pg____ Row____ Item#____	Part____ Pg____ Row____ Item#____	Part____ Pg____ Row____ Item#____	Part____ Pg____ Row____ Item#____
Criterion / # Items									
Students									

Material Analysis and Adaptation Form

Program ______________________ Side 1

Area	Problem	Solution
A. Curriculum		
___ (A-Obj) Objectives	______	(A-Obj) Write behavior objectives? ___
___ (A-Prer) Prerequisites	______	(A-Prer) Teach prerequisite? ___
	______	Circumvent prerequisites? ___
___ (A-Seq) Sequence	______	(A-Seq) Resequence the activities? ___
	______	Use only selected steps? ___
___ 'A-Cont) Content	______	(A-Cont) Fill in step gaps ___
	______	Skip steps? ___
		Delete irrelevant steps? ___
B. Measurement		
___ (B-Pre) Preassessment	______	(B-Pre) Adapt test from this program? ___
	______	Adapt another test? ___
	______	(See Chapter 6)
___ (B-Prog) Progress/	______	(B-Prog) Prepare probes? ___
Mastery Assessment	______	Adapt from this program? ___
	______	(See Chapter 6)
___ (B-Vis) Visual	______	(B-Vis) Use material management ___
Display	______	chart? ___
	______	Use graph? ___
___ (B-Crit) Mastery	______	(B-Crit) Specify accuracy criteria? ___
Criteria	______	Specify rate? ___
	______	Specify consistency?
	______	Other? ___

Material Analysis and Adaptation Form (cont.)

Side 2

C. Instruction

____ (C-Prac) Practice	____________	(C-Prac) Break up activities into smaller sections? ____
	____________	Add practice activities? ____
____ (C-Dir) Learner Directions	____________	(C-Dir) Write directions? ____
	____________	Add demonstrations? ____
	____________	Other? ____
____ (C-Prog) Programming or Prompting	____________	(C-Prog) Change presentation mode? ____
	____________	Organize successive approximations? ____
____ (C-Teach) Teacher Activity	____________	(C-Teach) Manage materials? ____
	____________	Use roving tutorial ____
	____________	Add individual tutoring ____
	____________	Add pupil tutoring ____
____ (C-Reinf) Reinforcement	____________	(C-Reinf) Contingent teacher attention? ____
	____________	Point system? ____
	____________	Contracting? ____
	____________	Tangibles? ____
____ (C-Redir) Redirection or Correction	____________	(C-Redir) Practice same material again? ____
	____________	Practice in alternative material? ____
	____________	Provide teacher directed instruction? ____
		Reanalyze material? ____

CHILD-BASED MATERIALS EVALUATION TEACHER CHECKLIST

Name of Program ______________________________

Sequence of Tasks	Comments	Date Accomplished
1 Select Material Program		
2 Conduct a Materials Analysis		
3 State Purpose of CBME		
4 Select Sample to Test		
5 Select (or prepare) Child Measurement System		
6 Select Students		

CHILD-BASED MATERIALS EVALUATION TEACHER CHECKLIST (CONT'D.)

7 Assess Overall Classroom Program		
8 (Re) Schedule Each Student		
9 Implement CBME		
10a Assess Performance Data		
10b Assess CSR Adaptations		
11 Implement or Reject Materials		

Student Performance Summary Sheet

Program ______________ Publisher ____________________ Date Initiated ____________________ Completed ________________

Teacher ______________ Teaching Format ____________________________

UNIT SAMPLED	CHILD NAME	LENGTH		SCORE			AVERAGE
		Aver. Session	Days to Complete	Pretest	Intervention	Posttest	
1							Session & Days ______ Intervention ______ Posttest ______
2							Session & Days ______ Intervention ______ Posttest ______
3							Session & Days ______ Intervention ______ Posttest ______
4							Session & Days ______ Intervention ______ Posttest ______
5							Session & Days ______ Intervention ______ Posttest ______
TOTALS	______	______	______	______	______	______	
OVERALL AVERAGE	______	______	______	______	______	______	

Please Check:

Program Works __________ Program Does Not Work __________ Use ________ Do Not Use ________

Revise ______ Do Not Revise ______

Comments:

APPENDIX C

Skill Lists to Accompany a Materials-Management System

Math-Skill Profile Chart

A. NUMERATION

1. Terms

Select size (large-small).
Select length (long-short).
Define and select amount (how much more-less).

2. Number Recognition

Name or point to numerals 0-10.
Name or point to numerals to 30.
Name or point to numerals to 100.
Name or point to numerals to 1,000.
Identify printed names of numerals (one = 1).

3. Sequencing

Place numerals in order (orient which comes first 0-10).
Place numerals in order to 30.
Place numerals in order to 100.

4. Counting (oral)

Rote counting 1-10.
Rote counting to 20.
Rote counting to 100+.
Rote skip counting by 2's to 30.
Rote skip counting by 5's to 100.
Rote skip counting by 10's to 100.
Rote counting backwards by 1's from 10.
Rote counting backwards by 1's from 30.
Rote counting backwards by 1's from 100+.
Rote counting backwards by 2's from 30.

Rote counting backwards by 5's from 100.
Rote counting backwards by 10's from 100.

5. Counting things

Match equal numbers of objects.
Count 1-10 objects.
Count to 20 objects.
Count to 100 objects.
Count objects from a number to 20 by plussing.
Count objects backwards from a number (20).

6. Writing Numbers

Write numbers 1 to 10.
Write numbers to 20.
Write numbers to 100.

7. Place Value

Identify a number as 1's place.
Identify a number as 1's and 10's.
Convert tens to ones, 1's and 10's.
Convert 1's and 10's (numbers up to 99).
Convert 1's and 10's (numbers up to 999).

B. BASIC COMPUTATION

1. Math Facts

Addition facts (basic 100)—write answers to or call out.
Subtraction facts (basic 100)—write answers to or call out.
Multiplication facts (basic 100)—write answers to or call out.
Division facts—write answers to or call out.

2. Addition

Column addition, no carrying (write answers)
Column addition, with carrying (write answers)
2-place addition, no carrying (write answers)
2-place addition, with carrying (write answers)
3-place + addition, no carrying (write answers)
3-place + addition, with carrying (write answers)

3. Subtraction

2-place subtraction, no borrowing (write answers)
2-place subtraction, with borrowing (write answers)
3-place + subtraction, no borrowing (write answers)
3-place + subtraction, with borrowing (write answers)

4. Multiplication

2-place multiplication, no carrying (write answers)
2-place multiplication, with carrying (write answers)
3-place + multiplication, no carrying (write answers)
3-place + multiplication, with carrying (write answers)

5. Division

2-place division, no remainder (write answers)
3-place division, no remainder (write answers)
3 + place division, with remainder (write answers)

C. ADVANCED MATH

1. Fractions

Match parts to fractional numbers.
Add nonreducible fractions (simple).
Subtract nonreducible fractions (simple).
Multiply nonreducible fractions (simple).
Divide nonreducible fractions (simple).
Reduce fractions to lowest denominator.
Reduce and subtract fractions.
Reduce and multiply fractions.
Reduce and divide fractions.

2. Decimals

Match fractions to decimal equivalents.
Add decimal numbers.
Subtract decimal numbers.
Multiply decimal numbers.
Divide decimal numbers.

3. Percentages

Match fractions to percentages.
Match decimals to percentages.
Compute percentages.

D. APPLIED MATH

1. Time

Tell time by the hour.
Tell time by hours, half hours, five minutes.
Tell time to the hour and minute.
Tell time to the hour, minute, and second.
Read digital clock.

2. Length Measurement

Identify ruler parts.
Equate number of inches with feet.
Equate number of feet with yards.
Equate number of feet with miles.
Measure items by inches.
Measure items by inches and feet.
Measure items by yards, feet, and inches.
Measure items by inches and fractional parts of inches.
Convert units—inches to feet, feet to yards.

3. Metric Measurement

Identify ruler parts as meter, centimeter, millimeter.
Identify equal number of centimeters in meter.
Identify equal number of millimeters in centimeters.
Measure by centimeters.
Measure by meters.
Measure by millimeters.

4. Solid Measurement

Identify ounces, pounds, and tons.
Identify weight equivalents.
Measure in ounces, pounds, tons.

Identify gram, kilogram, metric tons.
Measure in grams, kilograms, metric tons.

5. Liquid Measurement

Identify ounce, cup, pint, quarts, gallons.
Identify liquid equivalents.
Measure in ounces, cups, pints, quarts, gallons.
Identify milliliter, liter, deciliter.
Measure in milliliter, deciliter, liter.

6. Money

Identify coins to half dollar.
Identify bills to $20.
Match coin equivalents to $1.
Match bill equivalents to $20.
Count coins in same unit.
Count coins in varied units.
Count bills to $20.
Give back change for $1 bill.
Give back change for $20 bill.
Make change for a purchase.
Money-management skills.

E. VERBAL PROBLEMS

1. Construct equations; compute basic fact problems.
2. Construct equations; compute second- and third-digit computations.
3. Construct equations; compute time problems.
4. Construct equations; compute distance problems.
5. Construct equations; compute money problems.
6. Construct equations; compute time, money, distance, combinations.

Reading-Skill Profile Chart

A. SOUND-SYMBOLS

Match same letters of the alphabet.
Match uppercase to lowercase letters.
Identify lowercase letters.

Identify uppercase letters.
Name long vowel sounds.
Name hard consonant sounds.
Name short vowel sounds.
Name soft consonant sounds.
Identify rhyming words when the ends rhyme.

B. WORD ATTACK

Identify (say) vowels when heard in words.
Identify (say) vowel dipthongs in words.
Identify (say) consonant blends.
Identify (say) consonant digraphs.
Identify (say) vowel sounds.
Identify silent letters in words.
Determine number of syllables in a word.
Identify roots in words.
Identify prefixes in each.
Identify suffixes in words.
Identify compound words.
Discriminate between plural and singular words.
Identify parts of speech (noun, verb, adj., adv.).

C. SIGHT WORDS

Level A, preprimary (call out)
Level B, primary (call out)
Level C, grades 1-1.5 (call out)
Level D, grades 1.5-2 (call out)
Level E, grades 2-2.5 (call out)
Level F, grades 2.5-3 (call out)
Level G, grades 3-3.5 (call out)
Level H, grades 3.5-4 (call out)
Level I, grade 5 (call out)
Level J, grade 6 (call out)

D. ORAL READING RATE

Sounds (Levels ABC), 30 sounds per minute
Sounds (Levels ABC), 60 sounds per minute
Sounds (Levels ABC), 90 sounds per minute
Sight words (Levels ABC), 30 words per minute

Sight words (Levels ABC), 60 words per minute
Sight words (Levels ABC), 90 words per minute
Sentences (Levels ABC), 60 words per minute
Sentences (Levels ABC), 90 words per minute
Sentences (Levels ABC), 125 words per minute
Paragraphs (Levels CDE), 60 words per minute
Paragraphs (Levels CDE), 90 words per minute
Paragraphs (Levels CDE), 125 words per minute
Passages (Levels FGHIJ), 90 words per minute
Passages (Levels FGHIJ), 125 words per minute
Passages (Levels FGHIJ), 150 words per minute

E. COMPREHENSION

Sentence Levels A&B answer vocabulary questions or give synonym.
Sentence Levels A&B answer fact questions.
Sentence Levels A&B answer inference questions.
Paragraph Levels CDE answer vocabulary questions, define or give synonym.
Paragraph Levels CDE answer fact questions.
Paragraph Levels CDE answer inference questions.
Passage Levels FGHIJ answer vocabulary questions, give synonym.
Passage Levels FGHIJ answer fact questions.
Passage Levels FGHIJ answer inference questions.

APPENDIX D

List of Publishers Who Publish Special Education Materials

ACI MEDIA, INC.
35 West 45th Street
New York, N.Y. 10036

ADDISON-WESLEY PUBLISHING
School Division
106 W. Station Street
Barrington, Ill. 60010

ALLYN AND BACON, INC.
470 Atlantic Avenue
Boston, Mass. 02210

ALPHAVENTURE
717 Fifth Avenue
New York, N.Y. 10022

GILBERT ALTSCHUL PROD., INC.
930 Pitner Avenue
Evanston, Ill. 60202

AMERICAN GUIDANCE SERVICE, INC.
Publishers Building
Circle Pines, MN 55014

AMERICAN TECHNICAL SOCIETY
5608 Stoney Island Ave.
Chicago, Ill. 60637

PAUL S. AMIDON & ASSOC., INC.
4329 Nicollet Avenue, S.
Minneapolis, MN 55409

ATC PUBLISHING CORP.
P. O. Box 5588
Lakeland, Florida 33803

BEAR FILMS
805 Smith Street
P. O. Box R
Baldwin, N.Y. 11510

BENCHMARK FILMS, INC.
145 Scarborough Rd.
Briarcliff Manor, N.Y. 10510

BENEFIC PRESS
10300 W. Roosevelt Rd.
Westchester, Ill. 60153

CHARLES A. BENNETT CO., INC.
809 W. Detweiller Drive
Peoria, Ill. 61614

BERGWALL PRODUCTIONS, INC.
839 Stewart Avenue
Garden City, N.Y. 11530

CHANNING L. BETE CO., INC.
45 Federal Street
Greenfield, Mass. 01301

DICK BLICK COMPANY
P. O. Box 1267
Galesburg, Ill. 61401

BOWMAR PUBLISHING CORP.
622 Rodier Drive
Glendale, CA 91201

CAREER AIDS, INC.
5024 Lankershim Blvd.
North Hollywood, CA 91601

CAREER INSTITUTE
(Subs. of Grolier, Inc.)
Sherman Turnpike
Danbury, CT 06816

CENTRON EDUCATIONAL FILMS
1621 W. Ninth Street
Lawrence, Kansas 66044

CHANGING TIMES EDUC. SERV.
1729 H Street N.W.
Washington, D.C. 20006

CHILDCRAFT EDUCATION CORP.
20 Kilmer Road
Edison, N.J. 08817

CLASSROOM WORLD PRODUCTIONS
22 Glenwood Avenue
Raleigh, N. C. 27602

CLEARVIEW, INC.
6666 N. Oliphant Avenue
Chicago, Ill. 60631

CONTINENTAL PRESS
520 E. Bainbridge Street
Elizabethtown, PA 17022

CONTINUING EDUCATION PUB.
P. O. Box 1491
Portland, Oregon 97207

CORONET INSTRUCTIONAL
65 East South Water St.
Chicago, Ill. 60601

CRAIG EDUCATION
(Div. of Craig Corp.)
921 W. Artesia Blvd., Box 5664
Compton, CA 90220

CREATIVE TEACHING ASSOCIATES
P. O. Box 7714
Fresno, CA 93727

CUISENAIRE CO. OF AMERICA
12 Church Street
New Rochelle, N.Y. 10850

CURRENT AFFAIRS/YOUNG WORLD
(Div. of Key Productions, Inc.)
24 Danbury Road
Wilton, CT 06896

DCA EDUCATIONAL PRODUCTS
424 Valley Road
Warrington, PA 18976

DEVELOPMENTAL LEARNING MATERIALS
7440 Natchez Ave.
Niles, Ill. 60648

DONARS PRODUCTIONS
P. O. Box 24
407 Lincoln Avenue
Loveland, CO 80537

DOUBLEDAY MULTIMEDIA
1371 Reynolds Avenue
Irvine, CA 92713

ECONOMY COMPANY
P. O. Box 25308
1901 North Walnut
Oklahoma City, OK 73125

EDMARK ASSOCIATES
13249 Northup Way
Bellevue, Wash. 98005

EDUCATIONAL ACTIVITIES, INC.
1937 Grand Avenue
Baldwin, N. Y. 11510

EDUCATIONAL DEVELOPMENT CORP.
4235 S. Memorial Avenue
Tulsa, OK 74145

EDUCATIONAL PERFORMANCE ASSOC.
563 Westview Avenue
Ridgefield, N.J. 07657

EDUCATIONAL PROGRESS
(Div. of Educational Dev. Corp.)
P.O. Box 45663
Tulsa, OK 74145

EDUCATIONAL PROJECTIONS CORP.
3070 Lake Terrace
Glenview, Ill. 60025

EDUCATIONAL RESOURCES DIV.
EDUCATIONAL DESIGN, INC.
47 West 13th Street
New York City, N.Y. 10011

EDUCATIONAL SOLUTIONS, INC.
80 Fifth Avenue
New York, N.Y. 10011

ELECTRO SYSTEMS, INC.
847 South High Street
Columbus, Ohio 43206

FEARON PUBLISHERS, INC.
6 Davis Drive
Belmont, CA 94002

FOLLETT PUBLISHING CO.
(Div. of Follett Corp.)

Educational Pub. Div.
1010 W. Washington Blvd.
Chicago, Ill. 60607

GFA ASSOC., INSTRUCTIONAL SYST.
P. O. Box 6404
Mobile, Ala. 36606

GINN AND COMPANY
(Div. of Xerox Education Group)
191 Spring Street
Lexington, Mass. 02173

GROLIER EDUCATIONAL CORP.
845 Third Avenue
New York, N.Y. 10022

HAWKINS AND ASSOCIATES
729 Delaware Avenue
Washington, D.C. 20013

HOFFMAN EDUCATIONAL SYSTEM
4423 Arden Drive
El Monte, CA 91006

HUBBARD PUBLISHING CO.
1946 Raymond Dr.
Northbrook, Ill. 60062

IDEAL AUDIO VISUAL SERVICE
4431 W. North Avenue
Milwaukee, Wisconsin 53208

IDEAL SCHOOL SUPPLY COMPANY
11000 S. Lavergne Avenue
Oak Lawn, Ill. 60453

INSTRUCTIONAL DYNAMICS, INC
450 E. Ohio Street
Chicago, Ill. 60611

INSTRUCTO CORPORATION
(Subs. of McGraw-Hill)
Paoli, PA 19301

INTERCULTURE ASSOCIATES, INC.
P. O. Box 277
Thompson, CT 06277

INTERPRETIVE EDUCATION
400 Bryant Street
Kalamazoo, Mich. 49001

JACOBY/STORM PRODUCTIONS, INC.
101 E. State St.
Westport, CT. 06880

JANUARY PRODUCTIONS, INC.
13-00 Plaza Road
Fair Lawn, N. J. 07410

LAUREL FILMS
P. O. Box 1852
Studio City, CA 91604

LEARN, INC.
113 Gaither Dr.
Mt. Laurel, N.J. 08057

LEARNING SYSTEMS PRESS, INC.
P.O. Box 2999
Lafayette, La. 70502

MAST DEVELOPMENT COMPANY
2212 E. 12 Street
Davenport, Iowa 52803

McGRAW-HILL BOOK COMPANY
1221 Avenue of the Americas
New York City, N.Y. 10020

CHARLES E. MERRILL PUB. CO.
1300 Alum Creek Dr.
Columbus, Ohio 43216

MIDWEST PUBLICATIONS CO.
P.O. Box 129
Troy, MI 48084

MILLER-BRODY PRODUCTIONS, INC.
Audio Visual Materials
342 Madison Avenue
New York City, N.Y. 10017

MIND, INC.
1 King's Highway North
Westport, CT 06880

MODERN CURRICULUM PRESS, INC.
13900 Prospect Road
Cleveland, OH 44136

MUTUAL EDUCATION AIDS
1953-1/2 Hillhurst Avenue
Los Angeles, CA 90027

NATIONAL EDUCATIONAL MEDIA
15760 Ventura Blvd.
Encino, CA 91436

NATIONAL TEACHING AIDS, INC.
120 Fulton Avenue
Garden City, N.Y. 11040

OLYMPUS PUBLISHING COMPANY
1670 E. 13 Street
Salt Lake City, UT 84117

PENNANT EDUCATIONAL MATERIALS
La Mesa, CA 92041

PERENNIAL EDUCATION, INC.
1825 Willow Road
Northfield, Ill. 60093

PHILIPS AUDIO VIDEO SYST. CORP.
91 McKee Drive
Mahwah, N.J. 07430

PRENTICE-HALL MEDIA, INC.
150 White Plains Road
Tarrytown, N.Y. 10591

PRENTKE-ROMICH
RFT 2, Box 191
Shreve, Ohio 44676

PROFESSIONAL ARTS, INC.
P. O. Box 8003
Stanford, CA 94305

PURDUE UNIV. ACHIEVEMENT
CTR. FOR CHILDREN
South Campus Courts, Bldg. E
West Lafayette, Ind. 47907

THE READING LABORATORY, INC.
55 Day Street
South Norwalk, CT 06854

REAL TIME MEDIA
429 N. Columbus Street
Alexandria, VA 22314

RESEARCH MEDIA, INC.
96 Mt. Auburn Street
Cambridge, Mass. 02138

RESEARCH PRESS
2612 N. Mattis
Champaign, Ill. 61820

FRANK RICHARDS CO.
324 1st Street
Liverpool, N.Y. 13088

SAALFIELD PUBLISHING COMPANY
Saalfield Square
Akron, OH 44301

WILLIAM H. SADLIER, INC.
11 Park Place
New York, N.Y. 10007

SCHOLASTIC BOOK SERVICES
(Div. of Scholastic Magazines)
50 W. 44 Street
New York, N.Y. 10036

SCIENCE RESEARCH ASSOCIATES
259 E. Erie Street
Chicago, Ill. 60611

SCHOOL-TECH, INC.
745 State Circle
Ann Arbor, MI 48104

SCOTT, FORESMAN AND COMPANY
1900 E. Lake Avenue
Glenview, Ill. 60025

SINGER EDUCATION DIVISION
(Div. of Singer Co.)
30 Rockefeller Plaza
New York, N.Y. 10020

SISTER KENNY INSTITUTE
1800 Chicago Avenue
Minneapolis, MN 55404

SOCIETY FOR VISUAL EDUCATION
(Div. of Singer Co.)
1345 Diversey Parkway
Chicago, Ill. 60614

SOUTH-WESTERN PUBLISHING
(Subs. of Scott, Foresman Co.)
5101 Madison Road
Cincinnati, OH 45227

SPELLBINDER, INC.
33 Bradford Street
Concord, Mass. 01742

STANWIX HOUSE, INC.
3020 Chartiers Avenue
Pittsburgh, PA 15204

STECK-VAUGHN COMPANY
(Subs. of Intext)
P. O. Box 2028
Austin, TX 78767

H. M. STONE PRODUCTIONS, INC.
6 E. 45th Street
New York, N.Y. 10017

STOUFFER PRODUCTIONS LTD.
300 South Spring St.
P. O. Box 15057
Aspen, CO 81611

TEACHERS PRESS
P. O. Box 3105
Orange, CA 92665

TEACHING AUDIAL & VISUALS, INC.
250 W. 57th Street
New York, N.Y. 10019

TEACHING RESOURCES CORP.
(A New York Times Company)
100 Boylston Street
Boston, MA 02116

TEACHING RESOURCES FILMS
(A New York Times Company)
2 Kisco Plaza
Mt. Kisco, N.Y. 10549

Index

B

C

E

F

G

H

I

J

K

L

M

N

Q

R

T